The Communication of Lea

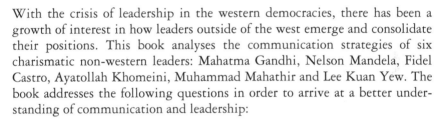

With the crisis of leadership in the western democracies, there has been a growth of interest in how leaders outside of the west emerge and consolidate their positions. This book analyses the communication strategies of six charismatic non-western leaders: Mahatma Gandhi, Nelson Mandela, Fidel Castro, Ayatollah Khomeini, Muhammad Mahathir and Lee Kuan Yew. The book addresses the following questions in order to arrive at a better understanding of communication and leadership:

- How do leaders communicate?
- Do leaders communicate more by words, or actions?
- Do leaders have unique communication strategies?
- Are leaders moral beings, or impostors?

The book describes how each of these leaders designed a unique style that integrated verbal and non-verbal modes of communication. It argues that leadership style is performed through the cumulative interaction of non-verbal modes – dress, body language, physical possessions, symbols and symbolic actions – with verbal strategies for communicating visions, values and legitimacy.

In order to understand how each of these leaders undertakes a dramatic 'performance' of leadership, Jonathan Charteris-Black uses Erving Goffman's notion of 'Front'. Noting the inherent similarities between the mutual dependency of actors with audiences and leaders with followers, the book suggests that leaders – like actors – use metaphors and symbols to satisfy followers' psychological and symbolic needs and that leadership is communicated through impression management, metaphor and media choices.

A fascinating and well executed study, this book will interest students and academics working on leadership, applied linguistics, communication studies and politics.

Jonathan Charteris-Black is Professor in Linguistics at the University of the West of England. He has published extensively in the areas of leadership communication, persuasive communication, political rhetoric, metaphor and corpus linguistics.

Routledge studies in linguistics

The Communication of Leadership
The design of leadership style

Jonathan Charteris-Black

Routledge
Taylor & Francis Group

LONDON AND NEW YORK

First published 2007
by Routledge
2 Park Square, Milton Park, Abingdon, Oxon, OX14 4RN

Simultaneously published in the USA and Canada
by Routledge
270 Madison Ave, New York NY 10016

Routledge is an imprint of the Taylor & Francis Group, an informa business

Transferred to Digital Printing 2008

© 2007 Jonathan Charteris-Black

Typeset in Garamond by Wearset Ltd, Boldon, Tyne and Wear

British Library Cataloguing in Publication Data
A catalogue record for this book is available from the British Library

Library of Congress Cataloging in Publication Data
A catalog record for this book has been requested

ISBN10: 0-415-37829-X (hbk)
ISBN10: 0-415-48650-5 (pbk)
ISBN10: 0-203-96829-8 (ebk)

ISBN13: 978-0-415-37829-1 (hbk)
ISBN13: 978-0-415-48650-7 (pbk)
ISBN13: 978-0-203-96829-1 (ebk)

To two inspirational leaders: Donard Britten and
Martin Trimnell

Contents

Illustrations

Plates

Figures

Tables

Acknowledgements

This work would have been impossible to write without the availability of some excellent web sites and I would like to thank the following: The Mahatma Gandhi Research and Media Service for their comprehensive collection of Gandhi's speeches and writings; the African National Congress for the web site containing Mandela's speeches, statements and writings; the Foreign Broadcast Information Service (a US government agency) for their Castro Speech database that contains English translations of his speeches; the Islamic Republic of Iran for their excellent speech database of Imam Khomeini and the Singapore government for their comprehensive 'Stars' speech archive that was invaluable for researching Lee Kuan Yew's speeches.

I would like to acknowledge the authors of the following biographies: Louis Fischer's *The Life of Mahatma Gandhi*; Anthony Sampson's *Mandela*; Tad Szulc's *Fidel: A Critical Portrait*; Leycester Coltman's *The Real Fidel Castro*; Khoo Boo Teik's *Paradoxes of Mahathirism: An Intellectual Biography of Mahathir Muhammad*; Michael Barr's *Lee Kuan Yew: The Beliefs Behind the Man* and Baqer Moin's *Khomeini: Life of the Ayatollah*. I would also acknowledge my debt to those leaders who have written autobiographies; in particular Nelson Mandela's *Long Walk to Freedom*; Mahatma Gandhi's *An Autobiography or My Experiments with Truth*; Lee Kuan Yew's *The Singapore Story*; and Mahathir's *The Malay Dilemma* and *The Challenge*.

I would like to thank my students on the University of Surrey MA in Linguistics (TESOL) programme who always enjoyed listening to speeches of leaders while developing their expertise as teachers of English. Finally, I would like to thank Dr Hugo Frey for providing helpful, supportive and insightful comments on draft chapters.

1 The magic of leadership

Overview

How do leaders communicate? Do they communicate more by what they say, or what they do? Are their communication strategies unique? Are they moral beings, or impostors? In this work I hope to answer such questions by analysing the verbal and non-verbal communication of six highly successful non-western leaders.[1] Verbal communication is their use of language – such as metaphors – and their non-verbal communication includes appearance, dress, gesture, the use of symbols and symbolic actions. An important finding is that verbal strategies are more effective when they interact with non-verbal ones. This is because multi-modal communication is more effective in evoking subliminal responses among followers and therefore is more likely to lead to the attribution of charismatic qualities. My overall intention is to enhance our understanding of how leadership is communicated.

In this chapter I first discuss the types of psychological need that leaders satisfy and some general theories of leadership. In particular, I consider transformational leadership and explain why it is relevant to investigating leadership across cultures. I develop two ideas that are important in our understanding of leadership – the creation of visions and values. I then consider charismatic leadership – in particular the relation between charisma, religion and myth – and the different circumstances in which charismatic leaders are likely to emerge. I argue that analysing transformational and charismatic leadership is vital to understanding how individual leadership style is designed.

In the following two chapters I examine the communication of leadership through the design of a leadership style that integrates a range of non-verbal and verbal strategies. I describe a number of non-verbal strategies for communicating leadership and how, verbally, metaphor is frequently used to create legitimacy by communicating visions and values, although there are culture-specific variations in the actual metaphors that are chosen. Charismatic leaders use symbols and metaphors to connect personal inner-visions with outer social realities. Metaphors are especially important in the communication of spiritual experience because they have the potential to erode barriers between religious and political spheres of action and satisfy the psycho-emotional needs of followers. But they have the potential to be more effective in the creation of charisma when they combine with non-verbal communication strategies such as symbols.

In each of the six following chapters I analyse the communication strategies of the following non-western leaders: Mahatma Gandhi, Nelson Mandela, Fidel Castro, Ayatollah Khomeini, Muhammad Mahathir and Lee Kuan Yew. The criterion for the selection of these leaders is that each attained an iconic status either by challenging western global dominance – typically in the form of colonialism – or by challenging a specific form of oppression that had its origin in the west (e.g. apartheid). I have included secular leaders (Fidel Castro and Lee Kuan Yew), spiritual leaders (Mahatma Gandhi and Ayatollah Khomeini) and leaders who had both a secular and a spiritual dimension to their leadership (Nelson Mandela and Muhammad Mahathir). Although the majority can be considered 'left-wing', I have also included those whose political thinking is more characteristic of the right (e.g. Lee Kuan Yew). As well as ideological breadth, I also have aimed for geographical range by including leaders from America, Africa, the Middle East and Asia. Finally, I wanted to choose leaders for whom communication was central to their success. Many other leaders could have satisfied these criteria equally well and so inevitably the choice is somewhat arbitrary.

In the final chapter I identify some of the shared communication characteristics of these leaders and consider how far these enable us to generalize about the role of language, metaphors and symbols in leadership communication. I claim that metaphoric and symbolic communication legitimizes leaders and that the adoption of metaphors and symbols that converge with the aspirations of followers allows them to dispose of unwanted identities and undergo psychological catharsis. I hope, through a series of detailed case studies like these, to arrive at an improved understanding of the leaders analysed and of leadership communication.

Perspectives on leadership

A recent definition of leadership is as follows: 'Leadership is a process whereby an individual influences a group of individuals to achieve a common goal';[2] since very few goals are achieved without common action, leadership is fundamental to the nature of society itself. Perhaps in a utopia we would be able to dispense with leaders altogether – such was the aim of Anarchism. One of the aims of Communism was that the Party would replace the need for individual leaders by itself representing the people's interests. Curiously, though, cults of personality seem to have surrounded Communist leaders even more than those in democracies where leaders are changed more easily. When we think of Communism, we think of leaders such as Lenin, Stalin and Mao. Similarly, religious societies also have a strong propensity to produce leaders. The Catholic Church has the Pope as its leader, and Islamic theocracies also show a predilection for charismatic leaders. Only Anarchism, because of its faith in fundamental human goodness, has re··· ·····ip because it relies on individuals becoming their ·aders are usually necessary because they generate a n the basis of social action.

p
se
tic
neε
imρ
ture
exteι
of exρ
whoɯ
they ɑ
matic
permits

is that to arrive at a degree of self-knowledge and ght involves a great deal of introspection, soul- to terms with the full range of tensions, contradic- iat arise from everyday experiences of life. There is a ce from individuals who are able to influence others to s seems to be equally true across time and across cul- evidence of inner qualities of aspirant leaders through ics such as confident behaviour, appearance and powers applies equally to secular and sacred leaders, or others for ιry between politics and religion is not relevant because ιportant distinction between the two.[3] A claim that charis- ιually share is to have access to ultimate truths – and this ιrs to escape from uncertainty and fear.

A gr
leadeι
as a s
analys
ers. Nc

ιl of research has been undertaken into providing a theory of ιis can broadly be divided into theories that analyse leadership characteristics, or traits, possessed by leaders, and those that interactive nature of the relationship between leaders and follow- ouse summarizes these as 'trait' and 'process' approaches to leadership.[4] Trait approaches fit with the popular view of leaders as people who possess exceptional characteristics. Based on an extensive survey of the early literature, Stogdill identified intelligence, alertness, insight, responsibility, initiative, persistence, self-confidence and sociability as the characteristics of great leaders.[5] Trait approaches go back to 'great man' theories of leadership, and have the attraction of simplicity over more complex 'process' approaches that consider leaders in the contexts of their situations and followers. However, trait approaches have sometimes encountered difficulty in arriving at an agreed list of traits and run the risk of oversimplification because they ignore the social situation. The interactive nature of leadership is such that leaders and followers are often jointly involved in creating each other.

It was this perspective that was incorporated into process approaches to leadership such as the situational approach, contingency theory and the path-goal approach. These are concerned with how leaders' behaviours may change according to factors in the situation such as followers' motivational levels. These approaches have the advantage of accommodating motivation theory by treating followers as part of the situation and also of exploring how leaders modify their behaviour in particular situations. They have practical outcomes in the form of offering advice to aspirant leaders and for this reason are often employed in management training programmes.

An approach that will be very influential in this work is the style approach. This approach integrates aspects of the trait and process approaches by proposing that the key feature of leadership is the actual behaviour of the leader in various contexts. It was initiated by researchers at Ohio State University and the University of Michigan who examined the interaction between two types of behaviour and their followers' responses. 'Task' behaviours concern the organisation and planning of work-related tasks while 'relationship' behaviours concern developing trust, commitment and mutual respect among followers. The successful leader needs to find the right balance between the task and relationship behaviours for a particular group of followers.

The value of the style approach is that – unlike the trait approach – it recognizes that personality traits are not sufficient in themselves but require expression through behaviour. In keeping with process approaches, it is dynamic because it recognizes that the particular blend of task and relationship behaviours varies according to the situation. This is especially important in an approach to leadership based on communication because one of the principles of successful communication is that it takes into account the setting and the audience. My notion of 'the design of leadership style' proposes a set of verbal and non-verbal strategies that resonate with followers.

In his classic study McGregor Burns first describes how:

> Leadership over human beings is exercised when persons with certain motives and purposes mobilize, in competition or conflict with others, institutional, political, psychological, and other resources so as to arouse, engage, and satisfy the motives of followers.[6]

Notice, first, that leadership can be treated in the abstract – that is, there is a common (or 'generic') idea of leadership that exists independently of both individual leaders and the particular social situations in which they operate. Therefore leaders can emerge in any type of social grouping – political, business, educational, military, religious, or leisure – and in *any* culture or society. Then notice that leaders have *their own* motives – they may be self-seeking or altruistic, and individuals compete with others for a limited number of leadership roles. In human society the struggle to become leader is the equivalent in the animal world to becoming the alpha male who is able to see off rivals in the search for sexual dominance. Next, notice the verbs: leaders are dynamic agents because they *mobilize, arouse, engage* and *satisfy*. Finally, notice the inter-connectedness of leaders and followers – leaders only exist because others follow.

The mutual dependency of leaders and followers is something commented on by Cronin:

> A leader has to resonate with followers. Part of being an effective leader is having excellent ideas, or a clear sense of direction, a sense of mission. But such ideas or vision are useless unless the would-be leader can communicate them and get them accepted by followers.[7]

And it is also highlighted in Burns' definition of leadership:

> I define leadership as leaders inducing followers to act for certain goals that represent the values and the motivations – the wants and needs, the aspirations and expectations – of both leaders and followers. And the genius of leadership lies in the manner in which leaders see and act on their own and their followers' values and motivations.[8]

Leaders satisfy and express their own psychological needs as well as those of their followers and therefore leadership equally concerns the inner values of leaders and the social values of followers. We will see in the next chapter that interaction between leaders and followers is vital to the effective communication of leadership.

Transformational and transactional leadership

A further approach to leadership that is central to this work is transformational leadership. This approach integrates characteristics of both the trait and process views on leadership and – like the style approach – is a theory that works effectively when describing leadership across a range of cultural and social settings. An important distinction that has dominated western leadership studies is the distinction between transactional and transformational leadership; this can be summarized as follows:

> *Transactional* leadership . . . occurs when one person takes the initiative in making contact with others for the purpose of an exchange of valued things.[9]

> *Transforming* leadership . . . occurs when one or more persons engage with others in such a way that leaders and followers raise one another to higher levels of motivation and morality.[10]

It is interesting to note that transactional leaders are concerned with exchange values while transformational leaders are concerned with ethical values. Implicit in these definitions is the claim that transformational leaders are more effective because they motivate followers by acting upon their higher order non-material needs, aspirations and desires rather than upon 'things'. The potential of transformational leaders to appeal to ethical values is a theme that is developed in subsequent discussions of Burns' transformational leaders. For example:

> Transformational leadership deals with the leader's effect on the followers' values, self-esteem, trust and confidence in the leader; and their motivation to perform 'above and beyond the call of duty'.[11]

Transformational leadership is measured by the *effect that leadership has on followers* as people are in some ways 'transformed' – whereas transactional leadership is measured in terms of materials that are exchanged. Therefore in the choice of terms there seems to be preferential treatment given to the transformational leader because of his capacity to *change* followers *for the better*. The positive connotation of transformational leaders is brought out by the use of the word 'higher' that occurs in nearly all definitions of such leaders and follows a 'conceptual metaphor':[12] GOOD IS UP, and DOWN IS BAD. Consider for example, the words that I have italicized in the following descriptions:

> Transformational processes usually involve the *upgrading* of needs. As a consequence of this *upgrading* of needs, subordinates and followers become self-directing and self-reinforcing.[13]

> The transformational leader's influence is based on the leader's ability to inspire and raise the consciousness of the followers by appealing to their *higher* ideals and values.[14]

> The transformational leader motivates participants to perform beyond expectations by ... altering or expanding participant's motivations to the *higher* orders of self-esteem and self-actualization.[15]

Transformational leaders are conceptualized in terms of a theory of motivation that describes the satisfaction of non-material needs and desires as 'higher' than the satisfaction of material needs and wants. In Maslow's theory of motivation the abstract need for self-actualization is considered to be 'higher' – and is at the tip of the pyramid.[16] Because transactional leadership is concerned with the exchange of things, it corresponds with the base of Maslow's pyramid where lower physical and material needs are satisfied. So in discussions of Burns' main categories of leader there is generally a preference for transformational over transactional leaders. Consider, for example, the powers attributed to transforming leaders by the italicized verbs in the following:

> The transforming or transcending leader is the person who ... so *engages* followers as to *bring* them to a heightened political and social consciousness and activity, and in the process *converts* many of those followers into leaders in their own right.[17]

In an empirical study Bass (1985) found the four factors that contributed to perceptions of leadership as transformational were: charismatic leadership, inspirational leadership, intellectual stimulation and individual consideration. The transforming leader subsequently became the primary focus of research interest in the leadership studies of the 1990s. In the discourse of leadership this is communicated by the use of terms that imply *both* change *and* improvement. Like a spiritual leader, the transformational leader moulds the souls of followers by inspiring them with zeal in pursuit of a vision. The traits of a transformational leader bear close resemblance to those of a charismatic leader:

> Regardless of the situation, charismatic leaders are likely to display high levels of emotional expressiveness, self-confidence, self-determination, and freedom from internal conflict and are likely to have a strong conviction of the moral righteousness of their beliefs.[18]

Transformational leadership appears to overlap with charismatic leadership. This may be because the distinction between transformational and transactional leadership has emerged in relation to models developed in management contexts while charismatic leadership occurs across a wider domain of social activities. We think of charismatic leaders in all walks of life, from evangelical or motivational speakers, football coaches, media celebrities and politicians. Importantly, charismatic leaders also emerge in a wide range of different cultural settings, whereas research into transformational leadership is restricted to western settings. Each of the leaders in this book is charismatic as much as he is transformational. Transformational leaders rely on the magical quality of leadership usually known as 'charisma' that will be explored later on in this chapter.

I propose a definition of a leader as someone who provides a sense of social purpose and motivates followers by providing explanations that correspond with unsatisfied needs. They are persuasive *because* they satisfy partially unsatisfied desires, hopes and aspirations. In the next sections I will explore how communication is used to arouse and satisfy the partially unsatisfied hopes and desires of followers. I will suggest that the primary means for the creation of a 'followership' is by communicating visions that correspond with underlying value systems and in the next two sections I will consider these two notions in more detail.

Visions and leadership

The concept of 'vision' has dominated the 'New Leadership studies'[19] and it has become a common assumption that leaders should also be visionaries. The ability to formulate, communicate and act upon visions has become a central component of leadership. A vision is an idealized state of affairs that does not exist at present but serves as a model or ideal for how they should be in the future. It represents a desired situation – a utopia or dream – and serves as a guide for present action and behaviour. In organizations visions are communicated in mission statements that encapsulate their desired states. While the New Leadership studies argue for the importance of 'visions', very few writers explain clearly what they mean by this; however, Bass provides a clue as to the essential meaning of 'vision':

Often this vision of the transformational leader involves symbolic solutions of conflicts which reconcile psychological contradictions inherent
in the experience of those influenced.[20]

A vision, then, projects an idealized situation that resolves the psychological
tensions and conflicts of followers. It satisfies their hopes and desires by offering an imagined solution to problems that are currently experienced. A vision
is an image that heals the psychological and material wounds that leaders and
followers share. It soothes present anxieties and offers hope for the future.
Nelson Mandela offered a vision of racial equality that would overcome the
conflict caused by apartheid. Gandhi offered a vision of an independent India
that would overcome the visible tensions endemic in colonial situations.
However, the challenges that they faced were rather less visible than those
faced by corporate leaders for whom tensions may be caused by market shifts.

Although the actual content of a vision may be determined by situational
factors, leaders need to have visions that they can communicate effectively in
order to convey a superior understanding of the situation. The ownership of
'visions' comprises a defining element by which individuals in all social
fields take on the status of leader. Religious leaders have a vision in which
peoples' actions and behaviour is a projection of their spiritual values, sports
leaders have a vision of winning a major competition. Business leaders have
a vision of particular markets that they will dominate and political leaders
have visions of nation-building:

> A vision is a target that beckons ... a vision always refers to a future
> state, a condition that does not presently exist and never existed before.
> With a vision, the leader provides the all-important bridge from the
> present to the future of the organization.[21]

A vision provides the focus of group energies towards a state of affairs that
will exist in the future and the very existence of the vision is intended to be
self-fulfilling and makes a state of affairs more likely to actually occur; it is
the equivalent of a destination in spatial terms. Without knowing *where* one
intends to *go* it is impossible ever to *arrive*. Indeed, the metaphor of travel is
often used in relation to understanding of vision: a vision provides a conceptual blueprint for a social unit. More important than whether or not these
visions are actually realized are perceptions and beliefs of whether or not
they have been, and aspirant leaders often claim that the visions of existing
leaders are unfulfilled.

Conger describes vision as 'the cornerstone of charismatic leadership' and
each of his four stages by which some individuals come to be regarded as
charismatic leaders contains reference to 'visions':[22]

1   Sensing opportunity and formulating a vision
2   Articulating the vision

3   Building trust in the vision
4   Achieving the vision – empowering others, creating self-belief, etc.

Visions, then, are the models that leaders build to represent how they will integrate their ideals, beliefs and aspirations with some fixed outcome. Vision:

> helps individuals distinguish between what's good and bad for the organization, and what it's worthwhile to want to achieve ... thus in a very real sense individual behaviour can be shaped, directed and, and coordinated by a shared and empowering vision of the future ... by focusing attention on a vision the leader operates on the *emotional and spiritual resources* of the organization, on its values, commitments and aspirations.[23]

It seems that visions resolve psychological tensions and conflicts most effectively when they correspond with the striving for good. Visions arise from the desire to make the world – or whichever part the social activity occurs in – a better place to live. They are by definition idealistic in nature because they describe situations that do not yet exist. On the assassination of Gandhi, Nehru gave one of the most profound descriptions of a leader acting upon followers' emotional and spiritual resources:

> The light has gone out of our lives and there is darkness everywhere and I don't quite know what to tell you and how to say it ... the light has gone out, I said, and yet I was wrong. For the light that shone in this country was no ordinary light. The light that has illumined this country for these many years will illumine this country for many more years, and a thousand years later that light will still be seen in this country, and the world will see it and it will give solace to innumerable hearts. For that light represented the living truth, and the eternal man was with us with his eternal truth reminding us of the right path, drawing us from error, taking this ancient country to freedom.

Of course, the vision that Gandhi had was of an independent India that was not ruled by a foreign power. Visions of national independence have been some of the most potent and influential in the emergence of great leaders of the twentieth century – including Nkrumah in Ghana, Nasser in Egypt, Mao Tse-tung in China, de Gaulle in France and Castro in Cuba. The crucial issue that all these leaders faced was in deciding the relationship between the vision of an independent country and the means that should be employed to attain this. However, Nehru employs the light metaphor to symbolize Gandhi because to see him was to understand him – there was no division between seeing and knowing. For Gandhi the principle of non-violence embodied the vision and therefore the means became the end.

In this convergence of means and ends Gandhi is exceptional since in other independence struggles force was considered a very necessary prerequisite for attaining the vision. Visions are generally end-focused goals: they do not prescribe the stages that are to be gone through in reaching the target. In Marxist-Leninism the means of attaining the perfect socialist society was through a class struggle that necessarily entailed violence. In some approaches to leadership within business contexts (such as franchising) the vision deliberately leaves the means by which preconceived ends are to be attained up to followers. This is based on the belief that by freeing outer parts of organization from imposed controls, the vision becomes more attainable than when the organization imposes the means.

Just as leaders articulate something for which we already have an inkling, so visions must combine the known with the unknown, as Handy puts it they must 'reframe the known scene to reconceptualize the obvious, connect the previously unconnected, dream a dream'.[24] Visions are persuasive precisely because they resolve tensions by integrating what is known with aspirations, hopes and desires of which we are only partially conscious. They are effective because they symbolize the human desire for the best of all possible worlds – it is for this reason they are often communicated by metaphors and symbols that describe the unknown, or partially known, using more familiar terms and signs.

Values and leadership

A vision is unlikely to be successful unless it complies with the values of a particular group. Followers will only believe in visions that are compatible with their value system. However, our understanding of the word 'value' is complicated by the fact that it may either be used to refer to exchange or monetary value or to refer to moral or ethical values. This is an important distinction that is generally overlooked in discussions of 'value' in the literature on leadership. For example, in his classic definition of leadership given above Burns refers twice to 'values'. It is evident that Burns is not referring to monetary value because when we talk about exchange value we do not use the plural form 'values'. Ethical values are necessary to cover a much wider range of human activities than the economic value of market transactions.

Values are socially agreed beliefs, opinions and judgements about what is good and bad, right and wrong, true and false. This definition of values assumes a pre-existing ethical scale with good and bad, right and wrong, true and false at the end points of this scale. Indeed when values are discussed in leadership studies it is the sense of ethical values that predominates; for example, Gardner identifies one of the tasks of a leader as affirming values and explains this as follows:

> In any healthy and reasonably coherent community people decide what things they will define as legal or illegal, virtuous or vicious, in good

taste or in bad. These values are embodied in the society's religious beliefs and its secular philosophy ... However expressed, values carry the message of shared purposes, standards, and conceptions of what is worth living and striving for; and they have immense motivating power ... The leaders whom we admire the most help us to revitalize our shared beliefs and values.[25]

Leaders' utopian visions will only appeal to followers if they correspond with what they believe to be good and bad and therefore determine which actions are evaluated as worthwhile or not worthwhile. In democratic contexts it is precisely because of a convergence of values that followers select their leaders in the first place. Zaleznik also argues that values are at the core of effective leadership:

> Leadership is meaningless without values. An organization or hierarchy can set its values and hope to develop leaders who will articulate them, but values cannot be imposed. They must correspond to the values latent in leaders and followers that can mesh with those of the organization.[26]

If the social function of visions is to get followers to act in certain ways, it is because effective communication of appropriate values motivates followers. By 'appropriate' I mean that followers will only choose to modify their behaviour if such changes are in line with their culturally-influenced world-view and belief system concerning truth and falsehood. This understanding of motivation corresponds with well-established theories of motivation, such as that offered by Maslow, in which the highest forms of motivation relate to higher order goals such as self-actualization. Visions are unlikely to be successful if they correspond only with the lower order satisfaction of physical and material needs; in order to engage they must necessarily embrace higher order needs. Values are precisely those aspirations that we have once our basic physical wants and needs have been satisfied. We may think of values as 'ethical desires'; they symbolize beliefs, opinions and judgements that appeal to non-physical wants and needs.

Given the importance of values in motivating human behaviour, leaders need to be in touch with followers' beliefs about what is good and bad because the absence of any convergence between the ethical desires of leaders and followers will mean that their visions will fail to motivate. Values cannot be imposed but must emerge from what is latent in followers and leaders. In the case of leaders of great protest movements there was convergence of values with visions; for Gandhi and Martin Luther King their values required them to use non-violent protest precisely because this symbolized a vision of a non-violent world in which people lived peacefully with each other. Dr King communicated this in his 'I have a dream' speech with the idealized cathartic symbol of children of all races eating at the same table. However, values are more typically described in terms of physical struggle and conflict.

Charismatic leadership

Definition and religious origins

The magical or religious power of leadership is central to the concept of charisma. The term 'charisma' – originating in the Greek 'a free gift of God's grace' – is defined by the German sociologist, Max Weber, as follows:

> The term 'charisma' will be applied to a certain quality of an individual personality by virtue of which he is considered extraordinary and treated as endowed with supernatural, superhuman or at least specifically exceptional powers or qualities. These are such as not to be accessible to the ordinary person, but are regarded as of divine origin or as exemplary, and on the basis of them the individual concerned is treated as a 'leader'.[27]

There are two components to this definition: first the charismatic leader is one whose powers and attributes are believed by followers to exceed what is normal and, second, these powers are attributed to a divine source. The first part of the definition also implies that the perception of charismatic attributes depends on the attitudes and beliefs of followers – rather than existing in any form that can be independently measured. The use of verbs such as 'is considered', 'treated as' and 'regarded as' concern the reactions of followers who are linguistically 'invisible'. As Bass puts it: 'As an attribute, charisma is in the eye of the beholder. Therefore, it is relative to the beholder';[28] it is known by its effects on followers:

> A charismatic leader induces a high degree of loyalty, commitment, and devotion in the followers; identification with the leader and the leader's mission; emulation of the leader's values, goals and behavior; a sense of self-esteem from relationships with the leader and the leader's mission; and an exceptionally high degree of trust in the leader and the correctness of the leader's beliefs.[29]

Although charisma is a mental state that exists in the perception of followers and can only be known through their reactions to an individual, there still has to be a basis for this reaction. The distinction between traits that are inferred by followers and actual traits is developed by some writers who deliberately highlight the insubstantial nature of charisma by contrasting the 'apparent' and the 'real':

> Often, the charismatic survives with more attention given the apparent than the real. Image of success and effectiveness is pursued. As long as the image of success and effectiveness as a leader can be sustained, the charismatic remains deified by his supporters.[30]

The distinction between actual and perceived traits also explains why leaders are abandoned if they lose their exceptional powers. One of the situations in which this occurs is if their vision no longer offers measurable benefits to followers. One can readily think of examples of leaders who have suffered this fate – in particular Winston Churchill who failed to be re-elected after leading Britain to victory in the Second World War and Margaret Thatcher who was dispensed with by the Conservative Party after winning three elections. In the case of Churchill, his vision as a wartime leader was no longer relevant after the war, while Thatcher seemed to have lost the magical ability to inspire and to motivate her party as her metaphors grew tired and stale. The charisma of Tony Blair became seriously tarnished after he lost trust because of the widespread belief (even within his own party) that he had used deception in arguing the case for a war against Iraq.

Sometimes the attempt to undermine charismatic status is a deliberate strategy by opponents. On the capture of Saddam Hussein – after a hunt lasting for several months – the Americans were keen to film, and release to global media sources, images of the erstwhile leader undergoing a lice inspection and a dental check-up. This (albeit minor) flouting of the Geneva Convention in relation to the treatment of prisoners of war was motivated by the desire to communicate symbolically his loss of status as a leader. This was done by showing him as experiencing the characteristic ailments of a convict 'on the run'. Similarly, the many references to being discovered in 'a hole in the ground' (rather than say 'a bunker') were intended to activate associations of animals burrowing underground – images that were also linked with Osama Bin Laden because of his extensive network of caves in Afghanistan. If charisma is a matter of representations – then it is also something that can be influenced for propaganda purposes.

The divine origin of 'charisma' remains very close to our understanding of the concept. Leaders who aspire to charismatic status often do so through behaviours that are deliberately intended to create mystique and evoke the emotional responses associated with intense religious experiences. Gardner and Avolio propose that leaders deliberately develop a set of impression-management techniques through which they construct an identity that will be interpreted as charismatic by followers:

> they use their superior acting abilities to orchestrate nonverbal and expressive behaviors that followers see as highly fluid, outwardly directed, and animated ... Whereas many such behaviors involve spontaneous displays of genuine emotion, others are scripted in advance or through improvisation to maximize their impact. Their inspirational effects are readily apparent from audience reactions. For instance, people describe the voices of charismatics as captivating and their eyes as magnetic and hypnotic (Bryman, 1992). Charismatics also project a powerful, confident, and dynamic presence through their body posture, speaking rate, gestures, smiles, eye contact, and touch (Bass, 1985).[31]

The spiritual-emotional appeal is intended to evoke the strong emotional responses of love and hate that characterize intense religious experience. For some leaders – such as Mahatma Gandhi – the divine origin of their charisma was its very essence. An opponent of Gandhi's said that he was God descended to earth and 'the gates of Heaven were waiting to receive him'.[32] Similarly, followers frequently noted the divine origin of Martin Luther King's special powers:

> In 1961, after hearing King calm an unruly crowd, the president of the Atlanta Chamber of Commerce remarked, 'I had heard him called "Little Jesus" in the black community. Now I understand why ... during the Selma crusade Stokely Carmichael commented that rural blacks regarded King "Like a God"'. Coretta King observed that, during his sojourn to Chicago the following year, ghetto dwellers regarded her husband 'almost like a Messiah'.[33]

There is evidence that leaders manage impressions in order to create an association with divinity. While reflecting on the stabbing wounds he had received after an attack at a Harlem book signing in 1958 King is claimed to have said: 'So like the Apostle Paul I can now humbly yet proudly say, I bear in my body the marks of the Lord Jesus'.[34] In fact, charismatic status arises from a reciprocal relationship in which the psycho-emotional needs of both leaders and followers are best satisfied by divine explanations. These enhance the strength of a movement by constructing the leader as protected by divine forces and guarantee the status of martyr in the event of premature death by assassination. We see the yearnings amongst followers to become leaders by becoming martyrs in the emergence of the cult of the suicide bomber; I describe this later in relation to charisma, social conditions and modernity.

Charisma and myth

The divine nature of charisma is something that has been attributed to leaders irrespective of whether or not they have claimed to be religious. Even charismatic leaders in Communist and other non-religious movements have intentionally sought to create subliminal associations of divine approval through symbols and symbolic behaviour; they have done this just as much as leaders such as Gandhi and Martin Luther King for whom political issues were religious ones. The main evidence for the subliminal appeal of non-religious leaders is in the deliberate creation of myths. A myth is some type of narrative that carries a symbolic meaning.

Mythic interpretations of charisma have much greater potential in non-western societies because of the importance of religious and pre-religious belief systems and the way these constitute a fundamental part of a cultural or national identity. It is noticeable that western leaders who are known to be religious – such as Tony Blair – have gone out of their way to *conceal* any explicit statement of their religious motivation by replacing it with a form of watered-down ethical discourse. This contrasted with George Bush who was quite prepared – at least initially – to present the War on Terror as 'a crusade'.[35] However, belief in magical powers and their physical transference to followers is more typically part of pre-scientific, pre-rational belief systems and is therefore more likely to occur outside the west:

> Heroic leadership plays a vital role in transitional and developing societies where even the more idolatrous form of heroic leadership may meet the special needs of both leaders and followers. The idols are usually motivated by powerful needs for affection, esteem, and self-actualization. They want and need an audience, and an audience needs them. Followers flock to see such heroes, crowd in to touch their hands or the hems of their garments.[36]

In order to exploit the divine essence of charisma the aspirant leader needs to demonstrate charismatic motivation. Though I will deal with the communication of charisma in the next chapter, here it is worth noting that leaders convey the impression of religious approval by showing their mission is based on inner-goals. Charismatic leaders give the impression of being motivated by something that resolves the inner conflicts experienced by followers – by huge forces that go beyond those of the human ego. As Gorky said of Lenin: 'His words always gave one the impression of the physical pressure of an irresistible truth'; he seemed to speak 'not of his own will, but by the will of history'. It is because of their high motivation that they have an almost magical effect on others, as Joel Joffe testified in relation to Mandela:

> Nelson Mandela emerged quite naturally as the leader. He has, in my view, all the attributes of a leader – the engaging personality, the ability, the stature, the calm, the diplomacy, the tact and the conviction. When I first met him, I found him attractive and interesting, but the time the case finished I regarded him as a really great man. I began to notice how his personality and stature impressed itself not just on the group of the accused, but on the prison and the prison staff themselves.[37]

While on the run 'they persuaded him to abandon his stylish clothes, but he still had his vanity: they could not get him to shave off his beard, which had become part of his revolutionary style'.[38] It is because their mythic aura influences others that charismatic leaders have the power to transform society:

The bearer of charisma enjoys loyalty by virtue of a mission believed to be embodied in him; this mission has not necessarily and not always been revolutionary, but in its most charismatic form it has inverted all value hierarchies and overthrown custom, law and tradition.[39]

The charismatic leader, then, is an agent of change: someone who dispenses with what is previously accepted as given and challenges the existing understanding of values. In this sense charismatic leaders are also transformational. Representing their cause as a mission implies that their motives are not for personal gain but for the spiritual betterment of mankind. In its extreme form the charismatic leader becomes a prophet and actually becomes the voice of God – a Mahdi or a Mahatma – whose very being is inherently divine. Weber's definition of charisma as divinely inspired is especially applicable to leaders operating beyond the west and is of particular importance in understanding the appeal of contemporary charismatic leaders. However, this needs to be modified in line with our understanding of the contexts in which political myths are likely to flourish.[40]

Psycho-sociological conditions for the emergence of charismatic leaders

Charismatic leaders are only likely to emerge when the sociological and psychological conditions are right. A mission is more likely to evoke a response from followers who are experiencing some form of distress – 'Whether psychic, physical, economic, ethical, religious, or political'.[41] Much of Weber's discussion of charisma concerns the extent to which it is necessary for there to be a set of pre-existing social conditions for charismatic leaders to emerge: do leaders *create* followers or *are they created* by them? This in fact anticipates the distinction between trait and process approaches to leadership discussed earlier. As with the nature/nurture dichotomy in other social and human sciences, it is often difficult to find a simplistic answer to this question since usually there is an ongoing interaction between individuals and their environment that makes problematic any attempt to separate them. Racial policies in South Africa provided the seedbed for the emergence of Mandela as a charismatic leader. The cult of the suicide bomber in the Middle East is partly driven by the desire of followers to become leaders in their own right because of an overwhelming frustration with the prevailing social, economic and political reality. In Palestine the status of the 'living martyr' guarantees that followers who have no previous claim to be leaders in their own right are treated as if they already possessed the hallmarks of charismatic leadership. The nature of charisma is in an interaction between the attributes and behaviours of leaders and the psychological responses of followers both of whom are influenced by prevailing social conditions.

In some cases the psychological responses occur in affluent societies because of individual psychopathology:

Followers are, in essence, fulfilling a pathological need rather than a healthy desire for role models from whom to learn and grow. There has been support for these dynamics in research on cults and certain political movements. For example, studies . . . have found followers of charismatic political and religious leaders to have lower self-esteem, a higher intolerance for indecision and crisis, greater feelings of helplessness, and more experiences of psychological distress than others.[42]

However, in non-western societies, where life is often influenced by social disruptions and those caused by natural and environmental circumstances, the psycho-emotional conditions for charismatic leaders to emerge are more pervasive:

> The charismatic is an idolized hero, a messiah and savior who appears in times of great distress. This salvation from distress is what therefore engenders the special emotional intensity of the charismatic response . . . followers respond to the charismatic leader with passionate loyalty because the salvation, or the promise of it, that he appears to embody represents the fulfilment of urgently felt needs.[43]

Emotional distress often creates a fertile soil from which charismatic leaders can emerge. I have already noted the ambiguity underlying the attitude towards leaders in Communism: societies based in government for 'The People' have often been those in which social conditions have created the psychological conditions for charismatic leaders to emerge. The concept of revolution is attractive when social and economic conditions create extreme physical, spiritual and emotional hardship. Castro emerged from the incompetence of Batista's government; apartheid created the emotional conditions for Mandela – just as the experience of colonization formed those for Gandhi and Mahathir. A Tsar who did not understand his people's suffering created the conditions for Russian Revolution just as the perceived insensitivity of the *ancien regime* created the climate for the French Revolution. It is because of the psycho-emotional distress caused by social dissatisfaction that followers look outside the bounds of conventional political behaviour for a solution to their problems.

Weber argued that the prophets of Ancient Judaism were socially marginal individuals who emerged *outside* of existing social structures.[44] Charismatic religious leaders all appear to have spent periods of their life in isolation from society in order to develop the type of inner self-knowledge and insights that subsequently became essential to their charisma. This is irrespective of particular historical or cultural settings and applies equally to Jesus, Muhammad or Buddha. Many charismatic leaders – Gandhi and Castro and especially Mandela – spent long periods of their lives in prison. Gandhi periodically withdrew from social life by going to live in his ashram and regularly observed a day of silence. However, their charisma was enhanced by their withdrawal:

:eared from public sight into jail leaving vivid images
: military commander who championed the people's
:l leader in full regalia proclaiming his African iden-
. need television – which the government would not
:outh African until 1976 – to capture the people's imagina-

Sometimes the charismatic leader becomes appealing to followers who are undergoing stress and distress after a period of exile from the homeland, or from normal society. Exile may also apply to social groups, for example, a particular political party that has not been elected for a long period of time.[46]

Travel on long journeys – as undertaken by Mao Tse-tung or of Buddha – can also provide a social detachment that permits the growth of inner knowledge. The mythic regenerative power of journeys is something that potentially has a universal appeal.[47] The conditions that encourage the emergence of charisma are ones where the psychological, physical or spiritual instability of a society find resonance with the message brought from the wilderness by a detached individual on a mission. The physical journey becomes a mythic journey that symbolizes the journey of the spirit after death. Great leaders are able to create symbols evoking emotional responses that integrate the social realities of followers with their own deep spiritual needs.

Charisma and modernity

A further important issue in Weber's notion of charisma is the question of how far a concept of charismatic leadership – with its roots in religion and magic – is applicable to modern situations and in diverse cultures. Is charisma restricted to specific emergent societies or is it a more universal notion that has contemporary relevance? In this section I support the view that charismatic leadership can occur in contemporary societies – particularly in non-western societies. Evidence for this is found in the flexibility of political and religious notions in our understanding of charisma. Charismatic leadership can be extended beyond the sphere of religion to political contexts. A good example of this is the extension of the word 'mission' to refer to core values and intentions in contexts other than that of religion where it originated (the term 'missionary' emerged from the original mission or 'sending' of the Holy Ghost). Now politicians have missions, as do the owners of football clubs, chief executives of companies and leaders of universities. The emergence of 'mission statements' clearly indicates the way a word that developed in a religious domain has been extended to modern secular organizations. Charismatic leadership, then, can emerge in *all* types of society – including modern society.

Contemporary uses of charisma occur when national leaders instil a sense of nationhood. Wartime leaders such as Churchill, Hitler, de Gaulle and

Mussolini employed a metonymic substitution of the 'leader for people and place' because the basis of their legitimacy was in becoming the voice of the nation. However, it does not seem that this type of charismatic leadership is restricted to developed western countries because an idealized concept of the nation has been very central in the emergence of developing states. There is a general tendency in political discourse for leaders associated with nationalist and independence movements – such as Nehru, Gandhi, Nkruma, Lumumba, Castro, Gadafi and Mandela – to use figures of speech that identify themselves as symbols of their people. Charismatic leaders of national independence movements create a discourse in which they become symbols of the people and claim the right to speak as their voice.

The case that charisma can be extended to analysis of modernizing societies is even stronger in non-western societies because potentially the boundary between other domains, such as religion and politics, is itself determined by prevailing cultural norms. In India religious concepts can easily become political ones; as a biographer of Gandhi summarizes: 'Gandhi's religion cannot be divorced from his politics. His religion made him political. His politics were religious'.[48]

However, the dangers of conceptually blending issues of religion and politics – Church and State – in a context of global culture can be seen in the modern notion of a War on Terror. This is dangerous precisely because it follows the same philosophy as that of *jihad* in which religion is equated with politics: if terrorism is conceptualized as war then this permits terrorist acts to be represented as acts of war. This of course paves the way for violence to be deemed an acceptable means for attaining religious objectives. The emergence of a clear boundary between various domains of social life in which matters of church and of state are kept separate is one of the hallmarks of western rationalism – although it is by no means the preserve of the west. Ali al-Husseini al-Sistani the Shi-ite leader of Iraq argues for a secular government – as long as it does not pass laws that are contrary to Islamic principles – rather than the theocractic state of Iran. Nevertheless, there has been a tendency in the current Islamic revolutions – for example the emergence of theocracies in Iran – to blend political with religious objectives. This has encouraged the emergence of charismatic leaders – such as Ayatollah Khomeini and Osama Bin Laden – for whom the central tenet is the inseparability of spiritual and political questions. The extent to which politics and religion can remain separate is relative to the social processes at work in a particular culture at a particular time.

Contemporary terrorism shows a need for followers to become leaders in their own right by taking on roles that place them in a position of making the ultimate sacrifice – that of their own life – often as a precondition for the killing and maiming of many others. The social conditions for the emergence of terrorist 'leaders' seem to be a psycho-spiritual intensity driven by a sense of frustration with the possibility of realizing objectives through democratic means or by conventional warfare and a conflict of personal identity. No distinction is made between politics and religion. The aspirant suicide bomber goes through a temporary period of withdrawal from his family and regular social life and this is marked linguistically by addressing them as a 'living martyr'. The social isolation prior to the attack symbolizes the enforced separation of charisma and is intended to create a charismatic appeal; through such rituals the boundary between follower and leader is erased as followers seek to become leaders.

Leadership and communication

The particular approach that I will take on leadership in this work is to answer the question: how do leaders communicate? The answer I will propose is primarily through metaphoric and symbolic communication. Great leaders tend to be great communicators – as Cronin argues: 'The effective creative leader is one who can give voice and form so that people say, "Ah yes – that's what I too have been feeling"'.[49] It is through providing metaphors and symbols that leaders are able to communicate the unconscious desires and yearnings of followers: the leader is therefore someone who can give some type of formation to as yet unexpressed desires. As Orwell puts it: 'If people cannot communicate well, they cannot think well, and if they cannot think well, others will do their thinking for them'.[50] The ability to communicate well is not in itself a sufficient condition for someone to become a leader but it is unlikely that we will find leaders in whom this ability is entirely absent. The focus of Chapter 2 will be on the communication of leadership, but I will raise some introductory issues here.

Leadership research has generally overlooked the details of *how* leadership is communicated and tended to focus on psychological perceptions rather than linguistic performance – what was actually said by leaders. The trait approach is mainly concerned with psychological concepts such as extroversion, determination, self-confidence and dominance, rather than with a theory of communication. However certain communication traits have been observed to correlate with successful leadership; for example, research has indicated that the person who talked the most in leaderless group discussion tended to emerge as leader.[51] Other important traits include the ability to enhance memorability of messages, such as 'If you're not helping, you're hindering',[52] giving consistent messages and the timing of messages – for example, whether they occur early on or towards the end of a group interaction.[53]

The process approach emphasizes the interaction between leaders and followers. This is more in keeping with the basic premises of communication theory that – in addition to a communication channel and a communication medium – messages require both a sender and a transmitter – so it is not possible to consider leadership communication without considering the effect on followers. However, it does not differentiate between specific communication skills and facets of general interpersonal competence – such as creating perceptions among followers of being trustworthy and empathetic, and demonstrating insight. It has not yet identified what features of communication may lead to such perceptions.

The so-called 'style approach' of the Ohio and Michigan State Studies examine the relationship between 'task' and 'relationship' behaviours of leaders and followers' responses. One finding here is that the amount, or *quantity*, of talk is more important in task-oriented leadership whereas the *quality* of talk is more important in relationship-orientated leadership.[54] A number of other studies have emphasized the quality of communication and identified styles that lead to good relationships such as persuasiveness, explicitness and rhetorical sensitivity. Other positive leadership communication styles include being informative (by clarity of communication) and being trustworthy (by listening and engaging with others).

Many elements of leadership communication are shared by trait, process and style theories, these include: the communication of vision, inspiration, role modelling, intellectual stimulation, appeals to higher-order needs, empowerment, high expectations, and collective identity.[55] In a sense all of these are concerned with making meaning but there is a need for a model that integrates these diverse means and explains how they may work in different cultural contexts. In the following chapter I will argue for a theory of communication that is flexible enough to apply across cultures and that I describe as the *design of leadership style*.

Summary

We look to our leaders to provide answers to the questions that are as yet unresolved in our minds. They are people who are able to give form to the aspirations of followers seeking a better world. Change is always necessary because followers are not fully satisfied either with themselves or with aspects of the world around them – but are *unsure* as to what changes are necessary to improve the situation. Leaders are change agents who communicate the changes that are necessary and explain why they should be made. They do this by creating symbols that embody value systems and are able to articulate hidden or suppressed yearnings of followers. Leaders therefore communicate the things followers already half-know. This is why the messages of transformational leaders are rarely unfamiliar or unrecognized. Such leaders are able to remove the heavy responsibility of thought and truth seeking by *becoming* the symbols of their followers' needs, wants and desires.

The foregoing discussion argues in favour of the notion of leadership as a universal human phenomenon but one whose particular forms and shapes will be determined by specific historical and cultural factors. All human society shows evidence of symbolic communication by leaders; however, the type of symbols that are chosen by leaders will vary according to specific settings and determine the style of a leader. Because charismatic leaders occur in both western and non-western settings, it is worthwhile investigating their attributes and behaviours as a universal phenomenon. These may include external qualities that have positive associations in human society such as physical attributes (vigour, health, stamina, voice and eyes) and other attributes such as self-confidence and skill in communication. However, the values placed on particular symbols and attributes will be influenced by culture-specific factors. A great deal of research into leadership has been undertaken in relation to western societies and I believe that an understanding of leadership may be enhanced by an examination of leaders outside the west. This will first involve closer examination of something that is necessary for all leaders: a high level of skill in communication.

2 Non-verbal communication and leadership

Introduction: a theory of leadership communication

Recent approaches to communication see it as an interactive process in which participants exchange meanings in specific contexts using the full range of communicative resources that are available to them. In recent linguistic theory 'meaning' is not something that pre-exists in words or depends on the predefined senses available in dictionaries or grammars, but something that emerges from the mutual understanding, frames of reference and schematic knowledge that is shared by speech participants in actual communication settings. Since language is simply one amongst a range of human resources that include gestures, images, bodily contacts and even smells, communication theory is concerned with semiotics – or the emergence of meaning through rule-governed sign systems. Communication embraces the full range of senses:

> Recent writing across the humanistic and social science disciplines, not least anthropology, now increasingly explore the role of emotion and expressiveness as universal features of human life, querying the assumption that humans are, or ever could be, purely cognitive, verbal and rational creatures. Linguistic expression is only one special form amongst an array of communication modes that draw on looks, sound, feel, smell, taste etc.[1]

A semiotic approach is well suited to a study of non-western leaders because it rejects a cultural-centric point of view in which literary-based cultures are assumed to be superior to orally-based ones. A major argument of this work is that leadership is performed through the interaction of a range of intentional strategies and modes of communication in which verbal behaviour is only *one* component in the design of leadership style.

Leaders can draw on semiotic resources other than language and there are potentially 'grammars' or rules for each of the various modes of communication (sight, sound, touch etc.); a semiotic theory of leadership communication explains how these are integrated into a particular 'design'. Verbal strategies include the communication of a consistent message over time, a personal vision, a system of values and – closely related to this – of the legitimacy of the leader and his supporters. A primary verbal strategy for such communication is metaphor. Non-verbal semiotic modes – such as appearance and action – create symbolic meaning; I propose that metaphors and symbols contribute to the design of leadership style by interacting with the conscious and unconscious needs of followers. Leadership design is the combination and integration of semiotic resources for relevant social situations.

I propose that leaders internally design a unique communicative style that differentiates them from rivals and is a prelude to leadership performance. Although the design of leadership style – incorporating a range of choices as regards rhetorical strategy, mode and media – is a necessary precondition for leadership communication, there is also the need for leaders to put on an external performance that enacts leadership. Through his interest in external observation, the American sociologist, Erving Goffman, developed the concept of 'Front' that he defines as 'that part of an individual's performance which regularly functions in a general and fixed fashion to define the situation for those who observe the performance'.[2] He divides personal front into 'appearance' and 'manner' and while appearance is one of the non-verbal modes in leadership design, another is 'performance' that concerns the manner of dramatic realization: 'the individual typically infuses his activity with signs which dramatically highlight and portray confirmatory facts that might otherwise remain apparent or obscure'.[3] I will argue that typically leaders communicate a particular style through dramatic performances that I describe as 'symbolic actions'.

Symbolic actions are forms of action that encourage the development of a myth; they are similar to what Gardner and Avolio refer to as 'the dramaturgical process whereby leaders and followers jointly construct their identities'.[4] Symbolic actions may communicate kinaesthetically, through proxemics (the use of space), through the use of touch, or through vocalic features such as prosody and intonation (and other non-linguistic aspects of speech). In leadership performance, symbolic action could entail undertaking some form of extreme action that requires great physical stamina and entails suffering on behalf of the leader. This type of action is effective in leadership communication because it implies that the needs and desires of followers are such that the leader is prepared to make huge sacrifices for them and therefore *shares* their needs and desires. Followers identify experientially with leaders because they imagine themselves making these sacrifices – if only they could. Symbolic actions therefore create what Schlenker describes as a 'situated identity' which is defined as 'a theory of self that is wittingly or unwittingly constructed in a particular social situation or relationship';[5] this is one in which leaders identify with followers and followers identify with leaders.

The distinction between 'design of leadership style' and 'leadership performance' through 'symbolic action' corresponds with Goffman's distinction between an inner and a social self and between 'back' and 'front stage'. Design corresponds with the leader's inner sense of distinctiveness while symbolic action corresponds with the social self that performs. I have modified his use of the dramaturgical metaphor of an external 'back stage' physical space for performances to a mental space for the preparation of strategies, roles and disguises that are a prerequisite for performance; I describe this mental space as 'leadership design'. His 'front stage' enactment is equivalent to performance by symbolic action. Within the frame of the dramaturgical metaphor, the design of leadership style is analogous to the activity of the playwright, the selection of communication strategies equates to the activity of the producer, while performance is analogous to the actor's role.

A dramaturgical model is attractive in the development of a theory of leadership communication because of the inherent similarities between the situations of actors/audiences and leaders/followers as regards their mutual dependency:

> A leader has to resonate with followers. Part of being an effective leader is having excellent ideas, or a clear sense of direction, a sense of mission. But such ideas or vision are useless unless the would-be leader can communicate them and get them accepted by followers.[6]

Of course an actor's performance, equally, has to resonate with – and gain acceptance from – audiences. The appeal of Ronald Reagan to Americans in the 1980s was that his stereotypical good looks evoked positive memories from romantic 1950s Hollywood movies. The urbane charm communicated by the smiling eyes, the carefully groomed hair, the broad grin and the relaxed conversational manner enhanced his appeal. The 1950s saw the emergence of Hollywood as a global centre of cinema and it also saw the emergence of McCarthyism. The appearance of a Hollywood film star therefore contributed to a leadership style appropriate to the last Cold War leader. Arnold Schwarzenegger, who successfully became governor of California, presents a quite contrasting appeal; his height, and large, muscular physique gives a stereotypical impression of masculinity that is reinforced by the deep bass voice. This enhanced his appeal to a voting population desperately in need of a strong leader who could deal with the countless problems of the state.

Other American politicians, who were not actors, also possessed 'film star' looks. It significantly contributed to the charisma of John F. Kennedy and promoters of another good-looking leader, Bill Clinton, designed a magical transfer of this charisma by continuously replaying video clips of a handshake with Kennedy. Both Clinton and Kennedy designed their appearance to generate a dynamic dramaturgical appeal. What drama and leadership share is that they communicate through diverse semiotic modes (language, sound, appearance, action etc.) and rely – to varying degrees – on metaphors and symbols to communicate subliminal messages; above all, they stand or fall on whether or not they find resonance with their audience of followers.

A simplified overview of my theory of leadership communication is summarized in Figure 2.1.

I will define leadership communication as follows: leadership communication is an interactive process in which a leader intentionally influences, and is influenced by, followers employing a range of verbal strategies and a variety of non-linguistic modes; it is comprised of a design stage and a performance stage. In the remainder of this chapter I will outline the non-verbal modes of leadership communication while the following one will analyse the verbal mode. However, I will first provide an overview of the verbal and non-verbal components of the model shown in Figure 2.1.

Metaphor

The primary verbal strategy for the design of leadership style is the creation and use of metaphor. Metaphor involves a transfer of the meanings of words by taking them out of their original and expected contexts and placing them in new and unexpected ones – leaders choose words that create semantic tensions between their original and novel contexts of use.[7] Metaphors communicate visions and values and create the impression of the leader's self-legitimacy and the illegitimacy of his rivals. Charismatic leaders communicate a highly personal view of the world through the systematic

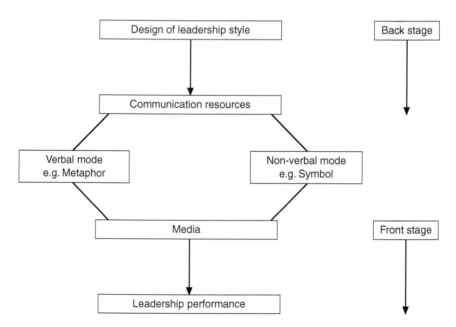

Figure 2.1 Model for leadership communication.

use of metaphor – often in combination with other rhetorical figures. Bennis
and Nanus have found empirical evidence of the importance of metaphors:

> We have found in our discussions with leaders that vision can often be
> communicated best by metaphors or models . . . In any communication,
> some distortion takes place, but the great leader seems to be able to find
> just the right metaphor that clarifies the idea and minimizes distortion.
> In fact, the right metaphor often transcends verbal communication
> altogether; like a good poem or song, it much more than mere words, It
> 'feels right', it appeals at the gut level, it resonates with the listener's
> own emotional needs, it somehow 'clicks'.[8]

What is important here is that leaders create ('find') *particular* metaphors
that latch into social meanings. Metaphors provide a conduit through which
followers may access their leader's world to find something that relates to
their innermost hopes, desires and aspirations – or to their deepest fears.
However, while the strategy of metaphor occurs across cultures, the actual
metaphors employed are highly dependent on the individual choices of
leaders that contribute to the unique design of leadership style. I will
discuss metaphor in more detail later in the analysis of the verbal mode in
the next chapter.

Symbol and myth

Leadership studies have noted the importance of symbols in communicating
leadership; for example, Bass observed how transforming leaders have
replaced existing symbols with new ones such as the swastika and the
hammer and sickle; he refers to Ataturk's outlawing of the fez as a symbol
of modernization, Roosevelt's New Deal, and de Gaulle's Cross of Lorraine
as a symbol for the old French virtues of honour, dignity and glory.[9] All
are examples of symbol change in which new symbols are designed to
replace old ones. On the basis of a study of 80 chief executives, Bennis found
that:

> they made extensive use of metaphor, symbolism, ceremonial, and
> insignia as ways of concretizing and transmitting their visions of what
> could be and committing their organizations to them.[10]

Why are symbols influential and persuasive in the design of leadership style?
Jung argued that cultural symbols 'Retain much of their original numinos-
ity or "spell" one is aware that they can evoke a deep emotional response in
some individuals, and this psychic charge makes them function in much the
same way as prejudices'.[11] Jung argues that scientific rationalism has dis-
placed symbols from their origins in man's relationship with nature onto the
individual psyche. Leaders are able to fill the sense of isolation that comes

from the loss of unconscious identity. The design of leadership style involves the individualization of communication by allowing metaphoric and symbolic elements to intermingle. While metaphors create tensions, symbols tend to overcome them – they are psychically healing. Style is most effective when it is coherent, that is, the metaphors and symbols fit together in performance to communicate a consistent message that appears to resist analysis.

Metaphors and symbols combine to produce myths. A myth is a story that provides an explanation of all the things for which explanations are necessary to resolve psychological tensions. These could be the origins of the universe, the causes of good and evil, the origin of the elements or anything else that is believed to be mysterious. Myth engages the hearer by providing a narrative that embodies a set of beliefs and expresses aspects of the unconscious. Myth symbolizes intangible experiences that are evocative because they are unconsciously linked either to life-affirming forces, or to death-confirming ones. Myth is therefore a two-sided response to the conscious and the unconscious. Its function in discourse is to explain the unknown and leaders use it to gain power because it removes uncertainty and therefore satisfies deep psychic needs for security and reassurance. Myth can be communicated by verbal strategies and non-verbal modes; the primary verbal strategy is through metaphors and the primary non-verbal mode is through symbols and through what I call the performance of symbolic action that I will explain later in this chapter.

Media

Media are the means employed for the dissemination of meaning. The development of modern media has enhanced the resources available for the performance of leadership. The radio permitted a much greater use of subtle prosodic features such as voice quality and texture; for example, Churchill's gravelly voice was important in communicating attributes essential to a war leader such as strength, conviction and reliability. The radio and the television are both domestic media and the leader is now invited into the privacy of the living room – creating opportunities for the design of intimacy. With the development of television, leaders' visual appearance – how they look, what they wear – has become another aspect of leadership design, and as Bass notes:

> Television has both helped and complicated the image-building and image-maintaining aspects of the charismatic leader's efforts. The brevity and selective editing capabilities can be used to protect the image, but the live camera is also a force for bringing reality into the living room. Events favorable to the image can be staged, but events unfavorable to the image can also dramatically show up as if the leader was face-to face with supporters.[12]

A number of British leaders have been unsuccessful because of unfavourable images: these include Michael Foot, Neil Kinnock and, more recently, Robin Cook. All are passionate and articulate verbal communicators but have not been naturally endowed with appearances conducive to positive media representations. This contrasts with others who have been shown to be highly skilled exponents of media design – such as Tony Blair, John F. Kennedy, Ronald Reagan and Bill Clinton. The effect of communication varies according to the media – the use of hand gesture is much more effect-ive outside a broadcasting studio because it appears exaggerated and there-fore distracting on television. Other non-linguistic modes of appearance, such as looks, dress and voice quality, communicate symbolically, but the particular blend will vary according to the media deployed by the leader. A general theory for leadership communication style will need to explore diverse semiotic modes. These modes include physical appearance, dress, body language, artefacts, symbolic action (all of which contribute to sym-bolic meaning), and verbal strategies. How particular leaders deploy com-munication modes in performance is influenced by cultural factors; for example, leaders will vary in the extent to which their symbols and metaphors evoke religious secondary meanings.

Given the importance of multi-modal communication skills, it is surprising how little research there has been specifically into the communi-cation skills of successful leaders – or any systematic analysis of the linguis-tic characteristics of persuasive leadership discourse across cultures. The most we have is fairly general statements such as the following: 'In order to present a charismatic image, they should be trained in four areas: modelling (the use of exemplary behaviour), appearance, body language, and verbal skills'.[13] A major objective of this work is to remedy this situation. The communication of leadership is a complex process involving the interaction of a number of different modes – of which the verbal, or linguistic, is only one. The design of a leadership style manifests itself both verbally and non-verbally – through metaphor and symbol, however the overall effect of design in performance is greater than each of the separate stylistic elements because their effect is cumulative. I will begin by analysing the various non-linguistic modes of communication style.

The non-linguistic communication of leadership

The non-linguistic modes of leadership communication are physical appearance, dress and body language, artefacts, symbols and symbolic communication.

Physical appearance

Physical appearance is a very important and under-researched mode of leadership communication; trait approaches have tended to focus on psychological rather than physiological or anatomical attributes, and therefore rather exaggerate the extent to which anyone can become a leader. Evidence of the importance of appearance in the creation of charisma can be found by the success that actors have had in entering politics – but not everyone can become an actor. When we think of actors who have been successful in politics – such as those mentioned above – it is easy to see how aspects of their appearance were designed to transfer associations created by their acting roles to their political image.

Moreover, the lure of appearance is not restricted to western cultures. In the Indian subcontinent there has also been an easy career move from the domains of acting and sport into politics. A good example here would be the Pakistani cricketer Imran Khan who became a significant charismatic political leader. Similarly, in India, the heroes of traditional Indian myths and the appeal of the heroic warriors of the Ramayana have influenced the attributes necessary for successful political leadership. A muscular build signifies strength, facial hair symbolizes virility and good looks signify high moral standing. Evidently, there are cultural variations – for example, a hirsute appearance has a much stronger association with positive physical and moral traits in Arabic and in Indian culture than it does in western or Asiatic culture where it may create suspicion. Though beards symbolize wisdom and knowledge (based on age and experience) in most traditional religious cultures, they have become more closely associated with religious fundamentalism: Osama bin Laden's beard is a powerful leader semiotic. Many early western visual representations of God show him with a beard and, while Abraham Lincoln, Disraeli and Lenin all had beards; facial hair has now become rare among western leaders.

A particular aspect of appearance that is commented on in the literature is the eyes and gaze of charismatic leaders.[14] 'The pipeline into our psyche'[15] and as Finnegan notes: 'hostility, anger, affection, welcome, accessibility, amusement, reserve, suspicion, embarrassment, boredom or love – all can be conveyed through the eyes'.[16] Very few successful politicians wear spectacles because they obscure the eyes and this is probably because the eyes communicate subliminally with followers. Charles Manson is said to have had hypnotic eyes and other religious leaders such as Bhagwan Shree Rajneesh are also claimed to have had magnetic eyes that could lock into the gaze of each individual. Eye size can be important and some leaders, such as Tony Benn are perceived as having large eyes.[17] The visible areas of whiteness around the eyes have an important evolutionary significance in making it easier for observers to track eye movements. Physical movements such as blinking become more noticeable and these apparently small physical gestures have gained in importance with the increased use of close-ups in television. Successful charismatic leaders such as Ronald Reagan, Tony Blair and Fidel Castro have always found it easy to look into the camera lens – and this has been of value in visual representations such as news photographs and political posters.

Further evidence of the importance of the eyes in the design of leadership is that a hypnotist asks his 'patient' to look into his eyes and in doing so is able to immerse him in an unconscious mental state that is detached from the world. It is the gaze that permits the follower-patient to establish a complete rapport with the leader- hypnotist – so long as he is unaware of the latter's intentions.[18] In many social situations the direction of the gaze indicates the relative social status of participants; with lowered eyes and brief glances indicating a lower status role. Awareness of the subliminal effect of the eyes was shown by the advertising agency Saatchi and Saatchi in the 1997 election campaign when they replaced Tony Blair's eyes with those of the devil. However, the intention to demonize the bespectacled John Major's opponent was not sufficiently subtle and clashed with the media image of Tony Blair as 'Bambi' – the baby deer, with large soft brown eyes: the message failed because it was not coherent with other visual messages that had already become established.

Appearance has, of course, become essential to the communication of charisma by leaders in the world of music, fashion and design; Michael Jackson's transformation of his original Negroid features to those of an apparently white American have been widely discussed – although at the same time an important issue has been the degree to which it has been intentional – he claims, for example, that the white pigmentation of his skin is the result of an illness; this raises the important point that while leaders may seek to manage impressions, the design of leadership style should never appear to be a conscious act or its magical effect is diminished: design should necessarily be invisible.

Dress and body language

Dress choice is another mode that communicates the design of leadership style. What is significant about the 'language' of dress is that – unlike other aspects of appearance – such as physical features – it is something that is readily transformed. Dress communicates messages for particular audiences and – like language – needs to be consistent with the image that is being designed for a particular communication setting. In western business circles dress is commonly used to provide subliminal – although not always well concealed – messages regarding the status and power of the wearer. The Crombie coat, the Hermes tie (with badge on the outer side) and double-cuffed shirts are all intended to represent status, wealth and power. In order to fit with his intended audience and message Tony Blair wore a bomber jacket before announcing the Allied attacks on Afghanistan in 2002. On a trip to Australia in 2002 he wore a Paul Smith shirt featuring naked women on the cuffs, and a blue Nicole Farhi jumper to indicate a 'laidback' attitude. The extent to which dress choice is effective in communicating its intended subliminal purpose is difficult to gauge – except when it clashes with the setting and indicates an error of style – so it is perhaps something that is easier to get wrong than to get right because of its normative role in communication: it creates identification with specific social groups and excludes others. Finnegan provides an example of such an error of dress judgement:

> Witness the furore over the 'disrespect' conveyed by the then leader of the Labour party Michael Foot when he attended a national cenotaph ceremony in duffel coat, not formal suit.[19]

In non-western contexts selection of dress is also a particularly powerful symbolic statement by leaders. Leaders of nations who wish to ally themselves with 'the west' chose formal western dress to symbolize reduced cultural difference. The standard attire of western businessmen – suit, collared shirt with cufflinks and tie – has spread to cultures where this dress was not traditionally worn by the powerful – such as Japan and Korea. By contrast, informal western or indigenous dress is chosen by leaders who have either sought to identify with global ideologies – such as Communism or Islam – or with native ethnic or religious traditions. African leaders may on occasion wear tribal dress, and Asian leaders may wear traditional dress to communicate an ethnic identity. In some cases western dress emphasizes historic identities – such as the gown and mortarboard of western academics, the ermine of royalty, or that worn by those with religious roles such as the Pope. However, we should differentiate between dress that communicates by reinforcing a traditional status arising from a position in an institutional hierarchy and dress that communicates because its choice forms part of a *unique*, or stylistic, leadership design.

Gandhi chose to wear the dress of the humble Indian peasant to symbolize his proximity to the common man, but it was not a requirement of an Indian political figure. Castro is usually seen wearing some type of military uniform – but not the smart type worn by westerners. In Mandela's 1994 election campaign: 'He would sometimes change his clothes three or four times a day – from a suit for a business breakfast, to an open shirt for a village crowd, to a woolly cardigan for a visit to the old people'.[20] By comparison, an aide of de Klerk's complained about him wearing the same golfing jacket – this was not intentional but rather because he did not understand symbolic communication. Nelson Mandela wears highly patterned Indonesian shirts to symbolize the cross-cultural appeal of his message of the essential brotherhood of man. In Islamic cultures traditional dress reinforces claims to be a traditional religious leader. The holy clothing, usually white and flowing, of the ayatollahs is believed to symbolize purity of intent and an affiliation with the unchanging values of the Koran.

Dress needs to be coherent with other aspects of appearance and with body language. For example, Osama Bin Laden used Islamic clothing and a noble bearing to communicate charisma to his followers. Video clips posted on the internet show him wearing elegant robes; he is not usually static but moving gracefully. This is a coherent image that is intentionally designed and performed through media presentation.

Artefacts

I define artefacts as material objects that are characteristically associated with a leader because they typify individual likes and preferences as well as social roles. They have become of increasing importance with the emergence of new approaches to material culture, for example in anthropology and in museology. Artefacts are important in a multi-modal approach to leadership because they are multi-sensory means by which leaders symbolize their individual style and convey messages about their values, taste, power and status; for example, the BlackBerry portable communication system is preferred by corporate executives seeking to communicate a high-status image. Conversely, the wearing of simple, rubber, charity wristbands symbolizes empathy with contemporary values by showing affiliation with the social cause of the charity concerned (and perhaps with charity in general). Their production value is low and they symbolize a rejection of status based on wealth.

In some cases the same artefacts may have different stylistic meanings depending on cultural associations. For Winston Churchill, the cigar signified a leader who had time to enjoy life's simple pleasures – and who was sufficiently in control to allow him small leisure-time luxuries. It also carried connotations of the untroubled leisured life of the upper classes because cigars were an expensive luxury item during wartime Britain; it was therefore a symbol of reassurance. For Fidel Castro the cigar is also a statement of hedonistic enjoyment of life's pleasures (thereby countering charges of Communism being opposed to pleasure). However, it also has another meaning of *opposing* high social status: the cigar symbolizes Cuba's economic independence as the producer of a product exported internationally because of its high reputation for quality. Stalin was regularly photographed smoking a pipe – again, as with Churchill, a reassuring image of a man with the ordinary pleasures of domestic life and worthy, therefore, of trust.

In charismatic leadership the artefacts belonging to a leader are sometimes considered to take on magical powers and are subsequently revered in museums or mausoleums. Gandhi's spinning wheel communicated both his own favoured personal pastime but also became both a spiritual and political symbol of Indian independence and was integrated into the national flag. Artefacts can also take on an ironic status of bathos – as, for example, the excessive clothing of Eva Peron, or Imelda Marcos's shoes. An artefact such as a walking stick can symbolize loss of former vigour, and – like physical characteristics such as baldness – satirists may exploit the symbolism of the artefact in political cartoons. African sculptors satirized their new colonial rulers by creating wooden effigies of them with red faces and wearing pith helmets.

In some cases artefacts combine with dress in communicating leadership – for example, in the wearing of medals and emblems. Brezhnev was often satirized for wearing a grand display of self-awarded medals. When Castro was about to embark on revolution at the age of 33 he:

was a Marxist and atheist, but he knew how to exploit the religious feelings of others, A medallion of the Virgin of Cober, Cuba's most revered image, was visible around his neck. He encouraged the legend that the Movement had started with twelve men. The temptation to create a parallel with Christ's apostles was too great to be resisted.[21]

This is a typical case of exploiting the magical potential of artefacts to become symbols in leadership performance as the leader adopts the positive associations of the artefact. The physically closer it is to his person, the more likely that transfer will occur – hence clothing or jewellery has special magical potential. Another type of magical dress is disguise: during his time in hiding in the early 1960s, Nelson Mandela became known as the 'Black Pimpernel' and took on a range of disguises to evade his eventual captors.

Symbols

A crucial non-linguistic mode in the design of leadership style is the creation and use of symbols. Carl Jung proposed that 'Whatever the unconscious may be, it is a natural phenomenon producing symbols that prove to be meaningful'.[22] A symbol is an entity that has a secondary meaning or signification – as Carl Jung puts it:

> Thus a word or an image is symbolic when it implies something more than its obvious and immediate meaning. It has a wider 'unconscious' aspect that is never precisely defined or fully explained.[23]

Leaders satisfy the unconscious needs of followers through providing them with symbolic meanings. For example, as well as a means of personal conveyance, a car usually symbolizes the attributes of its owner; similarly, dress or clothing, as well as keeping us warm (and preserving our modesty) often symbolizes something about the person wearing it: a shirt with the red cross of St George symbolizes a patriotic Englishman, a black and white chequered scarf symbolizes support for Palestine.

I propose that unlike metaphor, a symbol is *not* verbal and can be defined as any two or three-dimensional non-linguistic mode that has a secondary meaning. Because the meaning of a symbol is not the primary one, there is an inherent indirectness of meaning and its power often relies in its resistance to conscious analysis. The meaning and value placed on a particular symbol depends on its status in the culture: the wearing of a poppy in Britain communicates historical memory, and a conservative outlook, but placing a flower in the barrel of a soldier's gun symbolizes opposition to war that can be traced to the anti-Vietnam war 'flower power' movement in the United States. Symbols also therefore have a kinaesthetic dimension and form part of a dramatic ritual whose meaning is influenced by culture: Indian greeting rituals require presenting the guest with a garland of flowers. Symbols have long been important in political communication through the use of a range of media. Images can be lithographed onto silk, ribbons, rosettes, etc. and other materials such as metals, wood and plastic are used in making badges, buttons or jewellery.

Symbolic meanings arise by appealing to some form of conventional meaning – like drama, symbols 'tell' a certain type of 'story' because they latch onto social myths. Symbols permit followers' beliefs to merge with those of their leader (and with each others') as described in symbolic convergence theory:

> symbolic convergence theory[24] is based on the assumption that people view reality through a personal set of narratives, which represent 'the truth' of how the world is ... Once a group has accepted a shared set of narratives, it now also shares a symbol system and the views of its members have 'converged'.[25]

When groups of people share the same set of meanings, they share a common view of reality that corresponds with their common values, attitudes and beliefs and can form the basis for decisions and action.[26] This theory corresponds well with House's view of leadership as something that is attributed to leaders by followers[27] and with Gardner and Avolio's dramaturgical perspective on leadership.[28] Followers, like audiences, interact with leaders in the creation of an identity and I suggest that symbols play a crucial role in mediating this interrelationship.

Symbols – like metaphors – have the power to move followers but unlike metaphors (which can be extended or reversed) are resilient to change because they resist analysis:

> In terms of cognitive processing, symbols are influential for two important reasons. First symbols elicit strong emotions ... (based on) some enduring predisposition towards the symbol ... Second, symbols are likely to become chronically accessible constructs, which may make them impossible to counter or to modify.[29]

However, they can sometimes be modified – for example, the anti-war movement challenged the potential for implied support for war (and possible covert militarism) of the *red* poppy by designing a *white* poppy; but is not easy for symbols to become ironic because they tend to simplify:

> the condensation of complicated meaning into symbols fulfils citizens' need for cognitive reduction ... and relieves them of the burdens of the search for information and deliberative decision making.[30]

Symbols tend to invite acceptance rather than critical reflection by providing entry into a set of social meanings and inviting membership into the security of a group. This is a powerful form of leadership communication because it implies that it is the leader (usually with the assistance of a team – such as the Party, the executives, or professional meaning-makers) who will take on the responsibility of thinking and decision-making. The design of leadership style therefore requires attention to the creation of the symbols that will be employed to communicate leadership.

Symbolic action and performance

Examples of symbolic actions would include the following: kinaesthetic actions such as Mandela's raising of two clenched fists when greeting ANC supporters, or Gadafi driving a bulldozer into Libyan customs posts to symbolize the end of national frontiers within the greater Maghreb, or Khomeini's unexpectedly flight from Paris to Tehran in February 1979.[31] A symbolic action can be highly dramatic act – such as that of the eighteenth century Moroccan tyrant, Moulay Ismail: 'It is one of his common diversions, at one motion, to mount his horse, draw his cimiter, and cut off the head of the slave who holds his stirrup'.[32] As Goffman points out:

> Power of any kind must be clothed in effective means of displaying it, and will have different effects depending upon how it is dramatized . . . Thus the most objective form of naked power i.e. physical coercion, is often neither objective nor naked but rather functions as a display for persuading the audience; it is often a means of communication, not merely a means of action.[33]

As I have argued above, symbolic actions are the means by which messages conceived by the 'inner' leader as part of his leadership design are externally performed and are intended to create myths in the minds of followers.

Autocratic leaders adopt multiple roles – as sportsman, playboy, military leader – to symbolize their exemplary performance of dramatic roles and their exemplary symbolic actions are disseminated by the media. Multiple images of a leader engaged in physical motion – either in photographs or on television – represent him as a catalyst. Saddam Hussein established himself as all-powerful by appearing in popular everyday settings such as the market or the sports stadium, but the image was reinforced by ubiquitous visual representation in these roles. Multiplicity was accentuated by his dramaturgical use of actor-doubles – confusing the image with the reality. Marcel Mauss suggested that in modern societies the 'social self' was only able to express itself fully through a multiplicity of roles and situations that are unconnected.[34] They only become meaningful because they match with generic social roles and leaders communicate by symbolic actions that accumulate through the media to create myths of leadership. Symbolic actions are those where the leaders imagine ideal representations – as others might see them, through the lens of a camera.

Symbolic kinaesthetic actions tend to differ between cultures; western leaders communicate through displaying physical health and vigour. George W. Bush is regularly filmed while jogging or engaged in other physical activities such as wood-chopping on the ranch and British politicians rarely miss an opportunity to be seen kicking a football. They often seek to appear youthful and dynamic by participating in sporting activities. These images communicate an ancillary message that the leader is in good health and unlikely to be suffering an illness that could interfere with their leadership, rather than communicating divine motivation or magical influence. Physical energy can also be communicated through speed and intensity of movement. During the Cuban missile crisis Khruschev reinforced his image as a direct and dynamic leader – a man of the people with little concern for protocol – by removing a shoe and hammering it on the table to reinforce a point at a United Nations meeting.

Symbolic kinaesthetic actions may play quite different roles in designing leadership in non-western societies. For example, leaders may undertake a task that requires enormous physical endurance such as a fast, a very long march, or a vow of silence. Gandhi's fasting had a particular significance in a nation where many people were often hungry for much of the time. Long journeys by foot requiring physical endurance were also important to the charismatic appeal of leaders such as Mao Tse-tung. This is not because they communicated health but because going beyond what is physically possible for most ordinary mortals is a way of identifying with a divine motivation. Other types of symbolic action are common in most cultures; for example, being filmed at prayer can occur in any society where religion has a potent symbolic appeal.

The performance of another act of exceptional physical prowess and stamina that communicates a heroic status is the marathon swim. On 16 July 1966 at the age of 72 Mao Tse-tung leapt in to the Yangtze river and swam 15 kilometres apparently breaking all Olympic records for a swim of this length (until we realize the strength of the current). As he wrote 'for many years I thought about how to administer the revisionists in the party a shock . . . And finally I conceived this'. The effect on one of his followers was significant:

> Chairman, we have been following you for many years but did not know you were such a great swimmer, a man of such strong determination. When you were young you said 'struggle against heaven, struggle against earth, struggle against people – the happiness is endless.' This is really true. After swimming with you today, our happiness is endless. We have learned a great deal from the Chairman. I hope you continue to teach us more and criticize us more in the future.[35]

In fact, Mao was an obsessive outdoor swimmer and would challenge the anxieties of his security guards by embarking on ambitious swims with little prior warning. Prior to coming to power, Saddam Hussein evaded his captors by swimming across the River Tibus and then subsequently turned this event into an annual event in which supporters were encouraged to participate. Nelson Mandela rose at 5.30am to undertake an hour or more of intense physical exercise throughout his years in prison. Exceptional physical abilities contribute to the design of charismatic leadership style especially when they can be traced to divine origin and symbolize life, strength, energy, vigour and health.

Goffman argues that part of the performance of an individual concerns what is concealed from others as well as what is communicated to them, and that controlling what is communicated by concealment itself communicates social power.[36] Kenneth Burke also argued that audiences were held in a state of mystification in regard to the performer. This is especially the case with leaders: the greater the access to them, the more their mystique is potentially undermined. Leaders typically employ bodyguards, and, increasingly, communication, press and media relations' officers whose sole function is to reduce direct communication with them. Leaders set clearly defined boundaries around themselves and withdraw backstage to enhance their communication of authority. Gandhi periodically withdrew from social life by going to live in his ashram, regularly observing a day of silence, and this restriction on verbal communication was a form of non-verbal communication of spiritual control through symbolic action.

So far I have considered symbolic action in terms of representations and actions, but there is also an important dimension of leadership communication that is concerned with movement and location. A physical estrangement from society symbolizes death, but the return of the leader from isolation, exile or imprisonment symbolizes resurrection. The period of withdrawal in a natural or man-made wilderness is often the basis for Riesman's notion of the inner-directed leader:

> Such a leader has a highly developed and well populated inner life as a result of introjecting early objects and later identifying with objects, symbols, and ideals which have some connection to the introjects. The imagos, or internal audience exert a powerful influence on the leader, and form the basis for the ties he establishes with the masses.[37]

I propose that movement-related symbolic actions realize these internalized concepts. The return of the charismatic leader corresponds with the mythic pattern of a hero returning from a forced journey. The physical journey is a mythical one that symbolizes the journey of the spirit after death. This occurs in the Arthurian legend and in both the Christian idea of resurrection and the Muslim insurrectionary leaders known as the Mahdi. Travel on long journeys – as undertaken by Mao Tse-tung or Buddha – communicate a social detachment – permitting the growth of inner knowledge. The regenerative power of journeys is something that potentially has a universal, mythic appeal.

Leaders such as de Gaulle, Mandela and Lenin also underwent periods of enforced separation during which they were able to return as living embodiments of ideas they had developed while physically and socially removed. Both the separation and the return are to be considered as movement-based symbolic actions. The conditions that encourage the emergence of charisma are when the psychological, physical or spiritual instability of a society find resonance with the message brought from the wilderness by a detached individual on a mission. Great leaders undertake symbolic actions evoking emotional responses by integrating the social realities of followers with their own deep spiritual needs.

A further symbolic action that stimulates mythic beliefs among potential followers is a leader's ability to evade pursuers – by disguise and disappearance – and then, unexpectedly, reappear. By avoiding capture through changing appearance, the leader performs as if he has supernatural powers and arouses followers' numinous instincts; this is especially effective for *oppressed* followers. Disappearance has long been a tactic employed by charismatic guerrilla leaders to stimulate beliefs about their magical powers. It was used by Ho Chi Minh, Mao, Che Guevara, Castro and Mandela and is often employed by a leader who is undergoing exile or anticipates doing so in the future. Close knowledge of the terrain and the support of loyal followers makes magical disappearance much more feasible. Reappearances are used when leaders arrive unexpectedly at the site of conflict; such unexpectedness can raise the morale of followers as it suggests a strategist who is capable of the unexpected. Symbolic action – either kinaesthetic or movement-related – is therefore vital to the communication of leadership style, but there are significant differences between cultures as to the nature and effect of particular symbolic acts.

Summary

In this chapter I have argued that a range of multi-modal, verbal and non-linguistic communication modes contribute to the semiotics of leadership that I describe as the design of leadership style. I have suggested that metaphors and symbols are especially important in the creation of myths. I have identified a range of non-linguistic modes of communication including appearance, dress, artefacts, the creation of symbols, and symbolic actions and shown how cultural factors influence the forms these take. I have shown how symbolic actions can be kinaesthetic or movement-based and argued that symbolic meanings are formed by performances such as kinaesthetic actions or by withdrawal and disappearance since both can mystify followers. I have argued that a dramaturgical model is appropriate for leadership communication because leaders engage with followers in creating mutually dependent systems of meaning in exactly the same way as playwrights and producers engage with audiences. I have distinguished between a stage of internal reflection or 'design' from a 'performance' stage in which designs are realized.

We will see in the following chapters how leaders perform leadership communication by designing styles that are distinct; however, something that they all communicate is self-belief. If leadership is fundamentally a drama, then it is essential that the leader communicate self-belief so that the performance is interpreted as sincere and genuine – rather than spurious. Since language also contributes significantly to this, I will consider it in the next chapter.

3 Verbal communication, leadership and the media

Introduction

There is general agreement in the research into leadership that verbal communication skills contribute to success. In this chapter I identify strategies such as the use of metaphor, I explain why it is rhetorically effective and outline a method known as Critical Metaphor Analysis, I then explain the role of visions, values, legitimacy and myth in leadership communication before considering the role of the media; initially I consider some social psychological aspects of the stylistic features of leadership communication.

Social psychological approaches explore the interaction between a speaker's verbal behaviour and the audience's response through measuring observable evidence of approval such as applause. A number of strategies for evoking applause have been identified including favourable reference to 'us' and unfavourable reference to 'them', three-part lists, contrastive pairs, timing and gesture; these are all employed either to constrain, or to invite, audience applause.[1] For example, cross-cultural research shows that chanting regularly occurred in response to Ayatollah Khomeini's use of three-part-lists and contrasts in his speeches. Analytical approaches imply that there are a limited number of strategies that can attract audience approval; however, it seems more likely that the design of leadership styles requires – intentionally or unintentionally – a unique synthesis of strategies. A charismatic leader develops a style by finding a balance between the familiar and the novel, the verbal and the non-verbal and the numinous appeal of both may be rooted in the subconscious. The design of leadership communication therefore requires effective integration of the verbal and non-verbal.

In charismatic leadership, it is likely that speaking style is probably more important than what is actually said. Martin Luther King's style was characterized by exploiting the rhythmic and melodic potential of the human voice; his 'calm-to-storm' delivery and call and response exchanges[2] were rhetorical strategies developed over generations by black pulpit preachers for creating interaction with followers. Such techniques involved citing familiar phrases from hymns or quotations from the Bible to which the audience could respond; this creates a sense of expectancy as to when the next response opportunity will occur. The development of a style that had emerged as part of the cultural tradition of African-Americans, through the historical experience of slavery, was therefore vital in heightening the level of audience attentiveness. However, it was also by individual innovation in timing and voice quality that Dr King re-designed a culturally familiar vocal prosody into a unique leadership style.

The Iraqi Shi-ite leader Ayatollah Ali Sistani rarely talks above the level of a whisper, and this has a number of effects: it enhances his appeal as a man of the spirit and it ensures that the audience will have to strain to hear him. This style also differentiates him from the more aggressive ranting of other ayatollahs. One charismatic technique used by Tony Benn (probably unconsciously) is to interrupt audience applause by recommencing his speech *before the applause is fully spent*. Because the audience ceases to applaud in order to hear what he is saying, gratification is not fully expressed and so desire is dammed up – only to overflow once the opportunity is given. This design of communication style creates rhetorical tension through a build-up of unreleased emotion. One needs, then, in any consideration of the verbal communication of charisma to consider the specific strategies through which prosodic features, timing and gesture interact with what is actually said. This is an important component of the design of communication style.

Metaphor

I have defined a metaphor as 'a linguistic representation that results from the shift in the use of a word or phrase from a context or domain in which it is expected to occur to another context or domain where it is not expected to occur, thereby causing semantic tension'.[3] Metaphor implies that there is a *change* in the sense of words and therefore there are *two* domains: a source where the word normally occurs and a target where it does not. Crucially, metaphor is a matter of our *expectations* – based on our previous experience of language; therefore, it is a *relative* rather than an absolute concept. However, this definition applies to metaphor in general, whereas in political discourse there is also the choice between using a conventional and a novel metaphor, or some blend between the two, since, increasingly, the conventional intermingles with the subversive.

In fact, political leaders show a strong tendency to use metaphors from familiar source domains. Research I have undertaken of more than 2,000 metaphors used by western political leaders shows that journey metaphors and personifications account for over 37 per cent of these, and over 55 per cent come from only five domains.[4] However, within these very familiar domains, politicians often blend the familiar with the novel; for example, Tony Blair develops journey metaphors in nominal forms such as: 'journey of change', a 'journey of renewal', 'journey of modernization' and even a 'journey of convenience'. It has been argued that:

There is a very strong possibility that the use of metaphor is a deliberate tactic on the part of many leaders, thereby adding weight to the notion that powerful oratory is in large part stage-managed and an important ingredient of the social formation of charisma.[5]

I would add that the design of leadership style is often more effective when familiar metaphors are extended. For this reason it is important to consider the relationship between metaphor and leadership further.

Metaphors are particularly effective in communicating leadership because they integrate conscious with unconscious knowledge by drawing on what is known, to explain what is unknown or only partially known. They are familiar words often employed in new ways to provide insights and permit exploration of possibilities without final commitment to them. The essence of metaphor is a process of interaction that creates tension between the expected and unexpected, and a process of interpretation that arises when possible meanings are explored. Since expectations are subjective, the effect of metaphors is likely to vary between individuals making it somewhat unpredictable. Leaders are able to exploit this unpredictability to produce metaphors in which followers can invest their own meanings.

The domain of war arouses our emotions by creating a vital contrast between life and death; it activates the many powerful unconscious instincts, based in a desire for survival, that Freud described as the life and death instincts and the polarity of such opposites creates great tension. I have demonstrated how Margaret Thatcher very successfully exploited conflict metaphors for a heroic self-evaluation and a demonic evaluation of socialism.[6] Conflict metaphors are ubiquitous in British political discourse and are invariably associated with attributes that appeal to the emotions such as strength, courage and determination; this is why Tony Blair also uses them. Moreover, in a comparative study of English and German financial reporting we found that conflict metaphors were much more common in English than in German.[7] This alerts us to the potential for cultural differences – even within the west – implying the likelihood of even greater differences between unrelated cultures. Metaphor always has a persuasive role when it accesses an underlying social and cultural value system and part of leadership design is in selecting metaphors that are persuasive in a particular discourse context.

Metaphor represents a certain way of viewing the world that reflects a shared system of belief as to what the world is, and culture-specific beliefs about mankind's place in it. It offers a way of looking at the world that may differ from the way we normally look at it and offers some fresh insight. Leaders need to innovate by showing followers new ways of looking at problems and may draw on metaphor because of its combination of explaining new ideas with influencing the emotional response to them. It activates emotional associations in order to influence followers' beliefs, attitudes and values. Because we are more aware of the effect of changes in our emotional

state than what causes them, these associations are generally not ones followers are fully conscious of. Metaphor *provokes* affective responses by exploiting
the associative power of language; associations may be specific to a culture,
or they may be universal.

Gardner and Avolio explain why arousing positive feelings is vital to the
successful communication of leadership:

> Charismatic presentations to followers that produce self-enhancing iden-
> tification with the leader and/or his or her collective vision elicit high
> levels of emotional arousal among followers and positive affect for the
> leader; such positive affect is accentuated further when followers' self-
> esteem and self-efficacy are elevated by leader expressions of confidence
> in the followers.[8]

As well as heightening emotional impact, or pathos, metaphors are effective
in persuading because they can influence arguments by causing conceptual
shifts – by leading the audience to understand something in a new way.
Musolff explains this as follows:

> I propose to regard political metaphors as integral aspects of argumenta-
> tive reasoning, i.e. reasoning which typically aims to prove a contested
> issue and thus to legitimize a certain course of action, If metaphors can
> be deemed to lead to conclusions that 'bind' politicians and states, they
> must function in someway like warrants in an argument, i.e. they must
> appear to give a valid justification for using particular premises in order
> to arrive at a certain conclusion.[9]

The basis of the argumentative role for metaphors is the psychological
association between the attributes of the original referent of a metaphor (i.e.
of a word in its source domain) and those of the metaphor target. This
association must be transparent enough for the hearer to understand, but
different enough to create the semantic tension that is necessary for
metaphor to exist in the first place. The nature of the association is determined by culturally-specific values. As we have seen, physical conflict is positively evaluated in British culture where mental and physical strength and
sporting prowess are all positive. However, Buddhist culture, that places a
value on all forms of human life, may not evaluate conflict metaphors positively because they conflict with the ideal of harmony. Therefore, when these
metaphors are used, they transfer a set of culturally-based psychological
associations and beliefs.

The fact that metaphors also permit individual interpretation is very
important in the language of leaders who have not yet fully formulated fixed
objectives because they allow the integration of what is possible and hypo-
thetical with what is known from experience. Metaphors draw on the familiar to communicate the unfamiliar. Leaders who resonate with followers are

those who permit them to find something of *themselves* in the ideals offered by leaders. Their metaphors are rhetorically effective because they are specific enough to provide a sense of engagement with the values of an organization, psychologically attractive because they permit followers to dispose of their unwanted selves, and strategically effective because they do not prescribe the outcomes in advance.

The main claims I have made in this section are that metaphors form an important part of leadership design by activating unconscious and especially emotional needs, hopes and desires of followers but they also consciously communicate political arguments because associations carry with them a set of implied meanings. I have also suggested that one of the major rhetorical advantages that metaphors have for leaders is that they permit a high degree of rhetorical flexibility and do not commit leaders to fixed objectives. There is almost limitless potential for leaders to select metaphors that communicate a unique style and effective metaphors are sufficiently general for followers to place their own interpretations. The rhetorical advantages of metaphor stretch beyond particular cultural settings, though the actual metaphors used are influenced by knowledge of specific cultural and social values. It will be interesting to note how far non-western leaders share the same metaphors as western leaders and whether there are metaphors specific to individual leaders.

Critical Metaphor Analysis

Critical Metaphor Analysis is an approach to the analysis of metaphors that aims to represent the intentions underlying language use and is therefore important in analysing the design of leadership style.[10] It involves first identifying metaphors, then interpreting and explaining them. To assist in this process I employ the cognitive semantic approach originally described in Lakoff and Johnson's classic work *Metaphors We Live by*, and developed in their later work.[11] The basic claim of this approach is that most abstract concepts are in some way grounded in our bodily experience even though we may not be aware of this; therefore, thought is typically metaphorical and conceptual in nature. A conceptual metaphor takes the form *A is B* in which A is a metaphor target (an area of experience that is described by metaphor) and B is a metaphor vehicle (words or phrases from a particular lexical field that comprise the metaphor). For example, expressions in which the target UNDERSTANDING is described by a lexical item from the lexical field of SEEING – such as 'I see', 'the sense is clear', 'can you cast any light on this?', 'your meaning is transparent' – are evidence of a conceptual metaphor UNDERSTANDING IS SEEING. In this case, since vision is our primary sense it can be used metaphorically to refer to comprehension arising from all senses and knowledge sources. Conceptual metaphor represents the experiential basis that underlies a set of metaphors. Conceptual metaphors have effectively evolved from our sensory, motor, and – in more recent claims for the theory – neural systems and reflect the origin of metaphors in the inter-action between the human mind, the human body and everyday experience.

An issue for discussion is whether a conceptual metaphor – such as LEADERSHIP IS A JOURNEY – for which there is evidence in metaphori-cal expressions such as 'journey of renewal', 'the long march to freedom' or a 'roadmap for peace' – *predicts* leadership communication or whether it *retro-spectively explains* expressions used by leaders. The former is a much stronger claim than the latter because it implies that conceptual metaphors are inher-ent to leadership design, that is, leaders select conceptual metaphors in order to manipulate followers through conscious impression management, whereas the latter might simply be a way of classifying and analysing metaphor for, say, training purposes.

However, the distinction may not be particularly important in an applied sense, because as long as there is evidence that metaphors can be systematic-ally described and analysed using conceptual metaphors, then we have the basis for describing leadership communication. The value of such an approach for present purposes is that it allows us to identify, describe and explain similarities and differences in the language of leaders in different cultural set-tings. Interpretation of individual metaphors by identifying the conceptual metaphors and the extent to which metaphor choice is systematic is therefore a way of analysing the role of language in the design of leadership.

Identifying conceptual metaphors leads me to the third stage of Critical Metaphor Analysis – explaining language use. For example, identification of a conceptual metaphor such as POLITICS IS CONFLICT is a way of explaining figurative uses – it shows a proposition or assumption that underlies language use. It is also a way of explaining fundamental cultural differences in ideological outlook. For example, Gandhi developed an under-lying concept POLITICS IS NON-VIOLENCE that inverted the prevailing POLITICS IS CONFLICT concept that underlay much use of language by British colonial leaders. Critical Metaphor Analysis is, therefore, a form of analysis that enables us to explain *why* some metaphors are chosen – rather than others. I suggest that style in leadership communication is partially designed through the selection of metaphors.

When analysing political speeches using Critical Metaphor Analysis the cognitive semantic approach needs to be complemented with analysis of the verbal and non-verbal context of metaphor. Cognitive characteristics of metaphor cannot be treated in isolation from other persuasive features in the discourse context. Critical Metaphor Analysis provides us with a methodol-ogy for comparing leadership styles with the reservation that it may never be possible to explain the precise combination of every strategy that may lead to successful communication. In a sense, if the design of leadership commu-nication is too transparent, it loses its power to activate the unconscious, the spell is broken and the magic of leadership evaporates. There is a seamless quality to the metaphors of great leaders so that they appear natural and effortless.

The communication of visions and values

As noted in Chapter 1, the communication of visions has dominated the New Leadership studies. The word 'vision' occurs frequently in the discourse of leaders – particularly in current political speaking. A study that I undertook of post-Second World War British party political manifestos showed that there has been a shift from use of 'faith' to use of 'vision' when communicating a social ideal.[12] The origin of 'vision' is in the Latin 'video', sight, and many uses of the word retain this sense as in, for example, the literal senses attaching to eye tests and the anatomy of seeing. However, in relation to the communication of social ideals the word takes on a near opposite sense of 'something that appears to be seen *otherwise* than by ordinary sight'.[13] This shift in meaning in fact follows an underlying idea, or conceptual metaphor, that (as we saw in the last section) is very basic in English: UNDERSTANDING IS SEEING. The primacy of the sense of sight has led to it becoming synonymous with knowing and understanding. By metaphorical extension, therefore, visionary leaders have knowledge of how the future will be and can 'foresee' events; this enables them to resolve the conflicts and tensions that are currently experienced.

As we saw in Chapter 1, there is a very basic connection between visions and values: any communication of a better future that is uniquely foreseen by the leader must necessarily converge with followers' beliefs regarding what is right and wrong, true and false, good and bad. The language of leadership therefore either explicitly or implicitly evokes underlying notions of morality and ethics. The values that are communicated depend on the nature of the leader's vision, and while the vision is often communicated by a metaphor that uniquely belongs to the leader, its interpretation relies on the social appeal of the values that it assumes. Values provide the basis for the symbolic convergence of leaders' and followers' views of reality.

Leaders have a choice of language when it comes to the expression of visions and values; they can either express them using literal statements of right and wrong or they can use the subtler and potentially more persuasive means of metaphor. Why is it that metaphors are likely to be more influential in communicating values than literal utterances? First, let us think of some examples of literal statements of values; examples would include a law created by an appropriate institution, official statements of good practice, or a set of religious prescriptions such as the Ten Commandments or the Five Pillars of Islam. Although such formalizations reflect the moral code of a society and are necessary to underwrite its day-to-day practices they are unlikely to be effective in the language of leadership. This is because they are traditional institutionalized ethical formalizations that provide an objective framework for behaviour – rather than being persuasive or expressive forms. Choices here are very limited since laws can only be created, modified or abolished through institutionalized procedures. Literal statements are therefore less likely than metaphors to activate hidden, unrealized desires and the needs or emotions of followers.

Literal statements of values also commit leaders to the realization of their visions because they are transparently measurable. Since leaders can always be judged on the basis of their literal statements about values, they should only be used for actions for which there is a high degree of certainty as to their desirability and their feasibility. An example here would be the five commitments made by New Labour in its 1997 election campaign.[14] The advantage of appealing to *unconscious* needs and yearnings is that it is ultimately much more difficult to judge whether or not they have been satisfied! However, failure to satisfy these inner needs gives the impression that a leader has somehow *not* come up to expectation and has lost his or her magic.

The communication of legitimacy and myth

Weber distinguished between three types of authority: the rational, the traditional and the charismatic. When leaders represent themselves as the legitimate source of authority they are engaging in what is nowadays usually referred to as 'legitimization'.[15] For many, legitimacy is based on their position in an institution, whether they are political leaders who have been elected (legally or illegally), or organizational leaders who have gained their position through merit, through corruption, or through a combination of these. However, they will always lay claim to a superior vision (often based on a superior set of values) than their predecessors. In situations of social instability where traditional institutions are challenged and appeals to rationality are likely to be ineffective, charismatic leaders are more likely to emerge. Such leaders need to appear as extraordinary individuals whose solutions fit with the perceived problems of followers. As Conger argues, dissatisfaction with the status quo is central to the communication of charisma:

> The charismatic's verbal messages construct reality such that only the positive features of the future vision and only the negative features of the status quo are emphasized. The vision is therefore presented in clear specific terms as the most attractive and attainable alternative – the aim is to create among followers a disenchantment or discontentment with the status quo.[16]

Such dissatisfaction is more likely to occur in situations of social instability and since such situations are now more likely to arise in non-western societies, there is a greater potential for the legitimacy claims of leaders to appear charismatic in societies outside of the west.

Verbal self-legitimization occurs through a number of strategies including appeals to external sources of authority such as 'history', 'the people', 'the nation', 'God' or even 'the Revolution'. These verbal strategies often involve a complex blend of metonymy and metaphor – depending on the extent to which the leader claims to simply stand for, or represent, particular social entities and processes as opposed to the stronger rhetorical claim of actually *being* these entities and processes. The types of social entities that leaders may stand for are static concepts such as THE NATION, HISTORY, CHRISTIANITY or HINDUISM. Social processes are political movements that entail dynamic actions such as a revolutionary struggle, the struggle for human rights or for independence, freedom, democracy etc. The stronger legitimacy claim is conceptually based on metaphors such as THE LEADER IS THE NATION or THE LEADER IS THE HUMAN RIGHTS MOVEMENT. The stronger claim runs the risk of the cause dying with the leader because it is more individualized, whereas the milder claim reflects a more collectivist ideology in which the leader may be replaced by another who equally represents the valued social entity or process.

The essence of legitimization by political leaders is to communicate a perception of what is good and bad – a vision – in a way that followers share the implied value system. Legitimization is therefore an invitation to a shared perception of values. Once again metaphor is an important linguistic and cognitive resource employed by leaders for achieving this goal. For example, leaders who base their metaphors on the lexicon of conflict – as we have seen above – have the power to arouse emotions that are associated with physical combat; these include negative emotions such as pride, anger and resentment and positive ones such as strength, courage and determination. These emotions then evoke strong feelings because both 'the enemy' and heroic representations arouse the strong feelings of antipathy or loyalty that are generated by 'us' and 'them' representations. Political leaders are often effective at making the abstruse and abstract seem personal and responsive to enhance their legitimacy claims. Because metaphor relates abstract notions to our experience of concrete realities, it is an effective way of legitimizing ideology through myth creation.

Myth is especially effective in creating legitimacy because it is ultimately based on two of the deepest human emotions: love of life and fear of death. Critical examination of metaphors reveals the content of leadership myths and is therefore central to the claim that it *is* a myth rather than a reality. Since evaluation is central to legitimacy claims, analysis of the values implied by metaphors reveals the myths on which they are based. My analysis of Bill Clinton and Tony Blair showed evidence of a concept: GOOD GOVERNING IS CREATING when describing their own actions for valued entities by using verbs such as 'shape' and 'craft' and GOOD GOVERNING IS DESTROYING when using verbs such as 'root out' and 'stamp out' when describing their actions against entities that are not valued. In both cases the leaders represent themselves as dynamic agents who are mythically in control of the forces of creation and destruction.[17] As Freud has argued, the instincts of life and death underlie many of our psychological states and are therefore very significant in communicating legitimacy.

Taran contrasts the logic of myth with Aristotolian logic. Mythic thinking is synthetic, operates with images and allows contradictions, dramatization and cyclic, rather than linear, time. There may be a dramatic struggle between good and evil, the sacred and profane, the pure and the impure, between right and wrong. Cyclical time persuades followers that good events are unavoidable and is attractive in times of crisis. Myths may contain historically determined images such as: *Uncle Sam*, or *Mother Russia* etc. to communicate the idea of an emotionally unified nation. He finds that mythic thinking characterizes the discourse of the extreme political right and left, while Aristotolican logic typifies the centre; this is because political extremes seek to challenge existing discourse norms.[18]

Successful leaders rely on recurrent images to activate culturally-based ideas regarding what constitutes sources of fear and forms of social menace; the aim of leadership is to eliminate these sources of fear. This is effective because it satisfies the unconscious needs and desires of followers. Fear is, of course, very closely related to control since the more there is to fear, the greater the need for control. Leadership can be analysed in terms of some form of threat, some form of response to that threat and the emergence of a heroic leader. Heroic journeys form an inherent part of western culture that can be traced back to Homer's *The Odyssey*, the search for the Holy Grail in the Arthurian legends, medieval pilgrimages and crusades and, more recently, independent journeys of self-discovery. Myths therefore contribute to the design of a discourse of legitimization and we evaluate leaders' legitimacy claims on the basis of the subliminal associations aroused by their communication style.

Leadership and the media

An important issue relating to leadership in modern contexts is the question of whether modern communication media 'manufacture' charisma or whether it is in some way 'authentic', as implied by it being a free gift of God's grace. In the traditional understanding of charisma there is even a healing force that requires direct personal contact with the charismatic leader; in many non-western settings the traditional notion of charismatic leadership has prevailed and there is still belief in the magical powers arising from direct physical contact with a charismatic and faith in a quality that can be materially transferred to the follower. For example, in Moroccan culture the touch of a person endowed with God-given powers can transmit a powerful healing force known as *baraka*.

However, modern views emphasize the conscious role of impression management and these have come to the fore in the 1990s with the emergence of the public and media relations industry. There is evidence that the influence of the dark arts of the spin doctor has become ubiquitous and that innocence is now lost in the modern world of political communication. In modern western analyses of leadership there is a rational interpretation that sees even charismatic leadership as the effect of a combination of techniques of media control.[19] I refer to this contrast using the terms 'authentic' communication and 'design'. The distinction between the two viewpoints can be summarized as follows:

> the semblance of personal contact must be created through television, radio and newspapers. Simultaneously, these media create a charismatic figure out of the political leaders whom they project. Charismatic leaders are the products of the artifices or media experts and advertising exponents who consciously seek to train them in the art of striking oratory and to create an aura of an extraordinary person in order to enhance the likelihood of the imputation of charisma occurring. Modern charisma, according to this view, has more to do with stage management and advertising than with the personal and spontaneous context of charismatic leaders which provided Weber's focus.[20]

Atkinson also contrasts the traditional techniques of spellbinding oratory with the low-key conversational style that is effective in television broadcasting. He notes that the behaviour of large crowds in traditional oratory contrasts with the isolated and dispersed viewers of television and comments that:

> In the main our likes and dislikes derive directly from detailed observations of how a person speaks and responds in the course of everyday conversational encounters, observations which we are often hardly aware of making at the time, and which are hardly ever explicitly articulated with any degree of precision.[21]

His work predicted very accurately the important role of communication experts, advertising agencies, public relations and media consultants, press officers – and other professions that have become collectively known as 'spin doctors'. Tony Blair's political communication is a subtle blend of message content and, what I call leadership design, so that one is never quite sure which one is responding to. He has developed effectively the rhetorical strategy of 'sound bites':

> Effective political communication has always relied on easily understood slogans and phrases aimed at promoting and justifying the policy decisions of governments and their opponents. Radio, and subsequently television, provided politicians with an opportunity to explain their objectives to a mass audience in a personal and friendly way ... Therefore the most important point in any speech, broadcast or interview has to be delivered briskly and summarized as concisely as possible. Politicians want the public to remember their punch line.[22]

Blair also uses a great deal of style shifting by integrating the use of everyday phraseology in developing a personalized discourse style specifically for television broadcasting. This design strategy reduces the rhetorical distance between the leader and potential followers. He uses a similar informal strategy that mirrors popular conversational norms when speaking to a party conference audience in order to reduce the distance between leader and audience. In a study of his performance in political interviews Bull argues that he uses equivocation to be judged less face-threatening because direct face-damaging responses might reflect badly on either the Labour Party or on Blair's own integrity.[23] His use of imprecise language is central to his success as it avoids face-threat while presenting the best possible face for himself and his party. He argues that in terms of face-management his performance is highly skilled and communicates a 'rhetoric of modernization' in which the in-group is made as comprehensive as possible, while the out-group is made as restricted as possible. Blair defines issues so that greatest proportion of the audience identify with the in-group; this rhetoric attracts new supporters for the party while not alienating old ones. Design is a subtle, sophisticated and covert manipulative process that often defies easy analysis. In this view the understanding and effective mastery of modern media through leadership design can be magical in its *effect* – even when inherent charisma is absent.

In non-western situations we can differentiate between settings where there is explicit political control of the media – through propaganda – and those where more political freedom is permitted. In many non-western settings there is evidence of extensive control of the media machinery – for example, autocratic leaders such as Assad of Syria, Saddam Hussein and Gadafi, evidently employ propaganda. In western society there has been a huge shift from the relatively simple, persuasive use of the media in the pre-war and war period, to the highly sophisticated use I have described above in relation to Tony Blair and describe as the manufacture of charisma.

In settings where there is sufficient freedom to permit large meetings, the effect of leadership style is more measurable because the interaction between leader and follower leads to measurable responses in the form of shouting, clapping etc. One only has to listen to recordings of the speeches of Martin Luther King to appreciate the potency of interaction in creating charismatic effect. In other settings the message is communicated by implicit knowledge of how the media works rather than by explicit control. For example, neither Mandela nor Gandhi was in a position to control the media yet the whole world came to know of Mandela's nobility in imprisonment and the whole of India knew when Gandhi was fasting. Martin Luther King was able to use television to dramatize through what I have described as 'messianic discourse'.[24] His understanding of how the media worked was strategic in that the brutality of his opponents could be revealed on the screen. A more recent example is Osama bin Laden who has effectively exploited satellite television and the camcorder to design a heroic image and an impression of omnipotence in the Muslim world through publicising his ability to survive by disappearance and to endure physical hardship while living in a cave.

This was effective in countering the animal metaphors of George W. Bush, implied by words such as 'burrowing' and 'hunting' – he was simply a leader who had gone 'underground'.

All leaders face the challenge of making their own problems those of their followers and of projecting themselves into the unconscious minds of their followers. For these purposes the use of language is only one amongst a whole array of media strategies: their appearance in visual representation in posters, films, paintings, video recordings, web pages and text messages; their symbols, symbolic actions, dress, body language and verbal communication are also design issues. Successful use of the media is a universal prerequisite of effective leadership communication in both western and non-western settings. Therefore understanding the role of the media is also a very significant part of understanding leadership communication.

Summary

In this chapter I have argued that metaphor is vital to the design of leadership because – like symbol – it mediates between conscious, rational thought and unconscious mythical thought. Metaphors and symbols draw on the unconscious emotional associations of words, images and objects, the values of which are rooted in cultural knowledge. For this reason they potentially have a highly persuasive force because of the activation of conscious and unconscious resources to influence our intellectual and emotional response – both directly through presenting new concepts and indirectly by influencing how we feel about things. They therefore play a crucial social role in communicating leadership because they create a discourse of legitimization.

I have argued that metaphor does not work in isolation from symbols: to the contrary, I have outlined a range of symbolic strategies that may occur independently of metaphor. But metaphor becomes more persuasive when it is used in combination with symbol to create myth. When a political leader employs a rhetorical strategy in isolation the audience is quick to identify that there is an intentional strategy at work: they become aware of a manufacturer. However, when strategies occur seamlessly in combination with each other, the audience is more likely to be massaged by the speaker's design because the focus of attention is on processing the message itself rather than on how it is communicated. Leaders legitimize themselves most effectively through an interaction of verbal strategies with non-verbal modes, through metaphor and symbol, because the total effect is greater than when each occurs separately. Successful communication is the outcome of an interaction between linguistic and symbolic choices, contextual factors and the use of appropriate media that together I refer to as the design of leadership style.

4 Mahatma Gandhi
The soul of India

Introduction

In Chapter 1 I proposed that charismatic leaders are especially likely to emerge in non-western societies because of the prevalence of pre-rational, pre-scientific and religious belief systems. Perhaps the prototypical charismatic leader in modern times has been Gandhi who gained the saintly title of 'Mahatma' – or 'great soul' – through a lifelong devotion to transforming himself, his country and the whole of humanity. Gandhi's moral conviction ensured that his actions and words were equally consistent in communicating his ethical principles, and his leadership *transformed* followers; as one commented:

> Gandhi has in him the marvellous spiritual power to turn ordinary men around him into heroes and martyrs. In his presence one is ashamed to do anything unworthy and afraid of thinking anything unworthy.[1]

The best measure of charisma is surely through its *effect* on followers. His design of leadership style removed the invisible barrier between leader and followers: moral and non-egoistic personal actions such as fasting and meditation came to symbolize the solutions to India's problems. A leader who completely rejected his personal welfare gave followers a belief in their moral superiority. The self-confidence arising from this was a necessary prerequisite for political independence from the British colonial power. His rejection of materialism directed followers to a cultural domain in which they had superiority over the west: spiritual knowledge and religious conviction. This was especially communicative at a time when the cataclysmic clashes between western nations during the world wars were associated with a general decline in religious belief. The British politician Stafford Cripps noted:

> I know of no other man of any time or indeed in recent history who so forcefully and convincingly demonstrated the power of the spirit over materials things.[2]

An essential feature of transformational leadership is to remove the boundary between the private and the public, the individual and the social. It was because Gandhi demonstrated moral force through his own performance of leadership that his followers were inspired to imitate him by making politically necessary sacrifices. He created a mass following by connecting individual moral action with social outcomes. His vision was based in a refusal to analyse political, religious, economic, and dietary issues, as if they could be treated separately. He claimed that personal intellectual life and social action were interconnected by a common spiritual motivation:

> I claim that human mind or human society is not divided into water-tight compartments called social, political and religious. All act and react upon one another . . . I do not believe that the spiritual law works on a field of its own. On the contrary, it expresses itself only through the ordinary activities of life. It thus affects the economic, the social and the political fields.[3]

Gandhi's politics were, therefore, an inseparable part of his religion – just as his ethics were an inseparable part of his economics – and this is precisely why a political leader could be granted a title normally reserved for religious leaders. Further evidence of Gandhi's charisma was in his ability to remove distinctions that normally existed in Indian society: between Hindu and Muslim, between Brahmin and Untouchable. His rejection of existing boundaries is what motivated him to reject racial prejudice in South Africa and religious prejudice in India. Exceptional amongst all leaders of national independence movements was his rejection of any negative emotion towards the colonial power.

If there is one single belief that underlay Gandhi's leadership it was a belief in the power of love to melt the hearts of his opponents. His vision embraced groups that history had positioned as opponents: Muslims and Hindus, capitalists and workers, colonizers and colonized. It was the appeal to a vision of a unified humanity in which religious, social and racial boundaries would be overcome – that argues for him to be considered as the pre-eminent example of a charismatic leader. The basis of this idealistic appeal was a belief that man could create himself through correct action: 'In attempting to establish harmony between words, beliefs and acts Gandhi was attacking man's central problem. He was seeking the formula for mental health'.[4] For Gandhi the basis for social harmony lay in the creation of inner harmony.

As mentioned in Chapter 1, psychologically, underlying the evolution of a charismatic leader is the ability to resolve deep inner tensions through a period of withdrawal. The spiritual image we have of Gandhi – fasting in a loincloth – emerged from the psychopathology of a man who had experienced traumatic events in his early life. His mother was deeply religious and Gandhi always remembered that her 'saintliness' was manifested through regular extended fasts. Many of Gandhi's beliefs and political practices can be traced to her influence; for example, his concern with dietetics and the eventual use of fasting as a political weapon originated in her regular daily fasting that was part of the Jain tradition that she followed. He was only permitted to leave India to train as a lawyer when he overcame her resistance by swearing an oath not to touch wine, women and meat. Gandhi's concern with right practice and morality action can be traced to the psychological influence of his relation with his parents and, through them, to deep Indian cultural influences.

The confessional nature of Gandhi's autobiography and the fact that he reports on events that may have otherwise remained buried in the unconscious suggests that he was well aware of these tensions by the time he reached middle age. No doubt the long periods of his life that he spent in isolation – in prison and in his ashram where he regularly set aside a day in the week for complete silence – gave him the opportunity to undergo intense therapeutic self-reflection. This detachment from the material world enhanced his charismatic appeal as a leader with a profound inner-life. However, the very explicit way that he sought to demonstrate later in life that the forces that had earlier caused him so much anguish had been overcome leads us to question whether his inner psychological conflicts were ever fully resolved.[5]

Non-linguistic communication of charisma

Appearance and leadership style

It could be argued that Gandhi's charisma defies analysis, since analysis involves breaking things down into component parts. The appeal of Gandhi was not in how he looked (a rather small, undernourished man wearing spectacles) or what he wore (a simple loincloth). It was not in what he said, or what he wrote – his writings concern ethical discussions of truth, self-discipline, democracy etc. The appeal of Gandhi was the complete integrity of his being: everything he did – his actions (spinning), his eating habits (dieting and fasting), his daily social interactions – was completely *consistent* with an underlying ethical worldview. It was the completeness of his performance that communicated the self-knowledge and conviction of his design of leadership style. It gave followers the belief that what he did, wrote and said was right because it was governed by underlying principles derived from inner reflection (see Plate 1, p. 105). As Fischer puts it so eloquently:

> The Indian's heart aches for the lost glory of his country. Gandhi brought it balm. Gandhi in loincloth, imperturbable, prayerful, seated amid trees, not aping the British gentleman but resembling a saint of antiquity, reminded the nation that India has seen many conquerors and conquered them all by remaining true to itself. Gandhi kindles India's pride and faith, his magic wand became a ramrod.[6]

However, while I am aware of the risks in separating out the elements contributing to Gandhi's charisma, analysis of the design of leadership style requires separating the components of his charismatic appeal – even though such separations were probably not apparent to followers. I will begin by considering those non-verbal modes of communication through which he created symbolic meaning.

Dress

Gandhi rejected western dress and adopted the traditional dress of the rural Indian peasant – a loincloth made of homespun cloth (*khadi*). This conveyed a powerful political message of faith in the traditional values of India and removed any distinction between personal and national identity. It came to symbolize both his main political objective – Indian independence – and how this might be achieved through economic self-sufficiency. In this respect, dress contributed significantly to the creation of symbolic meaning and became a channel through which he communicated with the masses. Gandhi explained why he adopted the clothes of those from the lowest social levels – the Untouchables (who the British referred to as the 'Depressed classes'):

> In order . . . to set the example, I propose to discard . . . my *topi* and vest, and to content myself with only a loin-cloth and a *chaddar* whenever found necessary for the protection of the body.[7]

Transformational leadership often involves eliminating boundaries between leader and follower and Gandhi *performed* his belief in the values of his followers by removing any dress distinction between leader and follower.

Gandhi also required his followers to demonstrate symbolic acceptance of the political message that Indian independence relied on economic self-sufficiency by physically destroying all imported clothing. He invited followers to remove and burn their foreign hats, coats, shirts, trousers, underwear, socks etc.; sometimes men even stripped naked in public to communicate acceptance of the political message that social objectives were more important than the powerful cultural norms of modesty. Followers invariably came to visit Gandhi wearing homespun clothing as a way of re-affirming their loyalty.[8] The replacement of expensive clothes by simple indigenous clothing was a potent gesture that symbolized a transformation of values away from the imposed and foreign, towards the democratic and native.

Artefacts

Gandhi did not have a strong orientation to material culture: he gave money generously throughout his life to support his family and set up ashrams; he also avoided personal consumption other than the essential. His artefacts served to reinforce the philosophical and religious significance of his behaviour and appearance: they confirmed the message that the truth could only be attained by self-restraint. His personal artefacts – a bowl and spoon for eating, books and glasses for reading, a pair of sandals and a staff for walking – symbolized a rejection of the material in preference for the spiritual and political. The bowl and spoon represented fasting; the books, reflection; and the sandals and staff represented political leadership through marching.

An artefact that has become the prototypical symbol of Gandhi's leadership is the *charkha*, or spinning wheel – it even became the symbol of an independent India and remains today on the Indian national flag:

> Our present flag retains only the wheel as a symbol of the spinning wheel. This wheel is supposed to signify peace, progress and so forth, and that is all to the good, but when the tricolour was first thought of, its meaning was that all the people of India would live in harmony with one another and acquire non-violent strength through the spinning wheel.[9]

The spinning wheel symbolized independence from the British Empire through economic self-sufficiency and survival within a subsistence economy. Gandhi's descriptions of the *charka* describe its symbolic meaning through metaphors construing it as a living entity:

> The *Charkha*, therefore, is a useful and indispensable article for every home. It is the symbol of the nation's prosperity and, therefore, freedom. It is a symbol not of commercial war but of commercial peace. It bears not a message of ill-will towards the nations of the earth but of good-will and self-help ... For every revolution of the wheel spins peace, good-will and love and with all that, inasmuch as the loss of it brought about India's slavery, its voluntary revival with all its implications must mean India's freedom.[10]

Gandhi spent at least half an hour a day spinning for much of his life and saw the spinning wheel as a symbol that integrated spiritual and aesthetic objectives with political and economic ones. Spiritually, it symbolized Gandhi's core beliefs: 'The *Charkha* is an outward symbol of truth and non-violence'[11] and its spiritual attributes gave it a healing power:

> I believe that the yarn we spin is capable of mending the broken warp and woof of our life.[12]

> There is no *yajna* (sacrifice) greater than spinning calculated to bring peace to the troubled spirit, to soothe the distracted student's mind, to spiritualize his life.[13]

This spiritual healing power could be related to its aesthetic qualities: 'The music of the spinning wheel will be as balm to your soul'.[14] In political terms, it symbolized Indian independence:

> In my dream, in my sleep, while eating, I think of the spinning wheel. The spinning wheel is my sword. To me it is the symbol of India's liberty.[15]

But equally important was its symbolic value for economic autonomy:

> The spinning wheel and the spinning wheel alone will solve, if anything will solve, the problem of the deepening poverty of India.[16]

It was the spinning wheel that Gandhi saw as the gateway to his spiritual salvation. Perhaps its rotations correspond with Hindu beliefs in reincarnation and since what comes out is 'better' than what is fed in, it symbolizes self-improvement through effort. Certainly, if there were to be one single artefact by which Gandhi would wish to be remembered it is the spinning wheel. He once observed that: 'I feel as if I am spinning the destiny of India' implying that the spinning wheel combined spiritual, aesthetic qualities with political meaning. Its power as a symbol arises precisely because of a holistic significance arising from emotionally charged associations with spiritual, aesthetic, political and economic objectives; it therefore illustrates well how, in the design of leadership style, an artefact can communicate symbolic meaning.

Symbolic action and body language

Gandhi became politically aware of symbolic action in his early opposition to racial inequality in South Africa; in 1893 he dramatically walked out of the Durban Court after being requested by the English magistrate to remove his turban. Soon after, his refusal to give up a first class seat for which he had been sold a ticket led to his being thrown off a train. He believed fervently in fitting actions with beliefs and his great skill as a leader was that he was able to identify symbolic performances that communicated the moral strength of his beliefs. Initially, Gandhi was shy, but through experience and self-knowledge he developed a dramatic instinct that became a powerful instrument of political communication.

Perhaps the most significant of these symbolic actions was – ironically – a *non*-action: a refusal to eat or drink. He used the weapon of the fast in order to gain political control over outbreaks of violence in the build up to the partition of India and Pakistan – refusing to cease fasting until leaders had signed their agreement to end violence. These fasts were often successful: Untouchables were permitted for the first time into Hindu temples, enormous pressure was put on the British to make political concessions and there were far fewer deaths from inter-communal violence. Gandhi explained that he did not fast to coerce opponents but to strengthen or reform those who loved him: fasting can be seen as part of his philosophy of self-transformation through non-violent means. The spirit is transformed in proportion to the physical weight loss of the body and fasting became a form of communication through which followers could symbolically become leaders in their own right: it was something *any* follower could do – given the will and the motivation.

Symbolic action was central to communicating Gandhi's ideology because it entailed *not* reacting to violent attacks, *not* cooperating and *not* eating or drinking (fasting): *negative* actions were employed to attain *positive* political goals. One of the most memorable performances of symbolic action was the civil disobedience campaign that commenced in March 1930. Gandhi decided to disobey the Salt Laws that forbade Indians from making their own salt. Symbolic action was the absence of physical action: followers of non-violence refrained from instinctive response to attacks and thereby undermined the opponent's moral legitimacy. A leader who influences his opponents through symbolic action fundamentally changes their outlook; by acting in accordance with the principle of 'soul-force' he transforms, through suffering, himself, his followers and his opponents – and, in doing so, erodes any distinction between them.

Gandhi did not have a particularly powerful voice and was initially a very shy public speaker. However, as he was faced with addressing increasingly large audiences he learned to use body language to communicate symbolically with followers:

> During some speeches, he would lift his left hand and open up the five fingers. Taking the first finger between two fingers of his left hand he would shake it and say. 'This is equality for Untouchables,' and even those who could not hear him would ask for and get an explanation later on from those who had. Then the second finger: 'This is spinning'. The third finger was sobriety; no alcohol, no opium. The fourth was Hindu-Moslem friendship. The fifth was equality for women. The hand was bound to the body by the wrist. The wrist was non-violence. The five virtues, through non-violence, would free the body of each one of them and hence, India.[17]

Through this somatic communication Gandhi was able to use his own body to symbolize his core beliefs. Muslims use numbers mnemonically in the notion of the *five* pillars of Islam – this may have been influenced Gandhi.[18] By combining numbering with gesture Gandhi was able to communicate a complex philosophical position to illiterate audiences through a simple, but memorable performance.

Stylistic features of verbal communication

Gandhi preferred the native Indian languages for political communication – in particular Gujarati. Although, as a multilingual, he wrote, spoke and negotiated extensively in English,[19] for him it was the language of the mind – and as he grew in political maturity he became more aware of the need to communicate with followers in their own language. This was because he saw the native language as more effective in expressing affective and spiritual issues. He thought followers would not be motivated to act politically if their hearts did not follow their minds and the way to the heart was through the mother tongue. While, initially, he built his career in an English-speaking environment he became more and more aware that followers were most comfortable when communicating in their own language.

Gandhi was aware of the symbolic importance of language in creating national and cultural identity and had a strong feeling of personal and national pride in using indigenous languages rather than the language of a foreign ruler. Part of the design of his leadership style was an explicit resentment towards linguistic imperialism:

> When I find myself able to express my thoughts with more facility in English than in Gujarati, I tremble. Can those who insult their mother tongue do any good to their country? That the people of Gujarat should give up their own language for some other is unthinkable. If that is so, it would be no exaggeration to say that those who give up their language are traitors to their country and people.[20]

Gandhi saw linguistic independence as a prerequisite for political independence; he was highly critical of the dominance of English and had a strategy for redressing this:

> We have the shameful spectacle of Congressmen insisting on speaking in English and compelling others to do likewise for their sakes. The spell that English has cast on us is not yet broken. Being under it, we are impeding the progress of India towards her goal ... When the British yoke is lifted and we are independent, this infatuation with the English language will automatically go. In the meantime, let those who have realized the harm that this infatuation has done to the country, make it a point to use Hindustani or their mother tongue only.[21]

Gandhi's solution to the language problem was the use of local and regional languages. Awareness of the importance of language issues in relation to political rhetoric made language-switching an important signal of cultural heritage and at times Gandhi used his native language – Gujarati for public speaking. Problems of language also made him more aware of the symbolism of silent communication – as when he observed a regular weekly silent day in which the distractions of language were removed, permitting focus on the inner-life of the spirit.

An important characteristic of Gandhi's verbal style is his use of illustrative analogies to argue a particular point of view. This is probably a skill that he originally developed in legal training; he particularly liked to draw on concepts developed in western science for analysing the physical world to explain inner spiritual knowledge:

> I have learnt through bitter experience the one supreme lesson: to conserve my anger, and as heat conserved is transmuted into energy, even so our anger controlled can be transmuted into a power which can move the world.[22]

His analogies are frequently based on scientific concepts to counter the argument that his spiritual position might be interpreted as anti-scientific:

> I have always held that it is only when one sees one's own mistakes with a convex lens and does just the reverse in the case of others, that one is able to arrive at a just relative estimate of the two.[23]

At times, though, he would draw on knowledge of the natural world as the basis for analogy:

> We have not lived and toiled all these years that we should become barbarians as we appear to be becoming, looking at all the senseless bloodshed in Bengal, Bihar and the Punjab. But I feel that it is just an indication that, as we are throwing off the foreign yoke, all the dirt and froth is coming to the surface. When the Ganges is in flood, the water is turbid; the dirt comes to the surface. When the flood subsides, you see the clear, blue wear which soothes the eye, that is what I hope for and live for, I don't wish to see Indian humanity becoming barbarian.[24]

By describing inter-communal violence using an analogy based on natural force, Gandhi was implying that it was part of a natural process and equating culture with nature. Human commotion would be replaced by calm – just as there is a cyclical nature to natural processes. The political argument that social order will follow social chaos is communicated here by metaphor and the underlying conceptual metaphor, HUMAN FORCES ARE NATURAL FORCES, is a warrant for the argument that inter-communal violence would end. Metaphor is therefore part of the notion of *ahimsa* that will be discussed in the next section.

Verbal communication of vision and values

The communication of vision and values is fundamental to the design of leadership style and for Gandhi the two were inseparable: his vision was of a society that lived by spiritual values. This is evident from the two core values that communicated his leadership vision: *ahimsa*, or 'non-violence', and *satyagraha*, or 'truth'. Translation of these concepts is problematic and Gandhi preferred to keep to the native words for them. *Ahimsa* is a religiously based cultural concept that is central to his thinking; as he said: 'The most distinctive and largest contribution of Hinduism to India's culture is the doctrine of *ahimsa*'[25] and 'My life is dedicated to the service of India through the religion of non-violence which I believe to be the root of Hinduism'.[26] The concept originates in an ancient Jain commandment and means an *active* love rather than passively abstaining from violence – or being 'non-violent' as it is often translated. It is the complete opposite of *himsa* or "violence" which is conceived as passively giving in to an animal instinct. *Ahimsa* is a way of acting without harming others: though we may hate the harmful results of acts done by others, we must always love them out of a general respect for human dignity. Gandhi summarized the concept as follows:

> True *ahimsa* should mean a complete freedom from ill-will and anger and hate and an overflowing love for all.[27]

> *Ahimsa* means infinite love, which again means infinite capacity for suffering.[28]

The concept of *satyagraha* combines *satya* 'truth' or 'love' and *agraha* 'firmness' or 'force', to produce a literal translation of 'truth/love force'. However, Gandhi preferred the more dynamic translation of 'soul-force'; Gandhi invented the concept of *satyagraha* and described it as 'a relentless search for truth and a determination to search truth'.[29] When translating *satyagraha* as 'truth' we should recall that in Sanskrit there is a distinction between relative and absolute truth; however, *satyagraha* includes both relative truth of human words and deeds, and the absolute truth of God and the moral laws of the universe, which is why Gandhi preferred 'soul-force'.

The assumption of non-violent action is that the opponent is a moral being who will therefore be moved to end an injustice or to negotiate its end. Suffering will be eliminated by avoiding actions that arouse the desire for revenge:

> The former opponent becomes a friend. There are no losers, only winners. A truthful Satyagraha campaign, though it demands courage, self-discipline and humility on the part of the Satyagrahi, brings to bear tremendous moral pressure on the opponent and can bring about remarkable transformations.

Gandhi rejected the translation of *satyagrahi* as 'passive resistance' because it omitted an important aspect of the meaning:

> In passive resistance there is an idea of harassing the other party and there is a simultaneous readiness to undergo any hardships entailed upon us by such activity; while in Satyagraha there is not the remotest idea of injuring the opponent. Satyagraha postulates the conquest of the adversary by suffering in one's own person.[30]

Because it is an inherently moral concept, *satyagrahis* must always maintain a distinction between evil and the evil-doer – never confusing one with the other; as Gandhi explains: 'A *satyagrahi* must ceaselessly strive to realize and live truth. And he must never contemplate hurting anyone by thought, word or deed'.[31] *Satyagraha* is therefore 'the vindication of truth not by infliction of suffering on the opponent but on one's self'.[32]

In fact, the two principles of *satyagraha* and *ahimsa* are mutually dependent because *satyagraha* attempts to awaken an awareness of injustice among its perpetrators – but without harming or punishing them (because of the *ahimsa* principle). Followers must overcome evil with good, hatred with love, anger with patience, untruth with truth, and violence, or *himsa*, with *ahimsa*. Gandhi explained the relationship between the principles as follows: 'My religion is based on truth and non-violence. Truth is my God. Non-violence is the means of realizing Him'.[33] In this respect *satyagraha* was the theory on which the practice of *ahimsa* was based; because it was essentially an outer manifestation it required enormous courage: '*ahimsa* is an attribute of the brave. Cowardice and *ahimsa* don't go together any more than water and fire'.[34] Gandhi continued to espouse the power of *ahimsa* to overcome hatred right up to the terrible massacres prior to partition. Non-violence was fundamental to Gandhi's moral vision because – quite unique in twentieth century political leadership – it rejected any distinction between means and ends:

> They say 'means are after all means'. I would say 'means are after all everything'. As the means, so the end. There is no wall of separation between means and end. Indeed the Creator has given us control (and that too very limited) over means, none over the end. Realization of the goal is in exact proportion to that of the means. This is a proposition that admits of no exception.[35]

So non-violence was ultimately tied in with Gandhi's whole belief in *karma* – what goes around comes around. Gandhi believed that immoral means, such as violence, could not, by definition, produce moral ends, as means are ends in the making. For this reason it was the defining principle of his moral leadership: 'Non-violence is the first article of my faith. It is also the last article of my creed'.[36]

While *satyagraha* refers to a moral vision that legitimated his political behaviour, it was put into operation against British imperial rule by 'non-cooperation'. This is a refusal to participate in the functions of citizenship when the conscience no longer permits active support for a government that has become unjust and oppressive. Non-cooperation could involve withdrawal from government positions, renouncing government programs and services, and refusal to pay taxes. Although *satyagrahis* do not attack the wrong-doer, it is their responsibility not to promote or support wrong actions; therefore it was just as much a duty *not* to cooperate with an unjust government as it was to cooperate with a just one. Gandhi explained the relationship between moral values and political action as follows: 'non-co-operation and civil disobedience are but the different branches of the same tree called *satyagraha*'.[37] However, suffering was essential to both: 'To die without killing is the badge of a *satyagrahi*'.[38] This is why courage was so essential to the successful practice of *satyagraha* – it takes great bravery to embrace suffering. For Gandhi the concept of suffering was essential to the communication of values because it went beyond an appeal to reason by evoking empathy:

> I have come to this fundamental conclusion that if you want something really important to be done you must not merely satisfy the reason, you must move the heart also. The appeal of reason is more to the head but the penetration of the heart comes from suffering. It opens up the inner understanding in man. Suffering is the badge of the human race, not the sword.[39]

Here Gandhi communicates his understanding of suffering using the metaphor 'badge' and the metonym 'sword' – a sword causes suffering and is therefore from the same semantic domain, whereas a 'badge' is not from the domain of 'suffering' and is therefore a metaphor.

The above discussion of core culture-specific concepts shows that figurative language contributes to the communication of Gandhi's vision because of its capacity to move the feelings – and this is exactly the purpose of both *ahimsa* and *satyagraha*; as Gandhi explained:

> A *satyagrahi* is sometimes bound to use language which is capable of two meanings, provided both the meanings are obvious and necessary and there is no intention to deceive anyone.[40]

We can see the importance of metaphor in moving the feelings to communicate moral vision in the following:

> Having *flung aside the sword*, there is nothing except the *cup of love* which I can offer to those who oppose me. It is by *offering that cup* that I expect to draw them close to me.[41]

Metaphors to communicate the power of love were even used when discussing relations with the colonizing power:

> Let no one blame the unbending English nature, *The hardest fibre must melt in the fire of love* ... when British or other nature does not respond, *the fire is not strong enough*, if it is there at all.[42]

Metaphors were equally important in creating the emotional conditions for national unity: family metaphors were used to communicate the vision of a united India; India was 'Mother India' and Gandhi himself was *Bapu* or 'father'; once when asked 'how is your family?' He replied 'All of India is my family'.[43] Gandhi regularly referred to the partition of India as the 'Vivisection of the Mother' – the use of a human animate metaphor evokes strong emotions and argues for the legitimacy of a single unified India. His vision of unity was based in the view that all religions were equally worthy of respect: since human beings had created them, none could claim exclusive access to truth; he communicated this with a journey metaphor:

> *Religions are different roads* converging upon the same point. What does it matter that *we take different roads* so long as we reach the same goal?[44]

Gandhi also uses metaphors when evaluating political actions; a good example of this was when he prematurely called on the people of Kheda to commence a campaign of civil disobedience leading to many arrests. With typical self-criticism he evaluated this as 'a Himalayan miscalculation';[45] the metaphor gained wide currency and its rhetorical and emotional impact was heightened by hyperbole.

Critical metaphor analysis of Gandhi's communication of core concepts

An initial stage in the critical analysis of metaphors is to develop a system for their classification; there are two possible ways of organizing metaphors; the first is to classify the words that make them by the first or primary meanings of these words (their 'source domains') such as 'journey' or 'family' metaphors. An alternative approach is to classify metaphors by their secondary meanings – that is by what they mean when used as metaphors (their 'target domains'). I would like to illustrate both approaches by showing what source domains are used as metaphors for the target concept of *ahimsa* or 'non-violence' – as it is vital in Gandhi's design of leadership style.

Gandhi is well-known for short pithy sayings or epigrams that encapsulated his beliefs. A good example would be 'An eye for an eye only makes the whole world blind' – it builds on the knowledge status and stylistic shape of a proverb but contains a sense that is specific to his leadership vision. Epigrams compare with the status of slogans for other more secular leaders such as Castro and Mandela. Initially, I analysed a collection of Gandhi's quotations and epigrams that contained either *'ahimsa'* or its translation 'non-violence'.[46] I was first interested to find out how often metaphor was used and then to see what types of metaphor were used. On the basis of metaphors that occurred frequently, it was possible to infer underlying ideas (or conceptual metaphors) that account for the patterns of use in the full sample. I found that metaphor occurred in 95 (32 per cent) of 297 quotations and epigrams and that there were seven metaphor source domains in which five or more epigrams could be classified. Table 4.1 summarizes the findings for each conceptual metaphor.

Non-violence is war

Examples

> A non-violent *fight is sharp as the edge of a sword, sharpened* on *the whetstone of* heart.[47]

> A non-violent *warrior knows no leaving the battle.* He rushes into the mouth of *Himsa*, never even once harbouring an evil thought.[48]

> The *weapon* of non-violence does not need supermen or superwomen to wield it; even beings of common clay can use it and have used it before this with success.[49]

These sayings harness together adjectives and nouns with contradictory senses and are therefore oxymorons containing metaphors from the domain of violent combat or war, to refer to non-violence. This was the most common metaphor type, accounting for 20 per cent of all the metaphors

Table 4.1 Conceptual metaphors for Gandhi's metaphor target of non-violence

Source domain (17 total)	Conceptual metaphor	Number (>5)	%
War	NON-VIOLENCE IS WAR	19	20
Science	NON-VIOLENCE IS A SCIENCE	16	17
Person	NON-VIOLENCE IS A PERSON	16	17
Physical force	NON-VIOLENCE IS PHYSICAL FORCE	11	11
Law	NON-VIOLENCE IS A LAW	10	10
Plant	NON-VIOLENCE IS A PLANT	5	5
Journey	NON-VIOLENCE IS A JOURNEY	5	5
Other	NON-VIOLENCE IS LABOUR/ A MOUNTAIN/LIGHT etc.	14	15
Total		95	100

identified. Conceptually, Gandhi conceived of non-violence as a spiritual resource for opposing the force of violence. He used 'war' metaphors to argue that non-violence is more effective in achieving its political objective than physical combat. The hyperbolic rhetorical effect of these metaphors is enhanced, therefore, by the use of oxymorons.

Non-violence is a science

Examples

> The *science of war* leads one to dictatorship pure and simple; *science of non-violence* can alone lead one to pure democracy.[50]

> All society is *held together* by non-violence even as the earth is *held* in her position by *gravitation*.[51]

> *Ahimsa magnifies* one's own defects, and *minimizes* those of the opponent. It regards the mote in one's own eye as a beam and the beam in the opponent's eyes as a mote.[52]

These metaphors either refer overtly to non-violence as a science, or to a force or process that is associated with a scientific discovery such as gravitational force. They often refer to a scientific process or concept such as *acid test, electricity, velocity* etc. The argument is that non-violence is an empirical philosophy that produces tangible results. This was the second most common type of metaphor (along with personifications). They are rhetorically effective because they claim that the inner truths of the soul discovered by eastern philosophers are just as valid as the external scientific laws of western science (if not more so). They therefore appeal to cultural pride. As with war metaphors, they also contain an element of the unexpected by yoking together ideas that would conventionally be separated from each other.

Non-violence is a person

Examples

> True *ahimsa* should *wear a smile* even on a *deathbed* brought about by an assailant. It is only with *ahimsa* that we can *befriend* our opponents and *win their love*.[53]

> If our *ahimsa* is not of the brave but of the weak, it *will bend the knee* before *himsa*, and Gandhism deserves to be destroyed.[54]

In these metaphors – accounting for around 17 per cent of all metaphors for this target – *ahimsa* typically becomes the subject of a verb that would normally have a human subject rather than an abstract noun; such verbs are often from the domain of human emotions such as *fear*, *smile* etc. Personifications are rhetorically effective because they attribute to an abstract noun the emotional qualities that are experienced by people and are therefore effective in leadership because they communicate human empathy. Reference to human emotions is effective in communicating abstract notions because the aim of *ahimsa* is often to replace negative emotions such as fear by positive ones such as courage.

Non-violence is physical force

Examples

> Use truth *as your anvil*, non-violence *as your hammer* and anything that does not stand the test when it is brought to *the anvil of truth and hammered with ahimsa*, reject as non-Hindu.[55]

> Non-violence is the *greatest force* at the disposal of mankind.[56]

> I will not have the *power of non-violence* to be underestimated in order to cover my limitations or weaknesses.[57]

These metaphors are indicated by words such as *power*, *force* or *might* outside of a specifically military context. They are generally reifications since we normally think of these words in the context of the energy or strength that is required to move physical objects. They accounted for over 10 per cent of the metaphors and are rhetorically effective because they simplify understanding of *ahimsa* by explaining it as if it were a familiar physical reality.

Non-violence is a law

Examples

> Non-violence *is a universal law* acting under all circumstances.[58]

> When non-violence is accepted *as the law of life*, it must pervade the whole being and not be applied to isolated acts.[59]

In some cases there is also a rhetorical contrast between law and the breakdown of law implied by violence and war:

> When a man vowed to non-violence as *the law governing human beings* dares to refer to war, he can only do it so as to strain every nerve to avoid it.[60]

While in other cases there is some overlap with the idea of a scientific law:

> Unless you go on discovering new applications of *the law of non-violence*, you do not profit by it.[61]

These are similar to physical force metaphors but differ in that they appeal to the moral basis of *ahimsa* by referring to a law; the reason why this is treated as metaphor is because 'law' is a code of practice that has received legal sanction from the state. They are effective in political communication because they constitute legitimacy claims. They also account for around 10 per cent of the metaphors for non-violence.

Non-violence is a plant

Examples

> *Non-violence is a plant of slow growth, it grows* imperceptibly but surely.[62]

> Truth is self-evident, non-violence *matures fruit*. It is contained in Truth, but isn't self-evident.[63]

> *Love is a rare herb* that makes a friend even of a sworn enemy and *this herb glows* out of non-violence.[64]

These metaphors draw on the source domain of natural processes and include words such as *plant, grow, fruit* etc. These are commonly found in the Bible and are likely to be effective in political communication with illiterate rural people who rely on the land for survival. Gandhi's ashrams, such as Tolstoy Farm in South Africa, placed importance on cultivation as a means to self-sufficiency. We will also find that Nelson Mandela was keen on this type of metaphor.

Non-violence is a journey

Examples

> There is no hope for the aching world except through the narrow and *straight path of non-violence*.[65]

> The nation cannot be kept on the *non-violent path* by violence.[66]

In a study of metaphor in western politics I found journey metaphors to be the most common type of metaphor.[67] I have suggested that in political communication they are important as they imply social effort and participation in the social objectives that are predetermined by politicians; they are therefore effective in encouraging political unity.

Other metaphors for non-violence

Metaphor is likely to be most effective when it creates curiosity and interest; therefore, it is important that there is variety of metaphor in the design of leadership style. If metaphors are used too frequently their semantic tension is reduced and they eventually become conventional, or literal, ways of referring to something. Gandhi's rhetoric is more effective because he employs at least ten source domains to refer to non-violence – in addition to the ones discussed above; it is only possible to illustrate some of those here:

Non-violence is *the summit of bravery*.[68]

Non-violence is *the rock on which the whole structure of non-co-operation is built*.[69]

The alphabet of ahimsa is best learnt in domestic school and I can say from experience that if we secure success there, we are sure to do so everywhere else.[70]

These metaphors all seek to make non-violence more intelligible through reification – that is by construing it as a mountain, a foundation or as an alphabet. Some of these are persuasive because they are unexpected – such as when Gandhi draws on the domain of disease to communicate a positive evaluation:

If my non-violence is to be *contagious and infectious*, I must acquire greater control over my thoughts.[71]

Unexampled bravery, born of non-violence, coupled with strict honesty shown by a fair number of Muslims, was sure *to infect* the whole of India.[72]

Here he reverses the usual negative evaluation conveyed by a disease metaphor by highlighting an aspect of the source domain that would normally be suppressed in a positive evaluation – this is the idea that infections spread very rapidly. This novel use of a familiar metaphor communicates the idea that non-violence is a potent force because it can spread just as rapidly as violence. Gandhi believed that world peace was actually dependent on using non-violent means, it is not surprising that it forms a central part of his leadership communication.

The richness and diversity of metaphors used to communicate the concept of *ahimsa* is indicative of the personal, political and spiritual importance that he attached to it. In many respects it is a concept that accepted a political reality – given that the colonial power had taken control through force of arms and continued to maintain control through its potential for bringing military force to bear. Compared with the violence that arose from the end of colonialism in parts of Africa, it is a tribute to the relative success of non-violence that more lives were not lost in the struggle for Indian independence. Although if political 'vivisection' of India had been avoided the bloodshed would probably have been less. However, it may be considered as part of his legacy that the forces of peace have maintained their precarious hold on the two nations of India and Pakistan since their inception as separate states.

Verbal communication of legitimacy

In this section I will suggest that the two verbal strategies for communicating visions and values – the development of concepts and the use of metaphor (and frequently both in combination) – were also used for the communication of legitimacy. Gandhi's legitimacy claims for spiritual approaches to life and to living were communicated by metaphor; this is evident from the metaphors used to communicate spiritual legitimacy: words relating to light and darkness – as Gandhi wrote:

> Let those, therefore, who believe in non-violence as the only method of achieving real freedom, keep *the lamp of non-violence burning bright* in the midst of the present *impenetrable gloom.*[73]

Gandhi also drew on light and darkness metaphors to communicate his own personal spiritual struggles; for example, he wrote: 'I have never been in such *darkness* as I am in today … It is due to my limitations, my faith in *ahimsa has never been brighter* and yet I feel that there is something wanting in my technique'.[74]

It seems likely that Gandhi was influenced in this choice of metaphor by his reading of religious texts such as the *Bhavagad Gita* and the Bible. A study I undertook of four books of the Bible showed extensive evidence of conceptual metaphors such as; SPIRITUAL KNOWLEDGE IS LIGHT, and SPIRITUAL IGNORANCE IS DARKNESS.[75] Metaphors of light and darkness can be analysed as legitimacy claims because Gandhi's belief in the spiritual superiority of the east over the west was a fundamental part of his claim for the moral legitimacy of *Swaraj* (independence). We saw in Chapter 1 how Nehru referred to Gandhi's assassination with the phrase: 'The light has gone out of our lives'. Use of light metaphors by Nehru in this famous eulogy reminded hearers that metaphor had been a powerful strategy for the communication of legitimacy in Gandhi's leadership style.

Consider the metaphors that he used to discuss the major political issues of Untouchability, national independence and the question of a separate nation for India's Muslim population. I will first discuss the metaphors for Gandhi's views on Untouchability and then those that argued for the legitimacy of an independent India.

There is evidence of metaphor in around 50 per cent of Gandhi's sayings referring to Untouchability;[76] he described it as 'a monster', or 'a diseased plant', or personification is employed:

If untouchability *lives*, humanity must die.[77]

I would far rather that Hinduism died than that untouchability *lived*.[78]

As we have seen with the 'flood' metaphor to describe inter-communal violence, animate metaphors offer the political argument that if Untouchability is 'alive', then its lifespan is necessarily limited and it should therefore not be accepted as a permanent feature of the spiritual landscape of India.

There is evidence that Gandhi's opposition to Untouchability in the second part of his life was strongly influenced by the experience in the first part of his life of the race policy towards Indians in South Africa. Indians were excluded from hotels, from dining cars and sleepers on trains, from public baths and high schools. His political awareness of prejudice against Indians in South Africa seems to have been sparked by the metaphors used by supporters of apartheid to undermine their claims to be treatment as political equals. In both *The Green Pamphlet*[79] and in his press articles Gandhi refers to examples of metaphors for Indians:

And yet the Indian is the most *despised of creatures*; he may not ride in the tram-cars, nor sit in the same compartments of a railway carriage with the Europeans, hotel-keepers refuse him food or shelter and he is denied the privilege of the public bath![80]

In terms of constructing political arguments, animal metaphors were effective in supporting racial prejudice because they implied low value as when animals such as 'rabbits' were selected to communicate 'an excessive number' in the expression 'breed like rabbits'. Gandhi knew through his own experience that railway officials often treated Indians as beasts. This implied conceptually that INDIANS ARE ANIMALS and he explored the implications of this metaphor when he reminded his audience that a man had said at a meeting held in Durban that he 'was sorry we could not be shot like them'.[81] In arguing for Indian legitimacy, Gandhi used animal metaphors to heighten the emotional impact. For example, one argument in favour of independence was the role of Indians in the First World War (in which Gandhi had served in the ambulance corps):

Before the war broke out, the Colonials often used to taunt them by saying that, in times of danger, the Indians would scuttle off *like so many rabbits*, and such were the people who demanded privileges like them! But the war showed that the Indians *did not scuttle off*; they put their shoulders to the wheel and were prepared to take equal responsibility with others.

Here metaphors are used to contrast the cowardice that was anticipated with the reality of Indian behaviour. The idea that the Indian population was expanding and could overwhelm the white population was at the heart of the political perceptions of the white ruling elite in South Africa. An argument used to support the 1894 Bill to disenfranchise Indians in Natal was that 'the Indian vote might *swamp* the European'. In fact the word 'swamp' was commonly used in media reports, even when they supported the Indian cause:

> We are inclined to the belief therefore that the danger of the Indian vote *swamping* the European is a chimerical one. We do not consider the danger of being *swamped*, is at all a likely one.[82]

Other delegitimizing metaphors implied INDIANS ARE A DISEASE; these include:

> The Asiatic cancer, that has already eaten so deeply into the vitals of South Africa, ought to be resolutely eradicated.[83]

> The real canker that is eating into the very vitals of the community.[84]

And, in South Africa, Gandhi applied the same metaphor to his opponents:

> The hardship to which I was subjected was superficial – only a symptom of the *deep disease of colour prejudice*. I should try, if possible *to root out the disease* and suffer hardship in the process.[85]

There were obvious similarities in the conceptualization of social groups as sources of illness, or pests that could cause disease. Inspired originally by negative metaphors for the representation of Indians in South Africa, Gandhi turned these metaphors around – initially in the defence of Indian expatriates – and later, in India, in defence of another outlawed class, the Untouchables – by using metaphors based on the concept UNTOUCH-ABILITY IS A DISEASE:

> We are too near the scene of tragedy to realize that *this canker of untouch-ability* has travelled far beyond its prescribed limits and has sapped the very foundation of the whole nation.[86]

While negative representations legitimized Gandhi's policy on Untouchability, highly positive ones legitimized Indian independence (*Swaraj*); these included metaphors from the domain of nature, the family and music:

> Swaraj is a *hardy tree of patient growth*.[87]

Swaraj means ability to regard every inhabitant of India as our own *brother or sister*.[88]

There can be no Swaraj where there is *no harmony, no music*.[88]

He also used animal metaphors to describe the type of independence he sought for India: 'English rule without the Englishmen. You want the *tiger's nature without the tiger* . . . you would make India English . . . This is not the *Swaraj* I want'.[90] Similarly, he highlighted the negative qualities of British institutions using animal metaphors:

'There are in our country grand public roads, and palatial educational institutions,' said I to myself, 'but they are part of a system which crushes the nation. I should not have anything to do with them. They are like the *fabled snake with a brilliant jewel on its head, but which has fangs full of poison*'.[91]

The imperial power was mythically construed as a fierce and dangerous animal that should not be trusted. It was this representation that argued in favour of an independent India that was legitimate in so far as it demonstrated the opposite qualities. Gandhi regularly communicated his most important political messages by drawing on the emotional potential of metaphor; he also skilfully reversed the use of racist animal and disease metaphors that had been used to delegitimize Indians by using them to delegitimize the colonial power.

Leadership and the media

Gandhi was a prolific writer and sought to communicate his message through both the written and spoken word. He wrote for a range of publications – including *Harijan*, *Young India* and *Navajivan* – with an expressly political purpose; as he explains: 'Through these journals I now commenced to the best of my ability the work of educating the reading public in Satyagraha'. However, the circulation of both journals rose to only around 40,000 each at their peak.[92] This points to the major problem in political communication in India: with a population of 300,000,000 people – mostly illiterate – and with only 5,000 who had radios – how could a largely apolitical audience be politicized?

Gandhi's leadership design solution to this problem was through the symbolic action of fasting to communicate the most powerful political messages; it offered the most compelling means of activating existing communication technology – much of which was via word of mouth – through the extensive railway network of India. News of the Mahatma's fasts were printed in all the newspapers and those who read told those who did not. The cities knew, and peasants who travelled there to sell their produce heard the news; they carried it to the villages, where it would be corroborated by other travellers.

Gandhi undertook extended fasts at crucial political moments: in encouraging the textile workers of Ahmedabad to continue a strike; in bridging the conflict between Hindus and Muslims and, in 1932, he even went on a 'fast unto death' in opposition to the concept of a separate electorate for the Untouchables (*Harijans*). This won over Hindu leaders to this policy:

> From 13 September, when the fast was announced, to the afternoon of 26 September, when Gandhi drank his first orange juice, every change in Gandhi's physical condition, every word pronounced by anyone who had seen him, every journey of the least of the negotiators was broadcast to every corner of the country ... Hindus were reacting to a single throbbing wish: The Mahatma must not die.[93]

In terms of symbolic communication, Gandhi necessarily resorted to image and religious practice to reach those potential followers who were beyond the reach of the written word.

Summary

Shortly before his assassination Gandhi said 'My life is my message'.[94] By 'his life', he meant that all his actions, social interactions – the whole performance. This is effectively what Jung meant by 'individuation': there was no separation of the self and the ego and Gandhi became the Great Man that Jung believed all have within them. But Gandhi did not arrive at the point of self-realization without a psychic struggle – and here I will explore this further. I will briefly discuss some of the psychological tensions underlying Gandhi 'the man' to counterbalance the 'halo effect' that characterizes much writing about him; this is because they indicate how culturally imposed factors can be overcome in the design of leadership style.

In his autobiography – completed when he was 56 – Gandhi reports on a number of events that caused psychological tension later in life; the most significant of these was a strong feeling of sexual guilt. Gandhi was sexually active at a young age: he married when he was only 13 and it seems that they soon embarked on a sexual relationship since his wife became pregnant at the age of 15. In his frank explanations and rationalizations there is evidence that Gandhi had made great efforts to come to terms with deep-rooted feelings of sexual guilt. He comments on the relationship with his child bride: 'If with this devouring passion there had not been in me a burning attachment to duty, I should either have fallen a prey to disease and premature death, or have sunk into a burdensome existence'. He then refers repeatedly to his sexual desires as 'lustful': 'I was very anxious to teach her, but lustful love left me no time ... And when I awoke from the sleep of lust ... had my love for her been absolutely untainted with lust ... I have mentioned one circumstance that more or less saved me from the disasters of lustful love'.[95] From these references it is evident that at the age of 56 Gandhi still conceptualized his youthful desires as unnatural and immoral.

A similar guilt in relation to feelings and experiences with boys is evident in the chapter entitled 'Tragedy'. Here he describes a brief relationship with a friend of his elder brother; it was one that he was warned against by his mother, wife and eldest brother and was evidently based on admiration of physical behaviour:

> This friend's exploits cast a spell over me. He could run long distances and extraordinarily fast. He was an adept in high and long jumping. He could put with any amount of corporal punishment. He would often display his exploits to me and, as one is always dazzled when he sees in others the qualities that he lacks himself, I was dazzled by this friend's exploits.[96]

It is not clear exactly how far this relationship went – but evidently far enough for it to be a cause of later feelings of guilt: 'I am of the opinion that all exclusive intimacies are to be avoided; for man takes in vice far more readily that virtue ... I may be wrong, but my effort to cultivate an intimate friendship proved a failure'.[97]

The middle-aged Gandhi is apparently reliving the sexual guilt of his youth. First, he offers this alarmingly frank recollection of a failed visit to a brothel:

> My friend once took me to a brothel. He sent me in with the necessary instructions. It was all pre-arranged. The bill had already been paid. I went into the jaws of sin, but God in his Infinite mercy protected me against myself. I was almost struck blind and dumb in this den of vice. I sat near the woman on her bed, but I was tongue-tied. She naturally lost patience with me and showed me the door, with abuses and insults. I then felt as if my manhood had been injured, and wished to sink to the ground for shame.[98]

But he then evaluates it from the perspective of his older self: 'From a strictly ethical point of view, all these occasions must be regarded as moral lapses; for the carnal desire was there'. The guilt associated with his relatively early sexual experiences, and reinforced by strong cultural factors, was heightened by a very traumatic event that was probably the cause of much subsequent trauma. This was his participation in a sexual act at the very moment of his father's death: 'Every night whilst my hands were busy massaging my father's legs, my mind was hovering about (my wife's) bedroom – and that too at a time when religion, medical science and common sense alike forbade sexual intercourse'. He reminisced forty years later: 'if passion had not blinded me, I should have been spared the torture of separation from my father during his last moments'.[99] The baby that Gandhi believed to have been born from this particular coital union only survived for three days. He never attempted to deny the impact of the guilt attached to this crucial moment on his psychological development.

These early psycho-emotional experiences formed the basis for Gandhi's view that sexual behaviour was only permitted for the purpose of procreation. From 1906 he took a vow of celibacy (to become a *Brachmarya*) and apparently remained celibate until his death in 1948. During the latter part of his life, he decided that it was appropriate to test his self-control of sexual desire through a most dramatic performance of it: sleeping with young women without sexual arousal. This behaviour was controversial – leading to the resignation of his secretary – partly because it was unclear what benefits the female 'non-participants' gained from these nocturnal regimes of sexual discipline. I would suggest that the origin of Gandhi's need to control his wants and desires, and his belief that such control was the secret of human salvation, may be traced to psychopathological – and potentially Oedipal – traumas arising from early sexual experience. Gandhi's charisma originated in the struggle to resolve the tension between his 'natural' or biological desires, needs and impulses – his libido – and his understanding of what was permissible within the traditional religious belief systems of the culture in which he lived. The intensity of the personal, psychological conflicts was mirrored in the intensity of the social conflicts that it was his vision to resolve.

In this chapter we have seen that Gandhi's design of leadership style involved the interaction of a range of powerful symbolic and metaphoric semiotics: appearance, dress, artefacts and symbolic action were all consistent with the spiritual image that underlay his legitimacy. Verbally, he communicated the core vision statements of non-violence and soul-force through metaphors that reinforced the non-verbal message. Metaphor was crucial in creating the emotional impact of a message that combined the spiritual with the political: political issues and inter-communal strife would be resolved if people learnt to listen to their hearts. Gandhi sought to change behaviour that was based in the concepts HUMANS ARE ANIMALS and HUMAN BEHAVIOUR IS ANIMAL BEHAVIOUR, by using alternative metaphors to raise awareness of a new basis for legitimacy and adapting his opponents' metaphors for his own objectives. His use of metaphors was highly varied, including unexpected images that aroused curiosity and stimulated new ways of thinking about political and spiritual issues.

However, symbolic performances were equally, if not more, important in his leadership design; the creation of the spinning wheel as a national symbol was a powerful statement of legitimacy that combined political and aesthetic dimensions. Unlike most leaders who are characterized by a will to power, Gandhi's most effective political weapon was when he *withdrew* from power in extended periods of fasting. His inversion of western modes of leadership by appealing to the highest moral and spiritual forces in his own culture became a powerful, persuasive strategy in the design of leadership style. This should heighten our awareness of how a successful leadership style of performance combines universal with culturally specific strategies.

5 Nelson Mandela

Leader of the oppressed

Introduction

Nelson Mandela has been an archetypal transformational and charismatic leader because South Africa's relatively peaceful transition from the oppressive system of apartheid to democracy can be attributed directly to his leadership. If we recall that a defining characteristic of transformational leadership is the effect that a leader has on followers, then, undeniably, Nelson Mandela had a profound influence – both on followers and on representatives of the apartheid system. A tyrannical head of the Robben Island prison who was dismissed after Mandela's protests said on his departure: 'I just want to wish you people good luck' – reflecting this transforming influence.[1] Mandela saw the prison wardens as brutalized by the apartheid system and he 'could see beyond the brutalities, to the insecurities and psychological deformities of the wardens because he was already seeing the prison as a microcosm of a future South Africa, where reconciliation would be essential to survival'.[2] It was ultimately the combination of a clear vision grounded in a profound moral conviction that gave him the power to transform opponents. Mandela projected his own personal needs and aspirations onto those of a social group, sacrificing his domestic role as a father to become a symbolic father of first a nation and then of oppressed peoples everywhere.

A wide range of traits have been identified as contributing to Mandela's success including thinking creatively, being pragmatic, having a high self-regard, believing in a cause, motivation, self-discipline and skill in personal relations. His leadership has demonstrated decisiveness, a sense of direction and moral worth, the possession of a clear vision, and intelligence – including a prodigious memory. But, underlying these traits is an understanding of the processes of human relationships in a particular historical situation and a belief that forgiveness would always produce more long-term benefits than revenge. His leadership style has been designed on the basis of understanding the dynamics of conflict resolution and the benefits of conciliation in a historical setting that was highly conducive to conflict. Mandela's style, therefore, found the ideal balance between attending to the task of ending apartheid and developing relationships with those who had created the system, as well as with followers – to the extent that even former opponents could become followers.

We should recall that Mandela's style of leadership was not always the conciliatory one of the type we have come to associate with him. The view we have of Mandela today – as a leader who showed compassion and an almost spiritual understanding of the dynamics of hatred – was not the public perception at the time of his imprisonment, in December 1961:

> Mandela was now commander-in-chief of a burgeoning fighting force. He had the authority and prestige of a revolutionary leader taking on an unpopular military regime, in an age of revolutions when the forces of oppression seemed in retreat throughout Africa. All his previous roles – the boxer, the man-about-town, the lawyer, the family man – had been left behind by the new role of guerrilla leader underground.[3]

In frustration at the brutality of the government and the lack of political progress Mandela had given up his earlier views on non-violence and had travelled throughout Africa to raise resources for a violent campaign intended to bring about the downfall of the government. He was a hardened freedom fighter whose boxing experience encouraged him to look for the right opportunity to strike his opponent where he was most vulnerable.

We should recall that a transformational leader first acts on his or her own values and motivations, and undeniably Mandela was stimulated to do this by his experience of prison. He transformed his perception and understanding of his opponents as a prerequisite for establishing himself as a leader. We will recall that a clear understanding of the situation is essential to process approaches to leadership. He realized the importance of gaining an understanding of ordinary Afrikaans culture and used some of his time in prison to do this. He learnt the Afrikaans language (albeit retaining his Xhosa pronunciation), studied Afrikaans history and read Afrikaans literature. His understanding of *all* strands of opinion in South Africa permitted him to emerge as a *symbol* of national healing and as the only leader who had the charisma to inspire followers to believe in the possibility of a peaceful transition to democratic rule.

Charismatic leaders have usually resolved some type of internal conflict and this provides the basis for their emergence as leaders who seem to connect with the forces of history. While in prison Mandela was in a position to reflect on personal conflicts, resolve them and act upon these resolutions by developing the necessary actions and behaviour of a potential leader. Prison provided him with the opportunity to understand the process of human relationships. The limitations on social contact heightened their importance, and Mandela went out of his way to assist in the education of prisoners and used his expertise as a lawyer to resolve their specific legal problems. His belief in equality was enhanced by the prison experience. He developed self-discipline through a rigorous early morning exercise regime and his self-respect and pride as a black African was enhanced through contrast with the unethical behaviour and corruption of some white wardens. But, above all, prison allowed Mandela the time to reflect on personal psychological conflicts and how these were rooted in the position of blacks in South Africa.

Imprisonment allowed Nelson Mandela to detach himself from the immediate issues of political strategy that had dominated his life prior to imprisonment. In particular, writing developed his powers of self-reflection and he wrote much of his autobiography *Long Road to Freedom* while in prison. It is possible that this experience of separation from immediate political exigencies allowed him to develop the type of distance and objectivity needed to understand his own dramaturgical role as a performer of leadership:

> It is often desirable not to describe events, but to put the reader in an atmosphere where the whole drama was played out right inside the theatre, so that he can see with own eyes the actual stage, all the actors and their costumes. Follow their movements, listen to what they say and sing, and to study facial expressions and the spontaneous reaction of the audience as the drama unfolds.[4]

As implied by Gardner and Avolio's theory of leadership as performance, prison enabled Mandela to think of himself as a dramaturgical participant. As well as emerging as a prison leader by understanding the social setting in which the drama was enacted, Mandela designed a leadership style for which his personal attributes made him especially well-suited. As Joel Joffe – a fellow prisoner observed:

> Nelson Mandela emerged quite naturally as the leader. He has, in my view, all the attributes of a leader – the engaging personality, the ability, the stature, the calm, the diplomacy, the tact and the conviction. When I first met him, I found him attractive and interesting, by the time the case finished I regarded him as a really great man. I began to notice how his personality and stature impressed itself not just on the group of the accused, but on the prison and the prison staff themselves.[5]

It is significant that from early on Mandela was interested in the concept of leadership and while in prison he systematically studied politics and leadership. He took notes on the Boer War leaders and recorded quotes from leaders such as Montgomery ('Total war demands total fitness') and Truman ('A leader is a man who has the ability to get other people to do what they don't want to do, and like it').[6] As Bruno Mtolo noted: 'He did not have to show off to prove he was a leader, it was perfectly clear to anyone that he was. He was honest about everything which had to be done, and wanted it to be done in a simple way'.[7] Above all, Mandela understood the effect of his own behaviour on the behaviour and motivation of others. The importance of transformation in his design of leadership style shows in his use of this term in speeches made during his time as the first president of a democratic South Africa (my emphasis):

> Our first three years of freedom have demonstrated that our goals are achievable. Above all, South Africans have shown that by joining hands across all sectors of society and working together, even the most difficult problem can be overcome. And they have shown that South Africa's workers are a powerful and creative force for *transformation*.[8]

> *Transformation* is this government's reason for existence; and we shall not for a moment shirk our responsibility to the poor.[9]

> Within the intelligence services, it has become even more urgent to unearth the few rotten apples who arrogantly pursue an agenda counter to *transformation*.[10]

> As we reflect on the years of transition and beginnings of *transformation*, we have cause to draw inspiration from what South Africans can do. We dare to hope for a brighter future, because we are prepared to work for it.[11]

Evidently, he had an image of himself as a charismatic leader who would transform South Africa into a working democracy and, in so doing, make the world a better place to live in: without the self-knowledge he had developed in prison and an understanding of how to integrate this into the design of a leadership communication style, it is unlikely he could have achieved this goal.

Non-linguistic communication of charisma

Appearance and leadership style

There are many testimonies to the fact the Nelson Mandela looked and acted like a leader (see Plate 2, p. 106).[12] He has always been striking in appearance, physically very fit, full of energy and stamina and able to cut an imposing figure in most social situations. We should not forget that his leadership claims had an ancestry: he was the great-grandson of Ngubengcuka, a great king of the Tembu people, and grew up with the knowledge of this royal lineage. His father was a skilled orator who was sometimes referred to as the Prime Minister of Thembuland and once even took on the role of kingmaker.

In the early 1950s a black metropolitan culture was developing in Johannesburg, where – partly because of American cultural influences – blacks were emerging for the first time as cultural role models in the world of jazz, films and sports. 'Mandela had the confidence of a man-about-town, great presence and charm and a wide smile. But he kept his distance, as befitted an aristocrat rather than a commoner'.[13] Educated blacks were relatively rare at this time, and Mandela stood out from others because of his confidence and humility. He avoided the seamier side of the drinking clubs known as *shebeens*, developed a professional status as a lawyer, while carrying himself with the pride of an African tribal chief. He had the self-confidence to conduct his own defence at the Treason Trials where a British journalist described him as 'a large lawyer, untravelled but enormously well-read, slow speaking, nattily dressed' and 'a big bearded handsome man with a deep resonant voice'.[14]

However, Mandela's leadership style was founded on his ability to form close personal relations and his ease of social interaction implies a belief in the long-term value of developing and nurturing them. This has shown in his ability to create a rapport with individuals from any walk of life and in his faith in the virtues of simple, friendly human contact. In this respect his style has always been highly democratic – emphasizing the importance of building alliances and making friends rather than imposing his will on others. He has always shown a remarkable ability to see the others' point of view. In terms of leadership theory, Mandela may be said to practice a psychodynamic approach; in this approach it is important for leaders to understand both their own needs *and* the emotional responses of other people. The approach 'places emphasis on leaders obtaining insight into their personality characteristics and understanding the responses of subordinates, based on their personalities'.[15] Nelson Mandela knows himself well enough to understand how much he needs other people – while recognizing and responding to the signs of such needs in others.

What is exceptional about Mandela is his insight into the covert and unconscious desires of potential enemies; this enables him to offer them a cathartic experience in which they can dispose of unwanted identities and, on occasions, even become followers; as Sampson puts it:

> he had a relaxed charm which made almost anyone feel better after meeting him; but his magnanimity and lack of bitterness conveyed a moral seriousness, particularly to white South Africans, as if here were a priest at confessional, forgiving sins and giving blessings.[16]

Mandela's charisma is perhaps symbolized by a rather dramaturgical event that he describes as occurring when he joined a congregation of the Dutch Reform church in Pretoria one Sunday: 'The men all wanted to touch me. The women all wanted to kiss me. The children all wanted to hang on my legs'. While previously his guards were required to protect him from his enemies, 'This time they were there to protect me from being killed out of love'.[17] If transformational leadership is gauged by the effect on followers, there is surely no more dramatic measure of this than when former opponents become followers.

Dress

Nelson Mandela has always shown awareness of the importance of clothes in the creation of the persuasive and compelling image that contributes to the design of leadership style. As a young man he chose the same type of stylish metropolitan dress as preferred by other charismatic leaders of the time – such as Martin Luther King. When his friend Fatima Meer was told 'Some Indians said he was like Gandhi', she replied 'Gandhi took off his clothes. Nelson *loves* his clothes'.[18] But, as we will see later with Fidel Castro, he was also able transform a sophisticated professional image into a style that communicated the ideological message of a freedom fighter on the run:

> they persuaded him to abandon his stylish clothes, but he still had his vanity: they could not get him to shave off his beard, which had become part of his revolutionary style.[19]

He disguised himself variously as a gardener, a farm labourer and a mechanic; from this experience Mandela learnt that, as well communicating subliminal messages, his freedom relied on ensuring that his clothes fitted the performance setting. At his trial in October 1962 he dispensed with the suit and tie he had previously worn in the courtroom and created a dramatic stage entry wearing the traditional *Xhosa* leopard-skin known as a *kaross*. In his autobiography he reports the transforming effect this had:

> The crowd of supporters rose as one with raised fists clenched fists shouted '*Amandla!*' and '*Ngawethu!*' The *kaross* electrified the spectators, many of whom were friends and family . . . I had chosen traditional dress to emphasize that I was a black African walking into a white man's court. I was literally carrying on my back the history, culture and heritage of my people. That day, I felt myself to be the embodiment of African nationalism, the inheritor of Africa's difficult but noble past and her uncertain future. The *kaross* was also a sign of contempt for the niceties of white justice. I well know that the authorities would feel threatened by my *kaross* as so many whites felt threatened by the true culture of the African.[20]

By wearing the clothing of a traditional African chief, Mandela was laying claim to all the old tribal loyalties that formed the legitimacy for his rejection of apartheid. His use of clothing as a symbol reasserted cultural identity and was the performance of a leader who had inherited the leadership claims of his forefathers.

Dress also formed an immediate issue of dispute on his imprisonment because the prison authorities required black prisoners to wear shorts; Mandela was fully aware of the symbolic meaning of this rule:

Short trousers for Africans were meant to remind us that we were 'boys'. I put on the short trousers that day, but I vowed that I would not put up with them for long.[21]

Once elected as President of South Africa, he continued to show awareness of the symbolism of clothing – often wearing the floral batik silk shirts that were originally a gift from President Suharto of Indonesia. His clothes were not peripheral, they were central to his political life. Mandela understood the role of image creation in democracies by adjusting his dress to the specific situation and was also able to use clothes to communicate powerful political messages. In June 1995, after the Springboks won the World Cup final in Johannesburg, in their first tournament after the end of the anti-apartheid sports ban, Mandela walked onto the field wearing the Springbok jersey. As passion for rugby is deeply embedded in Afrikaner culture, this was a persuasive and symbolic gesture of reconciliation and nation-building: such semiotic messages are central in the design and performance of leadership style.

Artefacts

Little in Mandela's life has been conducive to the collection of material objects. After 18 years on Robben Island he was unexpectedly informed one day that he would be transferred. As he records in his autobiography: 'We were each given several large cardboard boxes in which to pack our things. Everything that I had accumulated in nearly two decades could fit into these boxes. We packed in a little more than half an hour'.[22] The things that he was deprived of most in prison were those on which he always placed highest value: letters from loved ones, books and newspapers (he read anything and everything). Otherwise, artefacts were primarily a means to an end – as, for example, those he needed for his main passion: gardening.

Symbolic action and body language

Mandela was very aware of symbolic gestures of defiance in his communication of leadership; these were acts that communicated the moral superiority of himself and his followers over their state opponents. His decision to defend himself in the treason trial was based on a feeling that he had acquired a new moral power; as he put it in his autobiography: 'I was the symbol of justice in the court of the oppressor, the representative of the great ideals of freedom, fairness and democracy in a society that dishonoured those virtues'.[23] By projecting himself first as a militant leader and then as one who was martyred he communicated a clear political message: 'it established him as the lost leader who had defied the system, hunted, underground and yet in the midst of the people'.[24] Mandela sought to activate the magic of leadership by appearing here and there like the spirit of an ancient chieftain. In this way myth creation became essential to the communication of charisma and was a source of inspiration to followers.

When he was in prison Mandela continued to encourage myth creation; the combined effect of the justice of his cause and his estrangement from his people communicated a leadership message. Like a meditating monk in his cell, he became a source of spiritual inspiration to continue the struggle, and perpetrated the myth of a leader whose very soul belonged to his people. This is why on his release he said:

> I greet you all in the name of peace, democracy and freedom for all. I stand here before you not as a prophet but as a humble servant of you, the people. Your tireless and heroic sacrifices have made it possible for me to be here today. I therefore place the remaining years of my life in your hands.[25]

Mandela has always known that existence in the minds of followers is crucial to political success; though in fact it was *he* who had made the heroic sacrifice, by reversing these roles he eliminated the distinction between leader and follower. Here was a leader who attained unity by performing as if he were one of his followers – surely the ultimate symbolic act of any charismatic leader. We can see the effect this had:

> For Mandela embodied a more elemental and universal myth, like a revolutionary opera or *The Odyssey*, depicting the triumph of the human spirit, the return of the lost leader. And his long isolation had allowed the myth to take off from the man. Leaving everything to the imagination: a dotted outline within which anyone could fill in their own detailed picture of a hero.[26]

Perhaps Mandela's most important attribute is his use of eye contact and facial expression to put people at ease and to ensure them that the relationship is of utmost value. His body language is also very important in relaxing people by walking over to them and making some form of physical contact. He deliberately undermines the distance given to charismatic leaders by admiring followers, often makes fun of his celebrity status by taking someone by the hand, looking the person in the eyes and engaging him or her in conversational pleasantries. He even rejected the symbolic status that followers gave to him: 'I am sorry if I am seen as a demi-god ... I am a peg on which to hang all the aspirations of the African National Congress'. At times he used body language as a way of disarming an opponent. He did this at the end of a televised debate in the 1994 election campaign when he reached out to take de Klerk's hand, his opponent admitted that 'suddenly what had been a certain points victory had been converted into a draw ... it was a masterful stroke'.[27] Mandela has never underestimated the importance of effective performance in front of a camera lens.

Stylistic features of verbal communication

Mandela's communication style may broadly be described as an inclusive, informal and democratic style in which choice of language is well-suited to the speech occasion. There is evidence of the underlying strategy in his auto-biography. In dialogic situations such as political debates and discussions, his style is modelled on that of a wise African tribal leader:

> As a leader, I have always followed the principles I first saw demonstra-ted by the regent at the Great Place. I have always endeavoured to listen to what each and every person in a discussion had to say before venturing my own opinion. Oftentimes, my own opinion will simply represent a consensus of what I heard in the discussion, I always remember the regent's axiom: a leader, he said, is like a shepherd. He stays behind the flock, letting the most nimble go on ahead, whereupon the others follow, not realising that all along they are being directed from behind.[28]

By concealing his own views within those of others, he was able to become the mouthpiece of a collective voice. On addressing 10,000 people for the first time, he describes his speech-making style as follows:

> I had never addressed such a great crowd before, and it was an exhilarat-ing experience. One cannot speak to a mass of people as one addresses an audience of two dozen. Yet I have always tried to take the same care to explain matters to great audiences as to small ones. I told the people they would make history and focus the attention of the world on South Africa. I emphasized that unity among the black people – Africans, Coloureds and Indians – in South Africa had at last become a reality.[29]

We will see later that Castro also adopted the style of *talking to* people rather than *lecturing at* them. Mandela's style is not excessively grandiloquent but concerned with giving the audience a feeling that they are involved in the joint creation of history. This sense of historical destiny was also a hallmark of Fidel Castro and Martin Luther King,[30] as well as that of western leaders such as Roosevelt and Churchill. The rhetoric was designed to embrace those who wished to join his side rather than to inflame those who would not:

> Whites are fellow South Africans . . . and we want them to feel safe and to know that we appreciate the contribution that they have made towards the development of this country. Any man or woman who abandons apartheid will be embraced in our struggle for a democratic, non-racial South Africa.[31]

Mandela's ability to overcome conflict was a crucial part of his communica-tion style since it offered the option of political accommodation if opponents were prepared to change.

Slogans are important instruments of persuasion for a political party because they provide the opportunity for social involvement in verbal statements of ideology in circumstances where solidarity is important. Slogans were particularly important in establishing a rapport between oppressed followers and a potentially martyred leadership in the period leading up to Mandela's arrest, trial and imprisonment. They also provided a means for political communication within prison itself and encouraged the feeling that the ANC movement extended both inside and outside of prison. Slogans became a vital verbal strategy for the drama of followership. Consider Mandela's own description of what took place in Robben Island prison:

> Each evening, seconds before lights were dimmed, as if in obedience to some silent command, the hum of voices would stop and the entire jail would become silent. Then, from a dozen places throughout the prison, men would yell '*Amandla*!' this would be met by hundreds of voices replying '*Ngawethu*!' Often we would start this call-and-response ourselves.[32]

Call and response is a well established interactive speech form for enhancing solidarity; it has its roots in both the work practices of slavery in North American and in Baptist religious discourse and was extensively used by supporters of Martin Luther King in the American Civil Rights movement. Mandela was well aware of the potential for slogans to communicate effective political messages; as he once commented 'A slogan is like a bullet, its effectiveness depends on matching the bore of the gun'.[33]

As we have seen in relation to Gandhi, language choice is also important in political communication. Mandela's frequent use of his native language, Xhosa, was particularly important in spoken fixed expressions (sayings, slogans, proverbs etc.); as with other African languages, it has a rich tradition of figurative phrases embodying traditional cultural perspectives and beliefs. Proverbs and sayings are the traditional means for knowledge transition between generations and are frequently used in settling legal disputes in traditional African settings. In 1961, when Mandela was arguing in support of a historic ANC proposal to abandon non-violence and to form its own military wing, he quoted the proverb '*Sebatana ha se bokwe ka diatla*' ('the attacks of the wild beast cannot be averted with only bare hands').[34] Then, in the treason trials, he described the South African government that was moving toward fascism as '*indlovu ayipatwa*' ('an elephant that cannot be touched').

The use of proverbs containing animal metaphors in political argumentation is of particular importance in African contexts and was not the exclusive preserve of any single politician. Significantly, Pik Botha used a hunting metaphor to describe the need to encourage a conciliatory point of view to racial difference: 'It does not matter whether you put the bullet through the white stripe or the black stripe, if you hit the animal, it will die'. And in the

1994 election campaign Mandela said in relation to de Klerk's National Party: 'We are dealing with a mouse. We in the ANC are like an elephant'.

Slogans and sayings often become persuasive in the verbal performance of leadership when they include metaphors. However, slogans do not necessarily employ metaphor – an equally important figure of speech in slogans is hyperbole; important ANC slogans were: 'We Won't Move' and 'Over Our Dead Bodies'. Castro described Mandela as 'one of the most extraordinary symbols of this era' and it is possible that the dramatic 'Over Our Dead Bodies' was modelled on Castro's 'Fatherland or Death, we will conquer'.[35] It has the same exhortatory intention of communicating inflexibility and self-belief and was intended to inspire and to encourage solidarity and a sense of historical destiny. However, at times, Mandela took a critical view on the effectiveness of slogans – especially when they did not correspond with political realities:

> 'Over Our Dead Bodies' was a dynamic slogan, but it proved as much a hindrance as a help. A slogan is a vital link between the organization and the masses it seeks to lead. It should synthesize a particular grievance into a succinct and pithy phrase, while mobilizing the people to combat it. Our slogan caught the imagination of the people, but it led them to believe that we would fight to the death to resist the removal. In fact, the ANC was not prepared to do that at all.[36]

Mandela generally preferred more conciliatory slogans and proverbs; for example, when considering the issue of whether the ANC should work within the system or be a revolutionary movement, he quoted the Sotho proverb 'A river is filled by little streams'.

Communication of vision and values

We saw in the critical metaphor analysis of Gandhi's core concepts that metaphor makes a significant contribution to the communication of visions and values and is a key characteristic in the design of leadership style; this is also the case with Mandela. In a corpus of 50,000 words taken from Mandela's speeches made over the period 1952–2004 for the purposes of this analysis I identified 252 metaphors (or around one every 200 words). The most common types of metaphor (as classified by source domain) were reifications (22 per cent), conflict metaphors (18 per cent), path-source (including journey) metaphors (16 per cent), and water metaphors (11 per cent). Previous studies I have undertaken of western politicians[37] show a high use of conflict metaphors (especially by Margaret Thatcher) and, as we saw in the last chapter, Gandhi used these in an inverted sense. An interesting feature of Mandela's conflict metaphors is that they are not evenly distributed and occur primarily in the speeches made *prior* to his release from prison in 1990. Mandela also uses domains such as farming and water metaphors more commonly than other politicians and this therefore contributes significantly to leadership style.

Mandela's rather special use of water metaphors can convey either a positive or a negative evaluation. When used with a positive sense, water metaphors typically profile the size of support given to the ANC:

> Ever since the arrest of Kotane, Dadoo and the others who defied the Suppression of Communism Act, there has been *a sudden upsurge in the rush to volunteer*.[38]

> The Government, alarmed at the *indomitable upsurge of national consciousness*, is doing everything in its power to crush our movement by removing the genuine representatives of the people from the organisations.[39]

> The processes in which South Africa and Southern Africa as a whole are engaged, beckon and urge us all that we *take this tide at the flood* and make of this region a living example of what all people of conscience would like the world to be.[40]

In a country in which tropical downpours are common, the use of water metaphors convey the idea that the force driving a political movement is a natural one – and contain the argument that because it is elemental it is also unstoppable.

Another argument communicated by water metaphors is that the ANC has popular support abroad – in 1962 Mandela left South Africa for the first time to tour countries that were involved in, or had recently attained, independence – Ethiopia, Tanzania, Algeria etc. – to obtain resources to commence armed resistance. This is how he described the resistance in one of his speeches:

> Camps were established at strategic points; heavy army vehicles carrying equipment and *supplies moved in a steady stream along the Reef*; helicopters hovered over African residential areas and trained searchlights on houses, yards, lands, and unlit areas.[41]

Later, when reflecting on the pressure of African opinion that had led western governments to introduce economic sanctions against the apartheid government, Mandela recalled:

> It was a time when *the tide of Africa's valiant struggle* and her liberation, *lapping at our own borders*, was consolidating black pride across the world and firing the determination of all those who were oppressed to take their destiny into their own hands.[42]

In these metaphor images there is a clever association between the political force within Africa (conceptualized as a tide) and the external force of overseas allies (conceptualized as the sea lapping on the shores of South Africa). There is some evidence here of an underlying concept that communicated a political vision: THE ANC IS A NATURAL FORCE. In terms of political communication this implies the irresistible expansion and growth of the ANC; we will also recall that Gandhi used a conceptual metaphor HUMAN FORCES ARE NATURAL FORCES to communicate a satisfactory outcome (the end of inter-communal violence). However, on other occasions, water metaphors could be employed with a negative sense implying lack of political control and loss of direction:

> We felt that the *country was drifting towards a civil war* in which Blacks and Whites would fight each other.[43]

Negative or cynical views about the future of South Africa:

> Worse still, we could turn some constituents into passive critics, *their own rationality drowned in the chorus of regret* that the past has passed.[44]

Or the effect of neo-liberal economic policies:

> Amongst the most pressing of these is the debt burden as well as the need to bring under control the vast movements of capital *which wash across the globe* without much social benefit, and with the capacity to undo years of industrialisation where it is most urgently needed.[45]

This shows that metaphors may profile quite different parts of the same source domain depending on the speaker's persuasive intention. Metaphors drawing on the natural environment frequently have a strong orientation to communicating deep, culturally-based outlooks. Winston Churchill employed sea metaphors in developing a heroic myth of Britain as a warrior nation that was essential to the survival of an island nation.[46] Evidently, since South Africa is also a country for which the sea has a powerful symbolic significance as a means of contact with the outside, Mandela frequently uses water metaphors in political persuasion. The difference is that for Churchill the enemy was without, whereas for Mandela the enemy was within.

The use of nature as a source domain may be traced to the fact that Mandela has always seen himself as a country boy. On his retirement he returned to the village of Qunu and even during his time at Pollsmoor he was permitted to cultivate a garden; as he writes:

> The Bible tells us that gardens preceded gardeners, but that was not the case at Pollsmoor, where I cultivated a garden that became my happiest diversions. It was my way of escaping from the monolithic concrete world that surrounded us ... each morning, I put on a straw hat and

rough gloves and worked in the garden for two hours. Every Sunday I would supply vegetables to the kitchen so that they could cook a special meal for the common-law prisoners. I also gave quite a lot of my harvest to the wardens who used to bring satchels to take away their fresh vegetables.[47]

Given his close identity with natural processes and the earth it is perhaps not surprising that may of his metaphors draw on this domain and he even used it to conceptualize his vision of what a leader is:

In some ways I saw the garden as a metaphor for certain aspects of my life. A leader must also tend his garden; he, too, sows seeds, and then watches, cultivates and harvests the result. Like the gardener, a leader must take responsibility for what he cultivates; he must mind his work, try to repel enemies, preserve what can be preserved and eliminate what cannot succeed.[48]

This is reminiscent of the naïve savant in Peter Sellers' film *Being There* in which a gardener becomes president of the USA when his literal statements about gardening are given metaphorical interpretations by aspirant followers. Mandela almost invariably conveys a positive evaluation of a situation with natural metaphors, and, on occasions, mixes these with other familiar metaphors from domains such as light and building that are commonly used by politicians for conveying optimistic messages. We see instances of these in italics in the following:

These millions of South Africans are joining hands to sustain their democratic achievement; and they will protect it like *the apple of their eye*. They are filled with hope about the *bright future that beckons*. They shall not be distracted by the *noise of a falling tree* amidst the dignified silence of *a new future starting to blossom*; because they know that: *The foundation has been laid; and the building has begun!*[49]

Sometimes his use of farming metaphors was used dramatically to win points in argument as in the following when the young Mandela was instructed by the Youth League to break up a communist meeting and said:

There are two bulls in this *kraal*, there is a black bull and a white bull. J.B. Marks says that the white bull must rule this *kraal*. I say that the black bull must rule. What do you say?

The crowd who had been supporting Marks responded 'The black bull, the black bull!'[50] Metaphors such as these are rhetorically effective because they provide analogies drawing on the daily life experience of followers.

On other occasions Mandela would use metaphors drawn from the urban world of industry and mechanization – we should remember that parts of South Africa had become the first industrialized parts of Africa. In particular, the shantytowns of Johannesburg provided strong sources of support for the ANC. Urban-based metaphors often implied strength and determination:

> For the guns that serve apartheid cannot render it unconquerable. Those who live by the gun shall perish by the gun. Unite! Mobilise! Fight On! Between the *anvil of united mass action and the hammer of armed struggle* we shall crush apartheid and white minority racist rule![51]

Outmoded methods of industrial production could give a negative evaluation of aspects of apartheid government:

> It is said that *the mills of God grind* exceedingly slowly, but even the Lord's *machinations* cannot compete with those of the South African judicial system.[52]

He frequently referred to apartheid as a 'system' and one of the important rhetorical goals of his use of mechanical metaphors was gradually to dissociate apartheid from the domain of animate beings. We see this in the following uses:

> If today all South Africans enjoy the rights of democracy; if they are able at last to address the *grinding poverty of a system* that denied them even the most basic amenities of life, it is also because of Cuba's selfless support for the struggle to free all of South Africa's people and the countries of our region from the inhumane and destructive *system of apartheid*.[53]

Apartheid was 'a system' because race categorization was used as the basis for social organization in every aspect of society, but in so doing it was treating humans as if they were inanimate objects. From these metaphors we can infer a conceptual metaphor APARTHEID IS A MAN-MADE MACHINE that contrasts with the conceptual metaphor THE ANC IS A NATURAL FORCE. In other instances traditional notions of industry argued that political progress was being made:

> *The wheel of life* is there, and national heroes from Autshumao to Luthuli, in fact the entire people of our country, have been working for it for more than three centuries, *It is clogged with dry wax and rust*, but we have managed to *make it creak* and *move backwards and forwards*.[54]

This metaphor is in some respects also a journey metaphor as it the idea of movement based on what is known in cognitive linguistics as SOURCE-

PATH-GOAL concept; in this respect ease of movement has a positive evaluation whereas blockage implies a negative evaluation as in the following:

> Neither should it ever happen that once more the *avenues to peaceful change are blocked* by usurpers who seek to take power away from the people, in pursuit of their own, ignoble purposes.[55]

In this schema, journey metaphors are often used to communicate the idea that the political vision is a destination and therefore political actions are a directional and purposeful journey towards that destination, as in the following:

> I salute the African National Congress. It has fulfilled our every expectation in its role as leader of the *great march to freedom*. Then at end of the speech: 'Our *march to freedom is irreversible*. We must not allow fear to stand in our way'.[56]

This has been described cognitively as PURPOSEFUL SOCIAL ACTIVITY IS TRAVELLING ALONG A PATH TOWARD A DESTINATION.[57] Often in such metaphors the political progress is measured in terms of spatial concepts such as speed:

> South Africa is in a momentous process of change, *blazing a trail towards a secure future*.[58]

These metaphors also commonly integrate the figure of antithesis or contrast:

> Thus we shall take *not just small steps, but giant leaps* to a bright future in a new millennium.[59]

I have described elsewhere the use of journey metaphors in the communication of political visions, especially by Martin Luther King, but also by other significant western political orators, including, most recently, Tony Blair.[60] It is significant, therefore, that Mandela used this metaphor source domain as the title for his autobiography *Long Walk to Freedom*:

> On the horizon lie the rural hills amongst which generations of South Africans began on that *long walk to freedom* that has taken our nation ever closer to the fulfilment of our dreams.[61]

Journey metaphors not only have a powerful intertextual reference to other freedom journeys but also activate deep-rooted mythical elements that have been described as follows:

A hero ventures forth from the world of common day into a region of supernatural wonder: fabulous forces are there encountered and a decisive victory is won: the hero comes back from this mysterious adventure with the power to bestow boons on his man.[62]

Here we can see an analogy with Mandela's life – although the worlds of Robben Island could hardly be called 'fabulous', a decisive victory seems to have been won there and the experience formed the basis of the peaceful solution that his leadership offered South Africa after his 'return'.

An important type of reification metaphor for communicating leadership vision is light/darkness; as with chiaroscuro, it can be employed to enhance a dramatic contrast. I have already mentioned how these metaphors are used extensively in the Bible and in the Koran – as well as by Gandhi – and also frequently combine with fire metaphors. We see an instance of this in the following:

Even in the grimmest times in prison, when my comrades and I were pushed to our limits, I would see a *glimmer of humanity* in one of our guards, perhaps just for a second, but it was enough to reassure me and keep me going. Man's *goodness is a flame that can be hidden but never extinguished.*[63]

The conceptual metaphor KNOWLEDGE IS LIGHT could be adapted to political communication when Mandela described the logic of Soviet dialectical materialism being: 'like a powerful searchlight on a dark night, which enables the traveller to see all around, to detect danger spots and the way forward'.[64]

As with journey metaphors there is often an evocation or often a direct allusion to the light and darkness metaphors of Martin Luther King:

Let the strivings of us all, prove Martin Luther King Junior to have been correct, when he said that humanity can no longer be tragically bound to the *starless midnight of racism* and war . . . *Let a new age dawn!*[65]

At times, though, in his deeper reflections, Mandela deliberately plays on the ironic potential for the use of dark/light metaphors to conceptualize racial issues. We find a salient instance of this when describing his time in hiding prior to his arrest in terms of living underground:

Living underground requires a seismic psychological shift. One has to plan every action, however small and seemingly insignificant. Nothing is innocent, in some ways, this was not much of an adaptation for a black man in South Africa. Under apartheid for a *black man lived a shadowy life* between legality and illegality, between openness and concealment. To be a black man in South Africa meant not to trust anything, which was not unlike *living underground* for one's entire life.[66]

In this metaphor notions of death and darkness are associated with the underground source of life: the roots of a plant. But perhaps, given that THE ANC IS A NATURAL FORCE, the idea of roots going underground has a positive connotation when referring to an *outlawed* political movement. The metaphor is especially potent when we consider that light deprivation is one of the worst results of long periods of imprisonment. As with other prisoners, Mandela's eyesight was permanently damaged by the contrast between the darkness of the prison and the blinding exposure entailed by prison work in a lime quarry:

> Worse than the heat at the quarry was the light. Our backs were protected from the sun by our shirts, but the sun's rays would be reflected into our eyes by the lime itself. The glare hurt our eyes and, along with the dust, made it difficult to see. Our eyes streamed and our faces became fixed in a permanent squint. It would take a long time after each day's work for our eyes to adjust to the light ... During the following weeks and months we requested sunglasses again and again. But it was to take us almost three years before we were allowed to have them and that was only when a sympathetic physician agreed that the glasses were necessary to preserve our eyesight.[67]

Interestingly, then, at times protection from a light source can be beneficial, especially in circumstances when daylight itself may not be positive because it does not permit freedom:

> A few days thereafter, he arranged for Michael Harmel to take me to Rivonia. I naturally found Rivonia an ideal place for the man who lived the life of an outlaw. Up to that time I had been compelled to live indoors during the daytime and could only venture out under cover of darkness.[68]

We should also recall in this respect that, of course, 'black' itself took on strong positive connotations in the discourse of the ANC as in expressions such as 'black consciousness':

> From the start, *black consciousness* articulated itself as 'an attitude of mind, a way of life'. In various forms and under various labels, before then and after, this attitude of mind and way of life have coursed through the veins of all the motive forces of struggle; it has fired the determination of leaders and the masses alike. The driving thrust of *black consciousness* was to forge pride and unity amongst all the oppressed.[69]

As with water metaphors, metaphors of darkness and light readily shift their evaluation according to the political argument that is being communicated within a specific cultural context and this is not predetermined by any universal value that is attached to 'lightness' and 'darkness'.

Communication of legitimacy

Nelson Mandela believed that his descent from royal lineage contributed to his legitimacy as a hereditary ruler of South Africa. He knew that the Afrikaners had gained their legitimacy by fighting a nationalist war against British colonial rule, and he interpreted the ANC struggle as a nationalist one against a system of colonial oppression, symbolized by apartheid. By finding parallels between the political struggles of South African blacks and the Afrikaners, he dramatically communicated the relevance of understanding the underlying historical situation to legitimacy claims. His leadership communication was designed on the basis of total belief in himself as the embodiment of this legitimacy; when defending racial equality in his self-defence speech, Mandela said that it was an ideal for which he was prepared to die. The communication of legitimacy was grounded in a personal moral conviction that a new multi-racial South Africa would be the outcome of an inevitable historical process:

> Perhaps it was history that ordained that it be here, at the Cape of Good Hope that we should lay the foundation stone of our new nation. For it was here at this Cape, over three centuries ago, that there began the fateful convergence of the peoples of Africa, Europe and Asia on these shores.[70]

Ending apartheid in South Africa was part of a broader global struggle for freedom from repression:

> We live with the hope that as she battles to remake herself, South Africa will be like a microcosm of the new world that is striving to be born.[71]

By relating the struggle of a political movement to pan-national issues such as colonialism and imperialism, Mandela was able to argue that the struggles of the ANC were legitimate because they were part of a broader humanitarian progress. We can infer from this a conceptual metaphor THE POLITICAL MOVEMENT (ANC) IS A MORAL FORCE. This was especially effective in winning the international support for the ANC that provided financial and ideological assistance. We see the claim for a historical legitimacy rooted in general humanitarian progress in the following:

> Because of their courage and persistence for many years, we can, today, even set the dates when all humanity will join together to celebrate one of the outstanding human victories of our century. When that moment comes, we shall, together, rejoice in a common victory over racism,

apartheid and white minority rule. That triumph will finally bring to a close a history of five hundred years of African colonisation that began with the establishment of the Portuguese Empire. Thus, it will mark a great step forward in history and also serve as a common pledge of the peoples of the world to fight racism wherever it occurs and whatever guise it assumes.[72]

The danger of developing political arguments in terms of general ideological terminology (colonialism, racism, imperialism etc.) is that it detaches itself from the personal and becomes part of an intellectual abstraction that is distanced from everyday personal hardships. One way to overcome this is through dramatic personification combined with offering as exemplar. In his eulogy to the murdered activist Steven Biko, Mandela personifies 'history', 'repression' and 'apartheid':

> *History called* upon Steve Biko at a time when the political pulse of our people had been rendered faint by banning, imprisonment, exile, murder and banishment. *Repression had swept* the country clear of all visible organisation of the people. But at *each turn of history, apartheid was bound to spawn* resistance; it was destined *to bring to life* the forces that would guarantee *its death*. It is the *dictate of history to bring to the fore the* kind of leaders who seize the moment, who cohere the wishes and aspirations of the oppressed.[73]

> To the extent that some of the apprehensions are imagined or based on opposition to change, to that extent we are convinced that *history will be the best teacher*.[74]

By personifying history and equating it with the anti-apartheid movement, Mandela is arguing that the ANC is a force that connects with the invisible 'natural' forces of human evolution. The legitimizing concept here seems to be THE ANC IS A HISTORICAL FORCE – as well as being a natural and a moral one.

The second strategy in designing legitimacy communication is to present himself as the legitimate symbol of black aspirations for equality, just as (we will see) Castro has represented himself as the symbol of the people's will, and of the revolution. Of course the legal processes of the apartheid government attempted to eliminate his legitimacy by taking him out of society with a life sentence; however, as part of his communication of leadership Mandela was able to design his imprisonment as a symbol for the imprisonment of a whole people:

> Freedom is indivisible; the chains on any one of my people were the chains on all of them. The chains on all my people were the chains on me.[75]

The indivisibility of leader and follower – that we have seen is a defining feature of charismatic leadership – was vital to his design of leadership communication because it implied a conceptual metonym LEADER FOR POLITICAL MOVEMENT (ANC). At first he designed himself as the symbol of the ANC, and later extended this design so that he became a symbol of a multi-racial South Africa. Mandela's legitimacy as a leader was primarily because he came to symbolize, personally, the moral worth of a multi-racial society based on reconciliation and forgiveness; this contrasted with the conflict and revenge that had characterized the experience of apartheid for many black and white South Africans. A dramatic appeal to universal values (in line with nature, morality and history) is common among charismatic leaders and was also used by Gandhi and Castro. Mandela based his legitimacy in universal principles of natural justice and his statement of it in his Nobel Prize acceptance speech alludes to both Martin Luther King and the declaration of human rights in the American constitution:

> The value of our shared reward will and must be measured by the joyful peace which will triumph. Because the common humanity that bonds both black and white into one human race, will have said to each one of us that we shall all live like the children of paradise. Thus shall we live, because we will have created a society which recognises that all people are born equal, with each entitled in equal measure to life, liberty, prosperity, human right and good governance.

He continues with direct reference to his own experience: 'Such a society shall never allow again that there should be prisoners of conscience nor that any person's human rights should be violated'.[76] Issues of universal morality and justice therefore become issues of how he personally was treated by the justice system. As well as symbolizing an oppressed people in a particular time and place, the leader also becomes a universal symbol of resistance to oppression. This is based on the extension of a conceptual metonym LEADER FOR POLITICAL MOVEMENT (ANC) to POLITICAL MOVEMENT (ANC) FOR ALL HUMAN RIGHTS and was implied by the legitimacy claims based on nature, morality and history. It was the personal moral development arising from his extended experience of prison that formed the basis for Mandela's general legitimacy claim to be a symbol of the universal human rights of the oppressed. As he put it:

> Prison was a kind of crucible that tested a man's character. Some men, under the pressure of incarceration, showed true mettle, while others revealed themselves as less than what they appeared to be.[77]

Prison itself provided the time for personal self-development and study:

In the struggle, Robben Island was known as 'the university' because of what we learned from each other.[78]

The metaphor 'the prison as university' was a way of usurping and challenging the state's intention that it should be a place of confinement. Since many prisoners went on to take degrees, the metaphoric way of thinking about the institution came to determine its reality. For Mandela, and others, prison was a lifelong learning experience. When his fellow inmate Kathrada said 'they can take us out of Robben Island, but they can't take Robben Island out of us'[79] he was referring to this broader education.

It is insightful to contrast legitimacy claims in Mandela's use of metaphors in speeches *prior to* imprisonment with those that characterized his speeches *after* imprisonment. The former are 'conflict' metaphors, while the latter draw on the domain of constructive activities (e.g. building) and journeys. Around three-quarters of his conflict metaphors occur in his speeches prior to imprisonment. In 1953 in his first major speech as president of Transvaal ANC he looked back on the Defiance Campaign when:

The entire country was transformed *into battle zones* where the forces of liberation were locked up in *immortal conflict* against those of reaction and evil. Our *flag flew in every battlefield* and thousands of our countrymen *rallied around it.* We held the initiative and the *forces of freedom* were *advancing on all fronts.*[80]

Although this was cited literally in the treason trial as evidence of Mandela's violent intentions, he explained that it was intended metaphorically.[81] As ANC representative to the Conference on Pan-African Freedom in Addis Ababa in January 1962, Mandela said in his address:

In most of these territories the *imperialist forces* have been considerably weakened and are unable to resist the demand for freedom and independence – thanks to the *powerful blows delivered by the freedom movements* . . . there can be no doubt that imperialism is *in full retreat* . . . It is a country torn from top to bottom by *fierce racial strife and conflict* and where the *blood of African patriots frequently flows.*[82]

Although blood did indeed flow in the struggles for independence, evidently some of the personifications here would normally be considered as hyperbole. Uses such as these become rare in the latter part of the corpus as his legitimacy as leader of South Africa became increasingly grounded in the symbolism of himself as the embodiment of forgiveness, reconciliation, peace and national unity. It was ultimately because Mandela was able to become a symbol of the human rights of the oppressed – irrespective of whether they were repressed for racial, social or ethnic reasons – that his political cause gained legitimacy in the world outside of South Africa.

Leadership and the media

Mandela was keenly aware of the importance of the media in the dissemination of leadership. This is mainly because it had played an important part in
publicising his imprisonment and spreading the anti-apartheid message
around the world – he subsequently made himself available to the media
because, under apartheid, the introduction of television was delayed until
1976 and then tightly controlled. Although the majority of newspapers
were white-owned, he thanked the press on his release from prison for
having not forgotten the ANC cause:

> In this regard, I wish to thank the media for its vigilance. While there
> may be instances where fingers were pointed at individuals without jus-
> tification, there are a good many examples where investigative journal-
> ism has helped us uncover the scoundrels – old and new – who prey on
> the public purse.[83]

But he was also aware of the power of the media to influence public opinion
in a way that could undermine his legitimacy:

> It is understandable that unscrupulous politicians, media commentators
> and those who wish to question the legitimacy of the democratic process
> as such will conjure up crises in their heads, where in reality there are no
> crises.[84]

He sought to influence the development of the media in the new democratic
South Africa:

> They are required as we strive to bring all power into the hands of the
> people; as we seek to shape a new media that appreciates the conditions
> and aspirations of the majority.[85]

Ultimately, the story of Nelson Mandela's life has always sold newspapers
because of its potential for dramatic representation and the media have been
quick to capitalize on its potential for communicating mythic themes that
cut across particular segments of their readership. His life experiences are a
drama with a universal appeal and he has therefore been fortunate enough,
usually, to have the media on his side, and clever enough to exploit this in
order to communicate his message to a global audience. His autobiography
continues to be an international bestseller. Increasingly, Mandela has
appeared in video clips shown on international television in connection with
any causes associated with the human rights of oppressed groups. His
Indonesian shirts, benign smile, age and appearance communicate his status
as an icon of the oppressed symbolizing their moral integrity – a latter-day
Martin Luther King. His performance of leadership communicates the

message that, ultimately, humanitarian causes are legitimate ones and, because of this, will be successful.

Summary

Nelson Mandela has been a highly successful charismatic leader; initially, this was because he offered a catharsis to a society that was in conflict with itself. Through personal example he demonstrated a process – based on inner reflection and understanding – through which someone could become a leader by changing his style of communication from one based on aggression towards one based on understanding the opponent's point of view. Like Gandhi and, as we will see in the next chapter, Castro, his moral leadership formed the basis for his political leadership and it was because he became a better person that he became a more effective leader:

> Mandela's basic appeal was not as a man of power, but as a moral leader who had stood for the fundamental principles and who gave hope for the future to all oppressed peopled and all countries torn by racial divisions. His dignity and wish for reconciliation gave him an influence beyond ordinary politics, which was the more surprising because he was not religious.[86]

It was only by effective leadership design that Mandela became a symbol, first of his own people, and, then, of humanity as a whole. His use of slogans and African expressions was important in communicating a sense of local historical destiny. But his conceptual metaphors – such as THE POLIT-ICAL MOVEMENT (ANC) IS A MORAL FORCE, A HISTORICAL FORCE and A NATURAL FORCE – were able to connect local political concerns in South Africa with those of the outside world and with a general historical improvement in human right. He drew strength from the civil rights struggle in the USA through metaphoric allusion to Martin Luther King because this connected spatially with another place. But, above all, he was happy to perform for the media to enable it to create a myth out of his life story so that he could never simply be forgotten as just another political prisoner. Though his story had its origins in a very specific historical-cultural situation, it became transformed into a dramatic myth of the power of the human will to overcome oppression.

Nelson Mandela's design of leadership style was communicated by repre-senting the anti-apartheid movement as part of a natural, moral and histor-ical process. He first designed himself as the legitimate symbol of the ANC, and then performed a role as the symbol of *all* human aspirations towards freedom and equality. This was cognitively based in the conceptual metonyms: LEADER FOR POLITICAL MOVEMENT (ANC) and POLIT-ICAL MOVEMENT (ANC) FOR ALL HUMAN RIGHTS; together these implied, therefore: LEADER FOR UNIVERSAL HUMAN RIGHTS.

Mandela's design of leadership style transformed him from being initially a party political leader, then a national leader, to becoming, symbolically, a leader of mankind – a truly global icon of leadership of the oppressed. In this respect he can be considered as the prototype of a transformational leader because we can define his leadership style both by the effect that it had on race relations in his own country *and* on the status and value placed in the modern world on ideas such as democracy, equality and freedom.

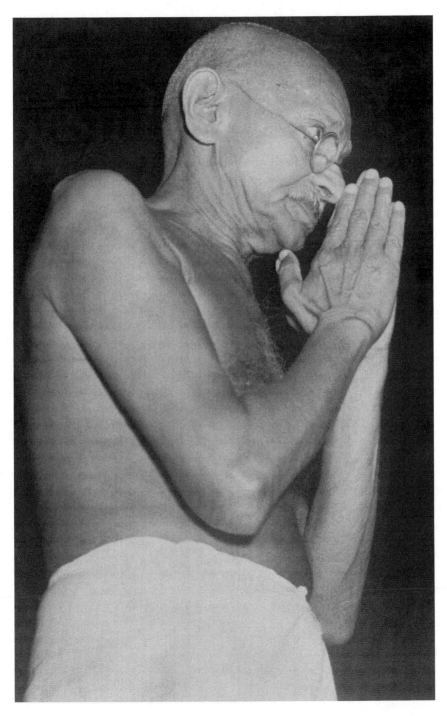

Plate 1 Mahatma Gandhi, praying, 2 December 1949 (© Bettmann/CORBIS).

Plate 2 Nelson Mandela, photographed around 1990, in Johannesburg, South Africa (© Hans Gedda/CORBIS).

Plate 3 Fidel Castro displaying a murder plot headline, 23 April 1959. Castro was in New York at the time; when asked about a reported assassination attempt, he replied: 'In Cuba, they had tanks, planes and they run away. So what are they going to do here? I sleep well and don't worry at all' (© Bettmann/CORBIS).

Plate 4 Ayatollah Ruhollah Khomeini shaking hands with a crowd, 3 February 1979. He had returned from exile on 1 February 1979 to take control of the revolutionary government (© Bettmann/CORBIS).

Plate 5 Ayatollah Ruhollah Khomeini praying in the garden of his villa at Pontchartrain, near Paris, where he was staying during his exile from Iran (© Bettmann/CORBIS).

Plate 6 Lee Kuan Yew speaking at a press conference on 4 September 1988 after winning a landslide victory in Singapore's general election, winning every seat except one (© CORBIS).

6   Fidel Castro

The Cuban Robin Hood

Introduction

The image of Fidel Castro – a big man with an unkempt beard wearing a peaked khaki cap and coarse military fatigues has become – along with those of Lenin, Mao, Che Guevara and Mao Tse-tung – a major global icon of communism. The fact that he is still a leader in the first decade of the twenty-first century is a prodigious feat of leadership skill. By 1962 the Cuban leader had already spent several years in exile, led a successful socialist rebellion, and fought off a US-sponsored invasion; since then he has resisted numerous assassination attempts and proven to be the greatest of political survivors. Though originally a pawn in a superpower struggle for global domination, since the collapse of the Soviet Union he has become a dramatic symbol of the moral courage of smaller nations in their struggle for survival as independent entities against usually aggressive and expansionist neighbours.

We may well ask how it is that the leader of a small island with a population of around ten million is still a thorn in the side of the most powerful nation in human history. In this chapter I propose that this is because he has designed a leadership style in which he identifies himself with Cuban national aspirations and these, in turn, have come to symbolize the cause of underdogs everywhere. This communication strategy – like that of Mandela and Gandhi – establishes an ethical legitimacy through adopting the cause of the underprivileged in societies dominated by apparently powerful and immoral forces; this satisfies the deep unconscious needs of followers for a heroic leader.

The ethical legitimacy of the underdog who heroically challenges the legitimacy claims of the powerful is evident in the following critique of the United States:

> I cannot understand how an opulent society like our neighbor's dare to speak of human rights, while 44 million people there have no right to medical care, where millions of citizens live in ghettos and countless beggars live under bridges; a society where there are millions of illiterates and semi-illiterates, where there are millions and millions of

unemployed and where prisons are filled with the children of the poorest and most deprived segments of the population ... Their hatred for Cuba stems from the unexpected resistance a small country has put up against this power and its allied powers which have plundered the planet. Cuba's presence is a pointing finger and proof that nations can fight, stand firm and win. Cuba's very presence is a humiliation for those who have imposed the most repugnant system of exploitation that has ever existed on Earth.[1]

Castro's rhetoric is intended to activate feelings of guilt by making Cuba symbolize a heroic alternative to the socioeconomic system led by the United States whose greed is represented as the cause of Third World suffering:

On your conscience, and on those of the leaders of the world's richest states, lies the genocide which is implicit in the death, every year, of more than 10 million children and tens of millions more people who could be saved. These deaths are the result of a vast assortment of pillage and robbery practiced against Third World countries through the unjust and no longer sustainable world economic order that the rich countries have imposed to the detriment of 80 percent of this planet's population.[2]

Castro establishes ethical legitimacy by identifying Cuban aspirations and interests with those of *all* Third World countries and his leadership style embraces all nations that are opposed to American global dominance. This internationalist perspective is ideologically motivated by the desire to counter the forces of globalization in which the market prices paid by consumers on one side of the world determine the fate of millions of producers on the other. As the leader of a state whose very existence is under constant threat he claims to draw on an inexhaustible supply of positive moral credentials that legitimize his role as a global Robin Hood struggling for natural justice. These credentials are based on broad Christian notions of equality and generosity in the allocation of resources and in support of oppressed people everywhere:

We are, in short, for all the noble aspirations of all the peoples. That is our position. We are, and always shall be for everything that is just: against colonialism, exploitation, monopolies, militarism, the armaments race, and warmongering. We shall always be against such things. That will be our position.[3]

The charismatic appeal of Castro has been noted by many of those who have met him. Perhaps none more so than Che Guevara. According to his lover, Hilda Gadea, Guevara felt himself drawn to Castro 'from the outset, moved by a feeling of romantic, adventurous sympathy, and by the conviction that it would be worth dying on an alien beach for such a pure ideal'. Followers were genuinely inspired by Fidel Castro and testimony to this is that they were prepared to put their faith in a creaking hulk – the *Granma* – to embark on a military escapade against Batista's corrupt and ruthless government for which they were singularly ill-equipped. Remarkably – and against all odds – they proved to be successful and nothing appeals like a successful underdog.

Non-linguistic communication of charisma

Appearance and leadership style

Fidel Castro has always had an actor's interest in appearance; as a young man he dressed fashionably in a dapper style and since then his physique, stamina and appearance have been crucial in the creation of a charismatic image as a forceful and robust leader. Subliminally, his physical height and presence have symbolized moral stature and political power. We can relate the symbolic appeal of his height to the underlying concept MORAL IS UPRIGHT; we find evidence of this in expressions such as 'pillar of society' and 'an upstanding member of society'. The positive association of the notion can be traced to the upright position of the healthy human body, and Castro's demanding work schedule – equalled only in the leaders covered in this book by that of Lee Kuan Yew – and longevity are evidence of the excellent health he has enjoyed for much of his life.

A biographer who knew Castro personally, presents this dramatic description of him as he advanced to Havana in January 1959:

> His semi-automatic rifle ... slung over his shoulder and his horn-rimmed spectacles perched on his Roman nose, Castro now presented the image of a warrior-philosopher king. This was precisely the way he intended to be seen and remembered for ever. The famous beard, the cigar-clenched in his teeth, and the olive-green combat fatigues (with a small medallion of the Virgin of Cobre on a chain around his neck conveniently visible under his open-collar blouse), these were the symbols of the Fidel Castro personality.[4]

When the rebel army entered Oriente in response to a call for a general strike, an important question relating to appearance was that of whether the rebels should shave off their beards. According to the Spanish journalist Meneses[5] the beards made the rebels more exotic – and certainly more photogenic – in addition, some rebels were concerned that by shaving they would become indistinguishable from the local population thereby endangering these innocent civilians from a police counterattack. Like the debates between the cast and the director as regards costume and make-up for a drama production, those more aware of symbolic communication won the argument and the beards were retained. Castro's beard achieved something of a legendary status: when the Sandinista delegation visited Cuba on the 26 July celebrations in 1980 Castro said:

> It has been said that the tyrant Somoza, when bidding farewell to the troops, asked them to at least bring him a hair from Castro's beard. [applause]. I have come here with a full beard. [applause]. to offer it to the victorious Nicaraguan people, even if only symbolically. [applause].

Further evidence of Castro's perception of his beard as a leadership symbol is testified by the fact that he has strongly discouraged other Cubans from wearing beards: this suggests that it contributes significantly to the design and performance of leadership style.[6]

The appearance of the eyes is especially important in communicating charisma – especially as regards their size, luminosity and intensity. Hilda Gadea noted of Castro that: 'when he spoke his eyes lit up with passion and with faith in the revolution'. Appearances are especially important in creating influential and persuasive impressions that linger in the mind in first meetings. The Cuban novelist, Terasa Casuso, described his first meeting with Castro in a Mexican gaol yard as follows:

> More than 50 Cubans were gathered in the large central courtyard . . . In the middle, tall and clear-shaven with close-cropped chestnut hair, dressed soberly and correctly in a brown suit, standing out from the rest by his look and his bearing, was their chief Fidel Castro. He gave one the impression of being noble, sure, deliberate – like a big Newfoundland dog . . . he looked eminently serene, and inspired confidence and a sense of security.

What is significant about this observation is that Castro's appearance marked him out from those around him and identified him as a leader. Everything about Castro's appearance contributed to the shared social perceptions of his followers and therefore to his leadership style.

Dress

Castro has consistently employed clothes as a powerful semiotic in the performance of leadership style. As a revolutionary leader he has typically worn the coarse military khaki of a Latin American soldier and the simple peaked military cap that photographs of him have made so familiar. A dramatic gesture regarding his military uniform is that he has always worn the insignia of a major. The military uniform with the modest insignia symbolizes an ongoing commitment to a revolution based in the ideal of equality. The relatively low position of military command implies that the relation with followers has not changed since he first came to power: the leader is simply another follower of the revolutionary ideal. As we will see later, this fits with a verbal message in which Castro symbolizes the revolution and the will of the people. In communism the leader must necessarily appear as the most prototypical of followers.

Because the image of a leader dressed in the olive green uniform of a guerrilla commander is well established, when Castro wears any other outfit he communicates a meaning that gains saliency from its variation from the norm. Soon after the revolution he caused a sensation in Cartegena by appearing in a long-sleeved shirt and, subsequently, in Paris his dark suit symbolized adaptation to the new post-Soviet political climate. Castro's dress has always played a role in performing leadership by communicating subliminally important political messages.

Two other dress performances are especially significant. The first is his use of local, traditional clothing when on overseas trips. As a leader who has modelled himself on the Cuban nationalist leader Martí, and has identified closely with Cuban history, he has known the importance of showing empathy with the political aspirations of all developing nations. The simplest way to communicate this is by wearing clothes that symbolize yearnings for a national cultural identity. Another semiotic performance is wearing the clothing of the sports that he is most passionate about: baseball and basketball. A number of images of Castro testify to his status as a big hitter in baseball. The image of a successful sportsman is associated with physical strength, stamina and courage – all qualities that may be transferred to the charismatic leader by the design of leadership style. Castro has also shown an awareness of the role of dress and taste in appealing to young audiences. The use of traditional, sports and modern styles shows the influence of cultural factors on the design of leadership style, whether nationally or ethnically defined cultures, or global in nature.

Artefacts

Apart from his cigar, for Fidel Castro the most significant, valued artefact that has come to symbolize the power of leadership is the gun. As a boy who resented early separation from his family it symbolized a source of protection and security and in school he always kept a pistol in his room. Later in the Sierra Maestra after leading the insurrection against Batista's government he kept a gun within arm's reach. At night he slept with a rifle on his chest and the barrel under his chin and finger on the trigger so that if the guerillas were taken by surprise he could evade capture and the humiliation of certain execution.[7] Still later, as head of government, he would put a weapon on the table when conferring and his most valued gift has always been a weapon. As summarized by one of his biographers:

> His life, as a child and a revolutionary, was one long love affair with firearms. His speeches were studded with reference to blood and to the prospects of violence and death. No man was complete without

weapons. They assured protection from enemies. They symbolized the power to impose one's will, the assertion of virility. Attack before you are attacked. Weaponless you are emasculated, helpless, effeminate. With a pistol the world is yours.[8]

The importance of the gun to Castro's perception of political power and leadership was because ultimately he agreed with Mao (as, we will see later, did Lee Kuan Yew) that 'political power grows out of the barrel of a gun';[9] we can see this philosophy in the following:

> As long as there is a man left with a gun, the seed of a guerrilla army remains! (applause) . . . There will be no surrenders, no defeats, because a man with a gun will always under any circumstances become a very dangerous man – a man with a gun, and even better if he has an automatic weapon, and better still if it happens to be an 'AKM' – such a man is extraordinarily dangerous for any aggressor.[10]

Castro had experienced as a rebel leader the crucial importance of weaponry in the attainment of political power:

> But we were very few. As we recently said in Manzanillo, we had seven rifles at the beginning. Among all of us there was not a single automatic weapon. We had a submachine gun. No, not even that. That submachine gun we found months later. We had seven bolt-action rifles . . . The enemy was very powerful, extremely powerful. They had some 70,000 to 80,000 men. We had to live those 25 months of war with seven rifles at the beginning to 3,000 armed men at the end.[11]

At times the attraction of guns was almost obsessive:

> The day had to come when the people would say: 'Enough! Out! Guns for the workers and the peasants! Machetes for the peasants! Guns for the students! Guns for the men! Guns for the women! Guns for the old people! Guns for the children! Guns for everyone!'[12]

This is perhaps a true reflection of the immediate importance of weaponry in the practice of a political revolution and in establishing the legitimacy of a new source of authority. In this respect, the gun became a metonym for the revolution itself. However, with maturity, and the establishment of himself and the revolution as sources of moral authority, there has been a gradual decrease in references to guns in his speeches. For example, in his speeches during the 1960s there are 18 references to 'gun' whereas in the 1980s I found only three references to 'gun' and in the 1990s none at all.

Symbolic action and body language

Fidel Castro has always designed a leadership image based on dynamism and action; in many ways this has come naturally because of his shear physical strength and energy. Symbolic performances that intended to appeal to new audiences include attending a Manic Street Preachers concert in Havana and unveiling a statue of John Lennon in Havana Park. Photographs of him rarely show him in a sitting position, typically he is standing and engaged in some type of physical action – whether it is public speaking, playing sports or travelling. Personal accounts and portrait photographs show evidence of animated facial expression, eye movement and physical proximity to the addressee. His speech deliveries are fully orchestrated by extensive use of hand gestures.

Two incidents reflect Castro's awareness of the semiotic potential of symbolic performances for the creation of dramatic effect in the design of leadership style. The first was in July 1947 when he was seeking to bring down Grau's government after it failed to support the Cayo Confites expedition.[13] He arranged for dramatic use of the very same bell that was struck by Carlos Manuel de Cespedes to signal the start of the 1st War of Cuban Independence. As the call to prayer in Christian culture, the bell has always been a potent symbol. He ordered that the bell was taken to the front of a mass demonstration and tolled while the crowd demanded Grau's resignation.[14] The bell communicated the meaning that the demonstrators were closely allied to Cuban independence and national spirit. Castro showed his awareness of the importance of symbolism in creating a political spectacle that would evoke an emotional response.

The second illustration of dramatic performance was when Castro was informed that his son Fidelito had been injured in a car accident while he was actually in the course of giving a TV interview. His permission was required for the boy to go to hospital for a major surgical operation, initially he procrastinated until the studio audience had to interrupt to insist that he went. His mother is said later to have told him 'You haven't changed. You are as irresponsible as ever'.[15] However, his refusal to go symbolized that the leader must be prepared to sacrifice personal interests and feelings to the greater cause of the revolution. Such sacrifices contribute significantly to the design of leadership style.

Although apparently heartless and irresponsible, this contrasted with the actions of previous Cuban leaders who had exploited their position of power to gain personal advantage for their families. Such leaders were the first to leave Cuba when events turned against them. Since Castro's leadership appeal was designed around ethical legitimacy, it was essential that he remained free of the accusation of putting his own needs – or those of his family – before those of the nation or the revolution – at least until he was exhorted to do so by the people!

Stylistic features of verbal communication

Fidel Castro has designed his leadership style through quantity: as a person-ality who is larger than life his rhetoric can be quantified by the length and number of his speeches. His speech 'History will absolve me' was over 26,000 words in length; some of his speeches have lasted more than nine hours; he has frequently made four-hour television appearances. A related and qualitat-ive reason for the shear quantity of his discourse is the conversational nature of his speech style; as he once put it: 'I discovered that the secret of public speaking was precisely not to give a speech, but rather to talk to the audi-ence'.[16] We have seen that a style of talking rather than lecturing to people was also characteristic of Mandela. However, the conversational style of a highly enthusiastic interlocutor leads to an extended verbal event.

A further stylistic feature that is also reminiscent of Mandela is the use of dramatic slogans. The word slogan originates from the Gaelic *slaughghairm* meaning 'army cry' or 'war cry' – as formerly used by Scottish clans. Like the bagpipe, the purpose was to exhort warriors to courageous acts that would lead to conquest on the battlefield. Slogans are powerful instruments of per-suasion across a range of language genres, from advertising to political cam-paigning. As with other speech forms, such as proverbs, they contain a number of features likely to make learning them easier; these include brevity, rhythm, repetition (of words and grammatical forms), alliteration and assonance. The primary purpose of slogans is to motivate followers by giving them a shared identity by finding a verbal form that communicates their shared ideological objectives.

Castro typically ends his speeches with his most favoured slogan: 'Father-land or death, we will win/conquer'. This was a shortened form of a slogan coined by the Independence leader Antonio Waceo: 'Anyone who intends to seize Cuba will soak the dust with his blood: Fatherland or death!' The role of this colourful slogan is to evoke emotions that eliminate fear of death and contrast any sense of personal loss with the nobility of the patriotic cause. There is evidence in Castro's explanation of the meaning of this slogan that he was fully aware of its motivating potential:

> What does this mean? This slogan means that no one of us cares if he dies provided his people lives, provided his fatherland lives, that no one of us minds giving his life for the fatherland, so that the fatherland can continue to live (applause and shouts of 'fatherland or death' and 'we will triumph'). And why do the people say 'we will triumph'? The people say this because even though many of us may fall, even though individually many of our compatriots, if the fatherland needs them, will sacrifice their lives, it will not be in vain, but it will be so that the fatherland can triumph! And for this reason each one of us says: 'Father-land or death!' And the people say 'We will triumph!' The fatherland says 'we will triumph!' (Shouts of 'we will triumph!').[17]

Castro here uses conversational strategies that encourage audience involvement such as questions and answers; effectively, the second part of this excerpt repeats the first part, leading to an extended discourse style with cyclical repetition that assists comprehension. Choice of an expression such as 'the fatherland' communicates a nationalist emotion that distinguishes the slogan from conventional Marxist–Leninist ideology. It is evident that Castro was fully aware of conventional Marxist slogans:

> Because in our determination to build communism, putting the emphasis on the slogan 'from each according to his capacity, to each according to his labor'.[18]

> If the unity of all progressive and revolutionary forces is the battle cry that Marx gave to the communists of each country, the unity of the international communist movement is the slogan of all the Marxists–Leninists. 'Workers of the world, unite' was the command of Marx and Engels.[19]

> We are reminded of the leader of the Soviet proletariat, who fought so much for peace: Lenin, whose slogan of 'Bread, peace, and land' converted that imperialist war into a socialist revolution.[20]

Castro takes a speech form that has the persuasive functions of creating social cohesion and encouraging vigorous forms of action and applies it to the Cuban context. The aim of his slogans was not so much to inspire class hatred (as it was in the Cultural Revolution in China) as to evoke historical memory of revolutionary struggle. His slogans communicate a heroic myth because they encourage an image of his supporters as people who were prepared to overcome their individual fears in the pursuit of patriotic social goals. In this respect they contribute to moral legitimacy since social and national survival is prioritized over individual survival.

The use of humour also contributes to Castro's design of leadership style; the informality of humour serves to reduce the rhetorical distance between leader and followers:

> I'll go to hell. The heat will be unbearable. But the pain won't be as bad as expecting too much from heaven, which always breaks its promises. When I arrive in hell, I'll meet Marx, Engels and Lenin. And you too, by the way, because capitalists also go to hell, especially when they enjoy life too much.[21]

> If a dog goes into a park to relieve itself, US satellites are observing it, photographing it and reporting it. Satellites are the entire world spying on everything.[22]

Such use of humour is a very important stylistic shift that makes the leader at one with his audience since laughter is a shared social experience. Jokes are a form of style shifting away from political, social and economic registers and counterbalance the didacticism that often characterizes other modes of revolutionary rhetoric. They provide an individualized and personal touch and show that underneath the high-minded revolutionary there is an instinctive perfomer. Jokes also provide relief from the tedium of the very lengthy speeches that we have seen characterize his communication style – Castro even occasionally mocks himself for the length of his speeches.

Communication of vision and values

Castro's leadership beliefs are communicated through his vision of a small independent state that practices the values of equality, justice and freedom. The ideal of social justice based in fundamental human equality draws simultaneously on Christianity and Marxism and is not far removed from the Liberation Theology that has become a predominant political force throughout South America. An important strategy for the communication of this vision is to contrast this ideal with the alternatives of colonialism and imperialism. As with the leaders analysed in earlier chapters, metaphors are a core characteristic in the design of leadership style. In Castro's vision the US is the embodiment of immoral forces and his favourite metaphor is to refer to the shark and the sardine when contrasting the greed and rapacity of imperialism with Cuba's moral integrity. It seems that this metaphor originated in a popular fable:

> To understand this problem of America, a book which explains the truculence of U.S. policy in our continent must be read. It is called 'The Fable of the Shark and the Sardine'. The shark is the Yankee empire; the sardines the weak American nations.[23]

There are several rhetorical characteristics of this metaphor that are worthy of note; it is one that draws on highly familiar areas of experience – both sardines and sharks thrive in the warm tropical sees of Cuba. Moreover, deep-sea fishing is his own favourite pastime and has also attracted others, such as Ernest Hemingway, to Cuba. Stylistically, there is a humorous element in evoking a child's fable to communicate a political argument. Conceptually, the contrast is one of size: in this metaphor size is associated with greed; but we also usually think of sharks as single operators while sardines typically move in shoals. This is an important aspect of the mapping of source domain onto the target of political relationships, as Castro has always sought allies amongst other smaller threatened nations – especially those in Latin America. This is evident in the following:

> The powerful country had violated the law against economic aggression; but when the time came to condemn the shark, the sardines met and condemned the other sardine. But this sardine was no longer a sardine.[24]

Here we can see that there is the political argument that smaller countries gain political power by forming alliances against larger ones. Fables are based on the conceptual metaphor PEOPLE ARE ANIMALS, interpreting the metaphor relies on working out the entities and behaviours in human relationships that correspond with the natural world. However, when applied in a political context the metaphor changes to COUNTRIES ARE ANIMALS and interpretation relies on working out correspondences between the behaviour of *social* entities and that of the animal kingdom. As well as the primary attributes of the shark – greed, strength and rapacity etc. – their typical behaviour also provides the argumentative potential of this metaphor:

> President Castro also spoke with CARACOL reporters about one of his favorite hobbies: underwater fishing. He answered some of the journalist's questions on this subject, especially questions about what a shark attack is like; for example, most of us believe that a shark attacks when it is hungry or when it smells or sees blood, but this is completely wrong in President Castro's opinion. He says that a shark attacks a man or a fish when they flee. However, in the case of a confrontation between a shark and a man, if the man stands his ground, the shark will flee . . . In his remarks on the behavior of sharks, President Castro was clearly alluding, although he did not say so, to Cuba's role in relation to the United States.[25]

Here the metaphor argues that Cuba intended to resist intimidation by the US in its policy of disrupting Cuba's political and economic life by economic blockade. It was the US policy of isolating Cuba that forced it to rely on the Soviet Union as the major political and trading partner. Underlying the metaphors 'the US is a greedy shark' and 'Cuba is a brave fish' is the conceptual metaphor: IMPERIALISM IS A RAPACIOUS ANIMAL, and it is this that forms an important component of Castro's political argument – as he argued on another occasion:

> If this country, vis-a-vis imperialism – which is a wild beast, a barracuda, a shark vulture with all its deft tricks, if this small country had ever shown fear and hesitation before the imperialists they would have devoured us.[26]

The metaphor again evokes feelings of heroism and courage in a dramatic struggle against a more powerful opponent. The metaphor could also be extended to evaluate shifts in political alliances, as when criticising those 'sardines' that have allied themselves with the 'shark':

> In a brief meeting with representatives of the Western press during a reception offered for his visiting colleague from Trinidad-Tobago, Eric

Williams, the Cuban prime minister described the TIAR as a shameful and indecent pact between the shark and the sardines. By means of that treaty, according to Castro, the shark is attempting to keep the sardines unarmed in order to train armies and maintain the dominance of trans-national enterprises. This led reporters to identify the shark as being the United States and the sardines the countries south of the Rio Grande.[27]

An important characteristic of the use of metaphors in the design of leadership style is that it is up to followers to interpret them. A joint act of meaning creation is effective in political argument because it stimulates the hearer to share the inferences of the leader. The act of metaphor interpretation bonds followers with leaders and such uses can have a transforming effect on followers.

The animal metaphor was not the only one employed by Castro to describe the relationship between the US and its smaller neighbours. He was quick to exploit the dramatic potential of another metaphor that satirises America's colonial aspirations – and one that ironically was coined by a President of the US:

John Adams had said Cuba was like an apple hanging from the Spanish tree, ready to fall into U.S. hands when ripe. Spanish power had wasted away in our country. Spain no longer had resources for keeping on with the war in Cuba. Spain was defeated. The apple was apparently ripe. And the U.S. Government stretched out its hand. A number of apples fell into its hands: Puerto Rico, the Philippines, and others.[28]

The conceptual metaphor SMALL COUNTRIES ARE RIPE FRUIT contains a political argument that they are ready for plucking by colonizers. In the formation of political arguments effective leaders are able to manipulate metaphors to serve their own rhetorical objectives. A good example of this is when Castro breathed life back into his favourite metaphor – now established as something of a political myth – by *rejecting* the view of Cuba as a powerless sardine:

If someone was able to write that bit about the shark swallowing the sardine, and a book with that title even appeared in the initial years of the revolution by an author who at that time had certain decorously progressive ideas, today you cannot talk about the shark and the sardine. Today you can talk about the shark and the fireball, and ask if the shark could swallow the fireball. [applause]. Today you can talk about the shark and steel, and ask if the shark could swallow that gigantic ball of steel which is the Cuban revolution today. [applause, chanting].[29]

The audience response here indicates the success of the inter-textual strategy of modifying and adapting an established metaphor. Similarly, he is able to exploit its potential of the conceptual metaphor SMALL COUNTRIES ARE RIPE FRUIT, by extending it further to develop a political argument:

> It is our historic privilege to have thwarted their dream of having the ripe apple fall into their lap. It will never fall, not like a ripe fruit, or like a rotten fruit. We have political maturity, revolutionary maturity. Those who wait with open mouths for the apple to fall will decompose before the apple becomes rotten. [Applause]. The empire will rot before the Cuban Revolution does. [Applause].[30]

Here he rejects the mapping of the ripening and rotting process onto Cuba by mapping these processes onto imperialists. Castro also communicates his moral vision with other types of animal metaphor based on the conceptual metaphor HUMAN BEHAVIOUR IS ANIMAL BEHAVIOUR:

> Cuba was the last country in America to free itself from Spanish colonial rule, to cast off, with due respect to the representative of Spain, the Spanish colonial yoke; and because it was the last, *it also had to fight more fiercely*. Spain had only one small possession left in America and it *defended it with tooth and nail*.[31]

In Castro's rhetorical flora and fauna, while small countries are ripe fruit or sardines and colonizing powers are rapacious humans or sharks, the capitalist is represented either as a beast:

> Ah, but a capitalist is *like a wild beast defending* his factory, defending raw materials, defending costs, defending everything, based on a ferocious contradiction with the worker, defending his interests as a capitalist . . . He is a *wild beast*, and he is efficient.[32]

Or as a parasite:

> All thieves, spies, henchmen, criminals, and smugglers in the world have employment assured with the Yankee Central Intelligence Agency, with imperialism. Of course this employment does not mean work, but rather being a mercenary, killing, robbing, lying, and *living as a parasite*. For the peasant and the honest man, work is not a punishment, but *for a parasite* the worst thing in the world is work.[33]

While capitalists can be vultures, beasts or parasites, counter-revolutionaries are invariably 'worms'. In the design of his leadership style animal metaphors become a coded form of discourse in which he arouses emotional states in the audience by mapping animal social attributes and behaviour onto human and social ones.

Analogy is another strategy for the communication of political vision and values in Castro's design of leadership style. A favoured analogy for depicting the relationship between Cuba and the US is the dramatic narrative of David and Goliath; the following instances occur over a wide period of time:

> But in this case, it became a struggle between David and Goliath: the struggle of a small people against the imperialist giant, whose vast hands can reach the peoples of all of the continents of the world.[34]

> It does not matter how big the Goliath of the North has grown because David has also grown bigger, morally and spiritually.[35]

> David is remembered because he fought against Goliath. Cubans will be remembered, who are an even smaller David against a much larger Goliath; will have to be remembered at least as much as David is remembered. If movies are made someplace other than Hollywood, or the United States, perhaps a few good movies will be made about the Cuban Revolution. [chuckles].[36]

> We could say that we are involved in that Biblical struggle, the struggle of David and Goliath. We need support because this battle has to be won morally and politically. Above all, by winning the moral battle, one wins everything.[37]

In Christian culture the biblical story of David and Goliath forms the prototype for the outcome of victory by a weaker combatant over a larger and more powerful one because of moral superiority and righteousness. David is the prototype of the heroic underdog representing courage based in self-righteousness when confronted by a large intimidating and unjust opponent. Its message is that faith and belief in a cause guarantee military success.

Castro was always quick in finding opportunities to take the moral high ground over his opponents and in locating the ethical basis for his political actions in the Bible. He is quick to find similarities between the behaviour of revolutionaries and Christians:

> Unscrupulous elements fail to understand the revolutionary meaning of the blood shed by Christ. They even want to undermine the traditional religious sentiment our people have for the Virgin of Charity because she is the virgin of all the Cubans, because she is the virgin of Sierra Maestra. This virgin saved the lives of three poor fishermen, among whom there certainly must have been a Negro. This should serve as an example to the hypocritical and farcical aristocrats who have been discriminating against the Negro. It is also well to remember that when Christ was looking for men to preach his doctrine, he did not look for 12 landholders but for 12 unlettered and humble men. These humble men whom Christ chose as his messengers are the men whom the revolution is helping.[38]

Castro's actions have shown a high level of morality; his public forgiveness of opponents and his rejection of international terrorism have provided him with the moral authority to condemn a country that has repeatedly practised state terrorism in eliminating other heads of state – including Castro. The CIA have made somewhere between six and 30 attempts to kill Castro and he has lost few opportunities to remind foreign journalists that this official agency of the US government has frequently sought his death (see Plate 3, p. 107). As Chomsky notes in his discussion of 9-11 in relation to just war theory:

> If the moral orthodoxy of the West accommodates the principles of universality, it follows that Cuba and Nicaragua (in fact, many others) can 'justifiably and morally resort to' far greater force against the US government. Uncontroversially, the US terrorist attacks and other illegal actions against Cuba and Nicaragua 'interfered with key values in the society attacked' far more dramatically than the case of 9-11 and were intended to do so.[39]

Castro is aware of what Lakoff (2002) refers to as the moral accounting metaphor – that good actions incur a form of 'moral credit' that subsequently needs to be 'paid off' by 'moral debtors'. And whatever financial insolvency Cuba faces, Castro has always been keen to ensure that his vision of a just society is upheld by being in possession of extensive moral credit. In this respect the vision of an independent Cuba is inseparable from the values on which it is based, and contributes significantly to his legitimacy in the design of leadership style.

Communication of legitimacy

Underlying Castro's communication of leadership style is a conviction in the legitimacy of his cause – conviction is the dynamo for his speeches and generates the stamina to speak for hours on end. Claims to ethical superiority are based on the alternating strategies of passing moral judgements on opponents and espousing the justice of his followers' cause. The source of their legitimacy is that they are engaged in a dramatic, morally justified struggle for the survival of a small country that is faced by a threatening, imperial, colonial enemy. The legitimacy of the struggle is, then, because it is one between good and evil that is based in claims of natural justice and as part of a historical process towards freedom. This sense of the historical legitimacy of his cause is most evident when he claims inspiration from the great nationalist leader Martí – as in the speech 'History will absolve me' that he made in self-defence at his trial following capture after the Moncada attacks in September 1953:

> Here is a regime afraid to bring an accused man before the court; a regime of blood and terror which shrank in fear of the moral conviction

of a defenceless man, a man unarmed, slandered, isolated . . . I warn you, I have only started . . . I know I will be silenced for many years. They will try to hide the truth by every possible means . . . But my voice will not be drowned. Strength gathers in my heart even when I feel most alone . . . To those who would call me a dreamer, I quote the words of Martí: 'A true man does not seek the path where advantage lies, but rather the path where duty lies, and this is the only practical man, whose dream of today will be the law of tomorrow, because he who has looked back on the essential course of history and has seen flaming and bleeding peoples in the cauldron of the ages knows that, without a single exception, the future lies on the side of duty'.

He identifies himself with other great national leaders and towards the end of the speech he makes clear the obligation that is placed on him and his followers as inheritors of a tradition of struggle against oppression:

> Still there is one argument more powerful than all the others. We are Cubans and to be Cuban implies a duty; not to fulfil that duty is a crime, is treason. We are proud of the history of our country; we learned it in school and have grown up hearing of freedom, justice and human rights. We were taught to venerate the glorious example of our heroes and martyrs. Céspedes, Agramonte, Maceo, Gómez and Martí were the first names engraved in our minds . . . We were taught that the 10th of October and the 24th of February are glorious anniversaries of national rejoicing because they mark days on which Cubans rebelled against the yoke of infamous tyranny . . . We were born in a free country that our parents bequeathed to us, and the Island will first sink into the sea before we consent to be the slaves of anyone . . . I come to the close of my defence plea but I will not end it as lawyers usually do, asking that the accused be freed. I cannot ask freedom for myself while my comrades are already suffering in the ignominious prison of the Isle of Pines. Send me there to join them and to share their fate. It is understandable that honest men should be dead or in prison in a Republic where the President is a criminal and a thief.

This narrative summary of Cuban history evokes memories of slavery and imprisonment culminating in an appeal of 'guilty'; this is rhetorically effective as it represents himself as a national freedom fighter and those who are likely to imprison him as colonial slave masters: good and evil are juxtaposed. After his imprisonment Castro developed a pamphlet from this speech in defence of the 26 July attacks on the Moncada barracks – suggesting that he saw this speech as a legitimacy statement. It has become the most sacred text for memorization in Cuban schools and – although it makes no mention of Marx, Lenin or socialism – provides the basis for legitimacy claims over the subsequent 50 years of Cuban history.

Castro's designed his leadership style around the motivation arising from a sense of ethical superiority and this can be conceptually represented as: THE REVOLUTION IS ETHICALLY PURE. This is because its underlying intentions are good ones:

> The first question those of us who undertook the revolution must ask ourselves is what our intentions were in doing so, and whether an ambition, an ignoble desire, was hidden in any of us. We must ask ourselves if each of the combatants in this revolution had a firm and heartfelt idea or thought because of some egotistical goal or in the pursuit of other unknown but inadmissible goals.[40]

These good intentions form the basis for ethically 'pure' behaviour:

> Not only did this serve the ends of the 26 July forces, but it also taught how it is necessary to deal with the enemy in war, because this was perhaps the first revolution in the world in which no prisoner of war was murdered, no wounded soldier abandoned, no man tortured, because this was the conduct maintained by the Rebel Army, and, moreover, this was the only revolution in the world which did not produce a single general.[41]

> This Revolution has left its indelible mark on the history of the world. [Applause]. It has absolutely nothing to be ashamed of, because its morals are as high as the stars and its behaviour has been unimpeachable.[42]

There is, then, a rhetorical contrast in Castro's communication of legitimacy between the morally pure Cuban revolution and morally impure American capitalism. This ethical contrast is also communicated by his use of metaphors based on sexual morality. This was developed initially during the United National General Assembly in 1960 in response to the media furore over that the Cuban delegation's decision to change accommodation to the black district of Harlem. This led to accusations regarding sexual morality in the local press, to which Castro was swift to respond:

> If we were the kind of men they try to depict at all costs, imperialism would not have lost all hope, as it did long ago, of somehow buying or seducing us. But, since they lost that hope a long time ago – though they never had reasons to sustain it – after having stated that the Cuban delegation lodged in a brothel, they should at least realize that imperialist financial capital is a prostitute that cannot seduce us – and not precisely the 'respectful' type of prostitute described by Jean Paul Sarte.[43]

Here his supporters are morally pure and incorruptible by the seductions of capitalism. As we saw with Gandhi, and also with his rejection of the ripe apple metaphor for Cuba, rhetorically skilled leaders are able to reverse the intention of opponent's metaphors so that they rebound on their originator.

Apart from claims to 'history', natural justice and religious morality there are two other very closely related sources of legitimacy: 'the people' and 'the revolution'. In many respects the post-revolutionary history of Cuba is concerned with the negotiation of relationships between these two entities. Consider these legitimacy statements in the speech made to the people of Santiago on 3 January 1959:

> We could achieve nothing by one uprising today and another tomorrow and another two years later and another three years after, because here in Cuba it is the people, and the people alone, who must decide who is to govern them. The military forces must unconditionally obey the people's orders and be at the disposal of the people, of the constitution and of the Laws of the Republic.

> Since those are the instructions given by the people of Santiago de Cuba, and since they represent the feelings of all the people of all Cuba, as soon as this meeting is over I will march with the veteran troops of Sierra Maestra, with the tanks and the artillery, toward the Capital in order to fulfil the will of people. We are here entirely at the request of the people. The mandate of the people is the only legal mandate at present. The President is elected by the people and not by a council in Colombia, meeting at four o'clock in the morning. The people have elected their President and this means that from this moment on the most powerful legal authority in the Republic has been established.

It is 'the people' that provide the basis for the legitimacy of 'the revolution' and one of Castro's major innovations in leadership design has been the channels of communication he has set up with 'the people'. In particular, the large public meeting where 'the people' are invited to make their feelings known in what he refers to as 'direct democracy'. The status of 'the people' is vital in this process; if we consider the speech made on 1 May 1960, he makes 191 references to the 'people' – this is one reference every 59 words. An important rhetorical reason for laying claim to 'the people' as a source of legitimacy in his speeches is because the speeches themselves are seen as more legitimate than other democratic processes such as elections. He rejects these because of negative experiences under previous regimes in Cuba and elsewhere in South America:

> Our enemies, our detractors, are calling for elections. Even a Latin American government leader stated recently that only those governments which are the product of an electoral process should be accepted into the OAS, as if a true revolution, like that in Cuba, could come to

power without the people ... as if the only democratic way of gaining power were through the electoral process, which has so often been prostituted in order to falsify the will and the interests of the people, and to bring to power those who were often the most inapt and the most cunning, not the most competent and the most honest.

For Castro it is 'the revolution' itself that provides an *alternative* source of legitimacy from elections; hence elections are corruptible in a way that the revolution is not:

As if, after so many fraudulent elections, as if after so much false and treasonable politics, as if, after so much corruption, it were possible to make the peoples believe that the only democratic procedure for a people is the electoral method, and that on the other hand, this procedure by means of which a people, not with pencils, but with their blood and the lives of 20,000 compatriots fighting without weapons against a professional and well armed army, trained and equipped by a powerful foreign country, destroyed the chains which enslaved them, simultaneously doing away with privilege, injustice, abuse and crime in our country forever, and initiating a true democratic era of progress, freedom and justice, was undemocratic.

A figure of speech that drives much of his rhetoric is to conceive of the revolution as a heroic agent and public meetings as the proper means through which it can remain alive:

They know we are waging a heroic struggle against the large foreign interests and they don't want us to win that struggle. They want to destroy the revolution by terror because they see that the revolution is a product of the people. We only express the will of the people. It has become necessary to defend the revolution. The need arises to defend the revolution and the people have the floor. [Shouts]. In the presence of my compatriots gathered here I say that I am going to consult the people about the restoration of the revolutionary courts. [Applause and shouts]. Let the citizens decide on this question and those who agree on the restoration of the revolutionary courts raise their hands. [Shouts].

The agency of the revolution as a dynamic force is sometimes communicated by making it the subject of journey metaphors:

As we say goodbye we make this promise: Cuba will not be intimidated; Cuba will not turn back; the revolution will not halt; the revolution will not turn back; the revolution will continue forward, victoriously; the revolution will continue going ahead without breaking step.

> Many who visit our country are surprised, amazed, and even ask them-
> selves what could be the explanation for this movement, force, momen-
> tum that the revolution is taking along this road on which we are
> marching and on which we are only beginning.[44]

If the revolution is a metaphorical journey, then it is the leader who becomes
the guide and provides the map. The concept of the revolution as a human
agent with aspirations and rights is very salient in Castro's 'Speech to intel-
lectuals' on 30 June 1961 where the italicized sections show it as the subject
of dynamic verbs:

> The *Revolution cannot reject* having all honest men and women march
> alone with it, whether writers or artists, or not. The *Revolution must
> aspire* to having everyone who has doubts become a revolutionary. The
> *Revolution must try to win* the major part of the people over to its ideas.
> *The Revolution must never renounce* having the majority of the people with
> it ... because *the Revolution has its rights also*, and the first *right of the
> Revolution is the right to exist*, and no one can stand against the *right of the
> Revolution to be and to exist*. No one can rightfully claim a right against
> the Revolution. Since *it takes* in the interests of the people and *signifies*
> the interests of the entire nation.

The argument here is that the revolution is a source of legitimacy because it
embodies the interests of the people and is in a relation of almost mystical
equivalence to the people and to the nation. To represent this I suggest a
double metonym in which REVOLUTION stands for THE PEOPLE and
THE PEOPLE for THE NATION. However, since it is the leader who
designs the relationship between the revolution, the people and the nation,
and as he symbolizes all of these, in metaphoric terms THE LEADER IS
THE REVOLUTION, THE LEADER IS THE PEOPLE and THE
LEADER IS THE NATION. The leader designs legitimacy through historically based appeals to the nation, the revolution and the people. Through his
power to express the desires of the people and the nation, the leader becomes
the legitimate voice of the revolution, implying a conceptual metaphor:
CASTRO IS THE CUBAN REVOLUTION.

Underlying the idea of the revolution as an active agent, with its own
rights, is the personification THE REVOLUTION IS A PERSON. This personification is very important in sustaining the metonyms and metaphors
that form the basis of Castro's claim to legitimacy because if the revolution
is a person, then the only person who can speak for it is the leader. The personification evokes contrasting representations of the revolution as either
fearless or vulnerable. These underlying metaphors sustain legitimacy claims
because they imply that the leader is both fearless and vulnerable. We can
see fearlessness if we substitute 'Fidel Castro' for 'the revolution'/'it' in the
following:

The revolution did not tremble or hesitate when the time came to give an exemplary punishment to the war criminals, as we had promised the people; to confiscate property stolen from the nation by corrupt rulers ... *It did not tremble or hesitate* when it decreed the deepest and most radical agrarian reform ever carried out in Latin America ... *It did not tremble or hesitate* to return a blow for every act of economic aggression by the United States, nationalizing one by one all the Yankee firms ... *It did not tremble or hesitate* when it became necessary to nationalize the entire banking industry, foreign commerce, and all the great capitalistic firms in the country. *It did not tremble or hesitate* to tear out racial discrimination by the roots and eradicate gambling, prostitution, drugs, and begging. [applause]. ... *It did not tremble or hesitate* in October 1962 when faced with the threat of invasion and nuclear war immediately after a crisis that occurred entirely as a consequence of the criminal Yankee aggressions etc.[45]

Here it is the leader who experiences and articulates the emotions of the personified revolution. The bravery of the revolution refers of course to both the leader and its followers; in this respect the metaphor CASTRO IS THE CUBAN REVOLUTION is a particular realization of the generic LEADER FOR SOCIAL PROCESS. Although the legitimacy of the revolution may originate in the leader's courage, bravery and military success, such legitimacy claims are communicated by the underlying propositions implied by the use of figurative language.

The same leadership communication style occurs when Castro represents the revolution as vulnerable and in need of protection:

Why are we able to destroy fortresses and convert them into schools instead of building more fortresses? Is it because *the revolution is not threatened*? Is it because *the revolution has no enemies*? Is it because there are *no plots against it*? Is it because we are not aware of the fact that we have fighting days ahead of us?[46]

At the same time it is essential to be prepared *to defend the gains of the revolution* and the country's independence against the treacherous and powerful enemy – U.S. imperialism.[47]

The claim that democracy without elections is legitimate is upheld by representing the revolution as fragile and threatened by those who are eager to witness its demise. The vulnerability of the revolution implies that it is like a child in need of protection by a father figure – one who represents History, the Fatherland, the People and the Revolution. Castro evokes these powerful sources of legitimacy and lays claim to this protective role; in this way, the leader becomes both the protected and the protector: both follower and leader. This ubiquity of roles is a characteristic stylistic feature in the design of charismatic leadership.

Leadership and the media

Castro can be acclaimed as one of the first charismatic non-western leaders to recognize the importance of the media in creating the basis for political power – both as a means for gaining power and for maintaining it. From the very early days when he established Radio Rebelde at his headquarters in the Sierra Maestra he has made use of the full range of available media – including radio, newspapers, magazines, television, printed books of interviews and, more recently, the internet. As leader of the guerrilla campaign in the Sierra Maestra he requested that an established foreign journalist be summoned to Cuba. It is somewhat ironic that it was an American – Herbert Matthews the foreign correspondent of the *New York Times* – who did more than anyone else to create a leadership myth around Castro through three lengthy articles on him in response to this request. He wrote on his first meeting:

> Taking him as one would by his physique and personality, this was quite a man – a powerful six-footer, olive-skinned, full-faced, with a straggly beard. He was dressed in olive-gray fatigue uniform and carried a rifle with a telescopic sight, of which he was very proud . . . The personality of the man is overpowering. It is easy to see that his men adored him and also to see why he has caught the imagination of the youth of Cuba all over the island. Here was an educated, dedicated, fanatic, a man of ideals, of courage, and of remarkable qualities of leadership.[48]

Matthews created a heroic myth around Castro that was designed to reach a wider audience. As Quirk notes:

> The American reporter, in only three articles, gave the Cuban people a charismatic leader with whom they could identify, a hero whom they could admire, and to whom they could turn when the revolution had defeated Fulgencio Batista. For more that three decades Fidel Castro's conception of himself and his public demeanour were determined by this image.[49]

The media potential of this image was designed to satisfy an international demand for more colourful and vigorous leaders. As Quirk continues:

> The public wanted new champions, and the young, flamboyant Cuban filled that need admirably. He was a revolutionary with an enormous ego and a flair for the spectacular. His unique style – his beard, his fatigue uniform, his long *sui generis* cigars, his famous rifle with its telescopic sight – made him instantly recognisable to millions. A few bold strokes by the cartoonist pen sufficed to identify him. Not to be outdone by the *New York Times* and *Look*, *Paris-Match* sent its own correspondent to Cuba to with instructions to interview the rebel leader.[50]

This is a clear statement of the integration of a complex range of symbolic semiotic modes in the design and performance of leadership style. Once the image was created, Castro has intentionally sustained this image-branding; he became aware of how the interests of the revolution could be served through a consistently revolutionary and romantic image created by a complex of interacting visual and verbal communicative modes. The verbal elements of leadership design blend the metaphors THE LEADER IS THE REVOLUTION/PEOPLE/NATION and CASTRO IS THE CUBAN REVOLUTION; and they establish legitimacy through metaphors such as THE REVOLUTION IS ETHICALLY PURE.

Castro's awareness of the importance of television in leadership perform-ance continued once he became Prime Minister of Cuba. He arranged for a panel of journalists to put questions to prisoners on live television. He real-ized that irrespective of what the prisoners said, the overall effect was likely to reflect well on him and to sustain the impression of being in dialogue with the people. The prisoners, though they might attack Castro for failing to hold elections, could not claim to have been ill-treated or intimidated. This stood in stark contrast to the use of TV media by subsequent leaders who have shown mistreated prisoners of war as a way of demonstrating power over their bodies. At one point Castro himself took over the question-ing, walking among the prisoners with a microphone like a talk-show host. 'Be honest', he said to one of the prisoners, 'Surely you recognise that you are the first prisoners in history who are allowed to argue with the head of the government you came to overthrow in front of the whole country and of the whole world!'.[51] Castro has been a creative exponent in the use of this media to occupy and command the moral high ground. News items carry live special reports on him. He uses television as a channel for communicating with Cubans in their own homes, this runs in parallel with the large polit-ical meetings that have been the traditional form for communicating polit-ical messages in Cuba. His speeches are broadcast live on television and re-broadcasted by the two national channels over the following days.

A major reason why he has provided a prolific media output – now including internet web sites – is to counter the powerful influence of the American domination of mass communication technology. He shares Chomsky's view of the global influence exerted through the influence of Hollywood, US news agencies, books, and magazines to instil the values of American culture.[52] His own media strategy has been to counter American influence through the design of a unique leadership style as a rebellious and heroic underdog, while for the largely Catholic domestic following he may be David battling Goliath, for his more secular global audience he is a Cuban Robin Hood.

Summary

In this chapter I have illustrated how the leadership design of Fidel Castro – his appearance, dress, gestures and symbolic actions have interacted to create a set of symbolic meanings for his followers. These symbolic meanings are reinforced verbally by the creation of ethical legitimacy through metaphors that contrast a large immoral entity – a shark, a Goliath or a rapacious individual – with a small, inherently moral entity – a sardine, a David or a Robin Hood. Legitimacy claims are further reinforced by metaphors based in conceptual metaphors such as THE REVOLUTION IS ETHICALLY PURE, THE REVOLUTION IS A PERSON/PEOPLE, COUNTRIES ARE ANIMALS and HUMAN BEHAVIOUR IS ANIMAL BEHAVIOUR. I have also explained how his leadership style identifies him with various valued entities that are potential sources of legitimacy; these are the Historical Process, the People, the Nation and the Revolution. This identification takes place linguistically as the leader becomes the voice that articulates the aspirations, desires and hopes of followers. I have represented this conceptually with the metonym LEADER FOR SOCIAL PROCESS and the metaphor CASTRO IS THE CUBAN REVOLUTION.

As a combatant for all that is ethically good, natural and just, engaged in a dramatic struggle with the evil, immoral 'empire' to the north, Castro performs the role of the heroic underdog – a Robin Hood. Yet, subliminally, his appearance suggests otherwise: he is a moral Goliath. He compensates for lack of material resources by drawing on vast reserves of courage, bravery, energy and moral virtue. The basis of his dramaturgical success, then, is in the tension created by the contrast between his stature – physically and morally larger than life – and the diminutive size of the country which he leads: its power and resources in relation to those of the United States. Such charismatic tension is highly effective in leadership design. He creates an omnipotent role for himself as guardian of everything that is to be valued – Cuban History, the People, the Revolution etc. – but in doing so he raises the crucial problem of charismatic leadership: the question of the succession. By identifying everything that is valued in the person of a leader – who has designed a leadership style as the unique, iconic image of the revolution, the great leader's demise risks the representation that the revolution is dead, thereby creating a vacuum that has the potential to be exploited by morally diminutive opponents.

7 Ayatollah Khomeini and divine leadership

Introduction

The importance of leadership is recognized in all Islamic societies and Iran in the 1960s was a society ripe for the emergence of an Islamic leader; Iranians were faced with the choice between a western style monarchy (originating in a *coup d'etat*) or a traditional Islamic model of leadership. The programme of the reformist monarch Muhammad Reza Shah, known as the 'White Revolution', was one of modernization while Ruhollah Khomeini symbolized a traditional Iranian form of charisma. His design of leadership style appealed to indigenous cultural forces by raising anxieties that national identity was threatened by the colonial exploitation of the United States and Britain. The western-dependent leadership of the Shah offered less to the needs and desires of many Iranians than a strong national leader with commanding moral authority and spiritual appeal.

In a society that was unsure of its place in the modern world – mainly through its experience of the external forces of colonialism and Marxism – the appeal of Shi'ism was that it had always offered Iranians a source of internal strength in times of insecurity:

> Khomeini employed the framework of an ideology that dated back thirteen centuries. Unlike Marxism, variations of which had been the dominant force behind revolutions elsewhere in the 20th century, the use of Islam involved no conversions or re-education. Khomeini used Shi'ite myths and beliefs to set the pace and to provide the flash points around which the revolution unfolded, just as he would use them again to provide the themes and justifications for many of his theocracy's actions.[1]

In order to understand leadership in this cultural context, it is necessary to consider the special nature of Shi'ite myths and beliefs as compared with the beliefs of Sunni Islam. A fundamental difference between the two branches lies in the special significance of the leader in Shi'ism. Whereas Sunnis permit leaders to emerge from all followers of Islam, Shias require them to be descended from the family of the prophet. The direct descendants of

Muhammad are known as Imams and are held to be imbued with the quality of charisma that is a prerequisite for Shi'ite leadership. The first Imam was the Prophet's cousin Ali; more importantly, his younger son, the second Imam, Hossein and his small force of followers were massacred at Karbala by a Sunni army numbering thousands. The tragedy of his martyrdom is commemorated every year on the tenth day of the Islamic month of Ashura. Shias commemorate the Battle of Karbala by symbolic acts of physical suffering and self-immolation that demonstrate their loyalty to Hossein by emulating his martyrdom.

The line of Muhammad – through Ali and Hossein – became extinct in 873 AD when the last Shi'ite imam, Al-Askari (who had no brothers) disappeared within days of inheriting the title at the age of four. The Shias found it difficult to accept that he had died, and found greater reassurance in the belief that he was merely 'hidden' and would return. When this failed to happen after several centuries, spiritual power passed to a council of twelve scholars known as 'the *ulama*' who elected a supreme imam. Shias believe that the supreme imam is a genuinely charismatic leader and this divine inheritance underlies his legitimacy. Moreover, the twelfth imam ('The Rightly-Guided One', Imam Muhammad al-Mahdí) is still alive but in a state of occultation and will reappear at a moment determined by Allah. He is the Awaited One whose return will spread justice throughout the world.[2] As Brumberg notes: 'The notion that the "Hidden Imam" will eventually reappear and restore justice to the world occupies a central place in the collective conscience of Iranian society'.[3]

Khomeini designed his leadership through encouraging the myth that he was this hidden imam and he latched into the Iranian collective unconscious by setting himself the divinely inspired task of delivering his country from oppression. As Brumberg continues: 'His lifelong immersion in mysticism, combined with an enduring fervor to defend his fellow Shi'ites against unjust rulers, endowed him with a genuine sense of his own divinity'.[4] The power of this myth is well described by an Iranian writer:

> Thus every event, very social gesture, also embodied a symbolic allegiance. The new regime had reached far beyond the romantic symbolism more or less prevalent in every political system to inhabit a realm of pure myth, with devastating consequences. The Islamic Republic was not merely modelled on the order established by the Prophet Muhammad during his reign over Arabia; it was the Prophet's rule itself. Iran's war with Iraq was the same as the war carried on by the third and most militant imam, Imam Hussein, against the infidels, and the Iranians were going to conquer Karbala, the holy city in Iraq where Imam Hussein's shrine was located. The Iranian battalions were named after the Prophet of the Twelve Shi'ite Saints ... and the military assaults against Iraq were invariable codenamed after Muhammad's celebrated battles. Ayatollah Khomeini was not a religious or political leader but an imam in his own right.[5]

Like others who have relied on messianic discourse, such as Martin Luther King, he developed an analogy based on the idea that THE PRESENT IS THE SPIRITUAL PAST, and a myth in which followers would only be delivered from oppression by a charismatic leader. Khomeini would deliver Iran from the Shah, just as Moses had delivered the Hebrews from the cruelty of Pharaoh, and Hossein had tried to deliver his people from the oppression of Sunni rule. Khomeini resurrected the myth that: 'Every day is Ashura and every place is Karbala'.[6] Throughout his life he inspired courage and heroism amongst his followers – based in the underlying conviction that it was better to die upholding what was right, than it was to live under a system of oppression. As he asked, and replied, rhetorically:

> The tyrannical regime imagines that I am very happy and satisfied with my life, and so they think they can threaten me. But what is this life that I lead? Death as soon as possible would be better than this life; then I might join the presence of the Most Noble One in the hereafter and be delivered from this life of misfortune.[7]

It was the expression of such charismatic statements that gave Khomeini's followers the belief that he was not of this earth but a divine reincarnation in the tradition of the 12 imams.

Non-linguistic communication of charisma

Appearance and leadership style

Khomeini's appearance exuded a divine aura that followers would expect of an imam and was therefore vital in his design of leadership style. Since his appeal to followers was primarily on the grounds of spirituality, it was important that there was nothing that conflicted with this image. It was particularly important to ensure an appearance consistent with the regularity that is a fundamental part of Islamic lifestyle – with its routine of ablutions, prayers and study – and one that evoked associations with the Prophet Muhammad himself. This entailed wearing the traditional non-western clothing of turban and loose gowns and other visual symbols associated with the Prophet, such as a beard (see Plate 5, p. 109). This was particularly the case during his exile in Bursa, Turkey, because of increased exposure to the eyes of strangers and the possibility of photographs of him being sent back to Iran. As with Castro, Mandela and Gandhi, the imprisoned or exiled leader always has the potential for heroic or charismatic return when conditions are favourable. Ali Cetiner – with whom Khomeini resided while in exile – was aware of Khomeini's design of leadership style:

> Khomeini's whole life was based on image. I believe that this was also part of his image. It was part of his cunning. Late, we noticed that he

was very careful to preserve an image, and did everything to conform to that image.[8]

Throughout his period of induction as a religious scholar Khomeini witnessed models of behaviour appropriate to the spiritual life since the life of a religious student entailed institutional living and constant exposure to the observations and evaluations of colleagues and students alike. Abnormalities would soon be detected and any attempt at deviation from the norms of traditional appearance would be interpreted as giving way to the corrosive forces of imperialism and westernization that threatened Islamic solidarity. His biographer indicates the impression he created after his release by the Shah:

> Tall and neatly dressed in his clerical garb, Khomeini's charisma was crystallized in his calm and deceptively inattentive gaze. His home became a place of pilgrimage for thousands of well-wishers from all over Iran, who were happy to merely achieve a glimpse of this awesome figure ... The fact that he managed to come out of the prison of 'Pharaoh' alive had given him the enigmatic quality of a Moses.[9]

In a time of transition and insecurity it was important that everything about Khomeini's leadership style was appropriate to a traditional Islamic leader and that his image sent the message that he was blessed with divine dignity and grace.

Dress

Nowhere is the symbolic meaning of clothes more significant than in traditional Islamic societies facing the challenge of modernity. The Koranic requirement to dress modestly is interpreted differently throughout the Muslim world, but all dress prescriptions imply that clothing is a culturally resonant semiotic through which powerful personal and social identities are communicated. The Islamic dress code requires modesty by concealing the human form and avoiding close fitting styles. Social restrictions on clothing in Muslim societies are often applied to women – especially regarding the wearing of the veil; a revolutionary slogan was: *A woman in a veil is protected like a pearl in an oyster shell*, and in the words of the exiled writer Azar Nafisi: 'The slogan, when it appeared, was usually accompanied by a drawing of a predatory half-open oyster shell revealing a glossy pearl inside'.[10] She describes her own experience of wearing traditional Muslim clothing:

> My constant obsession with the veil had made me buy a very wide black robe that covered me down to my ankles, with kimono like sleeves, wide and long. I had gotten into the habit of withdrawing my hands into the sleeves and pretended that I had no hands. Gradually, I pre-

tended that when I wore the robe, my whole body disappeared: my arms, breasts, stomach and legs melted and disappeared and what was left was a piece of cloth the shape of my body that moved here and there. Guided by some invisible force.[11]

The disappearance of the body is a powerful symbol of the effect of Islamic dress codes as it communicates underlying assumptions about the inherently sensual nature of the human body and its potential for temptation and sin.

At times, dress prescriptions have been applied equally forcefully on men to control the tendency for western clothing such as trousers, shirts with collars and hats with brims to replace traditional looser clothes and turbans. Hats have a special resonance because they are visible from afar and worn close to the centre of consciousness; the head touches the ground in Islamic prayer and the Muslim bares his head before God. Throughout the Muslim world the wearing of the turban has been associated with valuing the sacred and spiritual rather than the secular and material. As part of his efforts to create a modern secular state in Turkey, Ataturk had banned the wearing of the fez because of its semiotic resonance as an Islamic symbol.[12]

The dress choice of Khomeini and the Shah symbolized the contrast between modern and traditional styles of leadership. Khomeini wore traditional black robes and a black turban symbolizing descent from the Prophet while the Shah wore the most stylish, formal western clothing. Photographs show the Shah typically wearing the clothes of the highest social level – dark or white suits with collared shirts and ties for informal occasions and various military costumes for formal occasions – with all the paraphernalia of a high collar, sash, epaulettes, medals and a peaked military cap. His dress choice was at its most ostentatious for his coronation in 1967 and at the extravagant celebrations of the 2,500th anniversary of the Iranian monarchy in October 1971 near the tomb of Cyrus the Great, the founder of the Persian Empire.

This was intended as a magnificent state occasion and the Shah was adorned like an emperor on his gilded 'Peacock Throne' in a self-conscious symbolism intended to re-create the historical memory of Iran's pre-Islamic past. A huge tent city for foreign heads of state was erected below the ruins of Persepolis with luxurious furnishings, and food and wine imported from France. One of the most criticized expenses was for 30 gala uniforms for the members of the Imperial Household that were ordered from the French designer Lanvin. Civilian male guests were required to wear a white tie and decorative symbols and female guests were required to wear long dresses. Dress cannot be separated from a set of leadership semiotics designed to communicate ideology and this shows when ideological conflict is manifested through highly contrasting modes of dress.

Long, flowing garments that conceal the human form have been associated with an allegiance to the traditional values and way of life advocated by the Koran. Such dress signifies a rejection of the changes offered by

modernity and adherence to indigenous cultural values. Khomeini understood the political significance of rejecting the modernizing policies that the
Shah's father was importing from Turkey and the exploitation of such
symbols was crucial in his design of leadership. He rejected the imposition
of symbols of modernity by the persuasive argument that they were foreign:

> It is said that when this ungodly man went to Turkey and saw what
> misdeeds Ataturk had done there, he sent a telegram to his agents in
> Iran telling them to make the people wear uniform dress. At the time,
> he used the excuse that the farmers who worked out in the sun should
> wear a peaked cap so that they wouldn't be troubled by the sun –
> however, it was obvious that this was not the real reason for imposing
> this law. When he returned from his trip, then the pressures began in
> earnest. A series of intense pressures and outrageous atrocities followed
> the issuance of this Uniform Dress Law. The *'ulama* were tormented
> greatly because of this law, many of them were sent into exile and some
> of them were killed because of their objections to it.[13]

The Shah issued regulations for government officials concerning clothing.
The alien male dress codes that offended Khomeini were the neck- or bow-
tie, compulsory wearing of a hat and constraints on the colour and type of
shoes that were to be worn. Khomeini was even more outraged at the offence
to female modesty and the prohibition on women wearing the Islamic *hijab*:

> The second excuse used to bring pressure on the people came when he
> called for the unveiling of women, which again he did in imitation of
> the ungodly Ataturk, the unjust, armed Ataturk. What a shameful act
> this was. God only knows how this nation of Iran suffered when he
> forced the women to remove their veils. The veil of humanity was rent
> asunder. God knows which women he dishonoured in this way, which
> people he humiliated.[14]

Evidently, clothing was very much a life and death issue in the performance
of political leadership in Iran because it symbolized either a commitment
towards a future of change or a retrospective attachment to the values of the
past. Given the powerful symbolic meaning of dress in the ideological
struggle between the modern values of the Pahlavis and the traditional
values of Khomeini, it is not surprising that, when exiled in Turkey,
Khomeini was obliged to wear western-style clothing in public. As his
Turkish host attests:

> I had strict instructions from Ankara that he was not to be allowed out
> in his turban and robes, which were like a symbol of power for him. He
> saw himself as a powerful figure in that outfit. 'No' he said, 'I refuse to
> wear trousers'.[15]

Khomeini eventually did go out wearing trousers. However, once out of Turkey he reverted to traditional clothing and, in 1978 and 1979, demonstrators displayed huge images of him wearing his turban and robes communicating the widespread appeal of the traditional values symbolized by his leadership style. The symbolic contribution of dress to charisma continued right through to his burial:

> The body was set up on a temporary podium made of containers. Khomeini lay in an air-conditioned glass case covered in a white shroud, his feet pointing to Mecca. His black turban, indicating his religious status as a direct descendent of Prophet Muhammad, rested on his chest.[16]

Artefacts

As we have seen in relation to Gandhi, the spiritual appeal of the holy man is strengthened by a rejection of the material; however, we have some idea of Khomeini's favoured artefacts in the letters he wrote to his son Mustafa after exile to Turkey. He asked for clothing, in particular the *aba* (the robe the Muslim clerics wear over their dress), shirts and a towel, a prayer book and some textbooks to work on – the usual simple requirements of a scholar. There is also some evidence that he missed traditional Iranian food, as he wrote in one letter: 'Send me also some dried fruits, pistachio nuts and *gaz* (nougat)'.[17] For a man who, on his return to Iran after 14 years of exile, claimed to have felt no emotion (implying that Islam was a global rather than a national philosophy), as with attention-catching clothing, attachment to artefacts would symbolize a rejection of the spiritual. The ultimate form of such detachment is rejection of one's own body as a material object (as evident in its concealment by clothing) and a desire for the release of the spirit in death.

Symbolic action and body language

Khomeini's design of leadership was based on adherence to an ideal forged over time in Islamic culture; it was vital that behaviour was exemplary and followed Koranic requirements:

> The leader should have simplicity, dignity, manliness, honour, spiritual purity, justice and a noble character. His lifestyle should be simple and austere, devoid of all kinds of luxury, snobbery, haughtiness and wealth, a value system common with that of Khomeini and one which conferred great authority in pious society. The leader should also be held a worthy example of emulation to his followers and could be entitled 'imam'.[18]

It was equally vital that it was communicated by symbolic action; various personal accounts testify to the fact that there was little separation of

Khomeini's personal life from his social and political role; his comportment was in keeping with that of a good Muslim; he followed a very strict daily routine around regular prayer. Behaviour that was consistent with a religious leader became a form of symbolic action because it inspired followers. Khomeini's survival in exile had a more powerful symbolic meaning than any specific actions and his survival became a myth that evoked historical and spiritual resonance among his followers:

> To the masses Khomeini was no ordinary man. He had become an ideal, a living symbol of hope for millions who desperately wanted a leader who would personify their aspirations, restore their spirituality and who would bring freedom, independence and justice.[19]

In terms of the traditional style view of leadership, the distinction between task and relationship behaviour becomes unimportant because the holy nature of the task overrides relationships.

There are perhaps three events in Khomeini's life that can be used to illustrate symbolic action in the performance of leadership; the first of these was his return from exile (see Plate 4, p. 108):

> Khomeini's flight from Paris to Tehran was for many of his followers like the Prophet Muhammad's flight from Mecca to Medina in AD 622. In the new vocabulary developed by the Islamists, Khomeini was 'prophet-like,' the man who 'brought to an end the age of ignorance and introduced the light of Islam'.[20]

The seizure of the American embassy on 4 November 1979 was a further action that was initiated by followers and supported by Khomeini because of its symbolism; he came to regard the embassy occupation and the ensuing hostage crisis as the 'Second Islamic Revolution' and this is significant because it is an instance of a leader effectively *becoming* a follower: he had not initiated the seizure – but it was an outcome of the close dependence of the Shah on the United States that he had argued was the cause of all Iran's problems. In this respect a leader's symbolic action is often to *acquiesce* to the actions of followers when these actions are motivated by leadership communication. As one of the hostages summarizes:

> 'His style of leadership has always been to lead from the rear,' the embassy's political officer late recounted. 'Khomeini is inclined to look and see which way the winds are blowing, and then endorse the strongest current, or what appears to be the strongest current'.[21]

However, this appears to be something of a generalization since a final symbolic action in which Khomeini performed leadership was the utterance of the *fatwa* in 1988 exhorting Muslims to kill Salmon Rushdie for blasphemy.

In symbolic terms, the life of the revolution, and therefore of Islamic government, required the elimination of ideological enemies to Islam: bonds with followers were always strengthened through highly symbolic tasks such as religiously inspired assassination.

Of course, matters of life and death were a constant feature of life in Iran throughout the period in the aftermath of the revolution when opponents – such as the *Mojahedin* – were eliminated and then during the war with Iran. Both periods provided opportunities for heavily symbolic actions. During the war the poorly-trained troops known as the *Basij* ('the mobilized') – the majority of them children of often 13 years old or younger – were given red and yellow headbands that declared the greatness of God, or showed images of Khomeini. They were also given keys to hang around their necks: the keys symbolized automatic entry into heaven once they had been blown up rushing headlong into the minefields that needed to be cleared to permit the advance of regular forces. For followers of a divine leader, the sacrifice of one's life is a small gesture in exchange for proximity to God and the deaths of those who make this sacrifice become the ultimate symbolic statement of the faith, belief and conviction that charismatic leaders seek to instil.

Stylistic features of verbal communication

The inseparability of religion and politics was fundamental to Khomeini's rhetorical communication of leadership; it became the essential element in his view of Iranian national identity, because it implied that clerical leadership was a prerequisite for the survival of both Iran and Islam. Those who challenged this point of view were outsiders – imperialists seeking to impose alien cultural values. In his 12 lectures on Islamic Government made in 1970 he makes a mission statement legitimizing clerical leadership:

> This slogan of the separation of religion and politics and the demand that Islamic scholars not intervene in social and political affairs has been formulated and propagated by the imperialists; it is only the irreligious who repeat it. Were religion and politics separate in the time of the Prophet (peace and blessings by upon him)? Did there exist on one side, a group of clerics, and opposite it, a group of politicians and leaders? Were religion and politics separate in the time of the caliphs? ... or in the time of the Commander of the Faithful ... These slogans and claims have been advanced by the imperialists and their political agents in order to prevent religion from ordering this world and shaping Muslim society.[22]

Underlying Khomeini's claims for clerical leadership is the argument that Iran, and Islam, both need protection from invasion by the political forces of colonialism and imperialism that were inspired by Judaism and Christianity.

His rhetoric argues for the inseparability of religion and politics and the inseparability of Iran from Islam because this communicates his core leadership objective: the establishment of an Islamic state in Iran.

The idea of being overwhelmed by a numerically superior enemy had a dramatically emotional impact on Iranians because – as we have seen – it is anchored in the underlying Shi'ite myth of martyrdom. The symbolic tradition of Imam Hossein – originating in resistance to perceived oppression and thriving on opposition – was an ideology that offered a reservoir of moral authority on which Khomeini could draw:

> Hossein's defiant act contributed an important legacy to the Shi'ite community. As the ultimate martyr, having fought despite the foreknowledge that he would face a swift and bloody defeat, Hossein established the precedent of dying for belief rather than living with injustice. Revolt against tyranny, even if it meant sacrificing one's life in the process, became a duty to God.[23]

Khomeini represents Shi'ism as a bounded space – a type of moral cocoon needing protection from invasion – through the image of a fortress, and makes this rhetorically persuasive through the use of a question and answer pattern:

> So a crack has appeared in the protective wall surrounding Islam, despite your supposedly being its guardians. Then I ask you: 'Are you guarding the frontiers of Islam and the territorial integrity of the Islamic homeland?' To this your answer will be: 'No, our task is only prayer!'. This means that a piece of the wall has collapsed ... What kind of fortress is this? Each of the corners is occupied by some 'pillar of Islam' but all he can do is offer excuses when put to the test. Is that what we mean by 'fortress'?[24]

Even more insidiously, these invading forces operate both without and within Iran because the oppressions of the Pahlavi dynasty and its supporters depend on colonialism and imperialism. He argues that it is an absolute duty of the *fuqaha*[25] to protect the fortress from these internal and external dangers:

> The soil of the homeland is defenceless before them, and they grab freely whatever they want of it. The people are their slaves and are powerless to defend themselves. One ruler is a dictator by nature, malevolent and rancorous; another represses his wretched subjects ruthlessly, plundering by imposing on them all kinds of burdens ... Is it not strange – how can one not think it strange – that society is in the clutches of a cunning oppressor whose tax collectors are oppressors and whose governors feel no compassion or mercy toward believers under their rule?[26]

By creating a feeling of abandonment and isolation of 'the homeland', Khomeini creates an emotional climate in which followers look for the security and safety of an Islamic government. Images of protection of a native, innocent victim from an alien, rapacious aggressor drive his rhetoric; as Martin puts it:

> Overall an Islamic order that is just and serves the oppressed, the people and the country is contrasted in Khomeini's mind with the current order, which he describes as injustice and oppression by a band of robbers and swindlers who have taken the opportunity to oppress the people and build expensive edifices for their own use.[27]

Fear-arousing images of attack are contrasted with the comfort of an Islamic government providing psychological security because it encompasses every aspect of life:

> It regulates life from before birth, family life and life in society. It does not just involve prayer and pilgrimage ... Islam has a political agenda and provides for the administration of a country.[28]

A political system founded in the jurisdiction of a body of religious scholars or *fuqaha* would guarantee the moral integrity of a state in which political and moral purposes converge to create a paradise on earth. Only religious leadership – preferably under an imam – can provide the paternal protection that is necessary for the survival of Iranian society when threatened by these invasive forces. One can readily understand the appeal of such rhetoric to a people exposed to the insecurities caused by the rapid modernization and economic growth that arose from the oil boom of the 1970s and could readily be interpreted as a form of 'invasion'. It also can be traced to the need for security of a man who, as a boy, had lost his father to bandits in his first year of life.

However, the emotional force of Khomeini's rhetorical style does not rely exclusively on abstract ideology: the struggle between 'Islam' – symbolized by Iran – Christianity, imperialism, colonialism etc., but also in its highly *personalized* nature. We will see in the analysis of metaphor that he frequently heightens rhetorical effect by personalizing issues so that his followers evaluate individuals rather than ways of thinking or ideas; in particular the Shah, is represented as the embodiment of evil. One reason that political issues became dramatized is because culturally powerful metaphors were employed in a highly personalized form of verbal duelling between Khomeini and the Shah. For example, the Shah referred to his clerical opposition as:

> a numb and *dispirited snake and lice who float in their own dirt* ... If these sordid and vile elements with their reactionary friends do not awake from their sleep of ignorance, the fist of justice, like thunder, will be

struck at their head in whatever cloth they are, perhaps to terminate *their filthy and shameful life.*[29]

There is a modern Iranian myth that on one occasion the Shah sent a message to Khomeini warning him that if he continued to oppose him he would put on his father's boots and come to Qom to punish him. Khomeini is claimed to have replied: 'your father's boots are too big for your feet'.[30] This personalization of political discourse is unlike, say, Gandhi, or Mandela, who drew clear distinctions between individuals and the ideologies that underlay their behaviour.

There is further evidence of personalization and dramatization in the slogans that characterized political demonstrations in the revolutionary period. Typically, these contained the concepts of death and or war:

Whether we kill or are killed we are victorious!

We will fight! We will die! But we won't accept compromise!

But they were also frequently personal:

Death to the dictator, death to the dictator! God save you, Khomeini! Death to your bloodthirsty enemy!

Khomeini or Death.

These slogans were matched by the Shah's supporters when they chanted counter-slogans such as: 'Long Live the Shah'. In fact, there is little evidence that Khomeini himself used slogans, but they can certainly be treated as evidence that the personalization of political issues influenced followers in the Iranian revolution. The language that was used for political communication therefore determined the language through which followers expressed their beliefs and influenced their actions. There is evidence of the effect of slogans in creating the reality in the following personal testimony of a young English lecturer:

When in the States we had shouted Death to this or that, those deaths seemed to be more symbolic, more abstract, as if we were encouraged by the impossibility of our slogans to insist upon even more. But in Tehran in 1979, these slogans were turning into a reality with macabre precision. I felt helpless: all the dreams and slogans were coming true, and there was no escaping them.[31]

We can see from this that rhetorical communication that is a central element in the design of leadership style is not a peripheral issue of aesthetic concern but actually determines political and social reality.

Communication of vision and values

We have seen how Shi'ism provides an underlying cultural value system in which death and suffering in defence of the good is psychologically and spiritually justified. The rhetorical contrast, therefore, between life and death is not one in which life is necessarily good and death is necessarily evil – as is the case in western rhetoric. Admittedly, in times of conflict western leaders have evoked images of suffering – most memorably in Churchill's promise of blood, toil, sweat and tears – however, the norms of western political discourse are that life-supporting forces are inherently good. However, common to all leadership discourse is the effective use of dramatic moral contrasts in the communication of values. For Khomeini, contrast between good and evil covers all aspects of life – existential, historical, socio-political etc. – and he evaluates individuals, social groups, events and ideas in terms of the extreme end-points of these scales. The nature of these scales is summarized in Figure 7.1.

The protection of what is valued and legitimate – against what is devalued and illegitimate, operates at the levels of ideology, history and

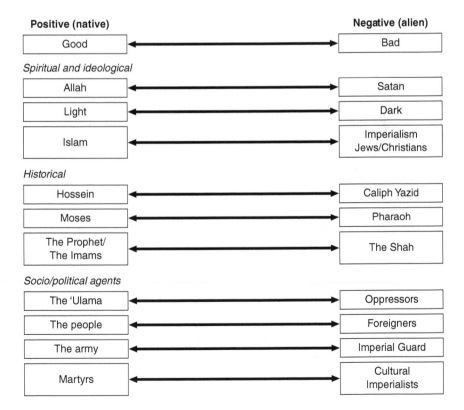

Figure 7.1 Khomeini's rhetorical scales for evaluation.

socio-political agency. The positioning to the extreme ends of the scale is because of his stylistic preference for antithesis and hyperbole.

Values are also communicated through metaphors that activate culturally-based associations. For example, referring to foreign social agents as 'animals', following a conceptual metaphor PEOPLE ARE ANIMALS (that we found evidence for in Castro's rhetoric), implies a strong negative evaluation in a culture that places low value on animals:

> This weaponry baffles us so they have to bring in American advisers and experts to show us what to do with it. But these experts won't show us how to operate it. *They are such animals*, they will not be satisfied with this.[32]

> We have nothing to say to those whose powers of perception are so limited that they regard the wearing of European hats, *the cast-offs of the wild beasts of Europe* as a sign of national progress.[33]

Here the metaphor intends to reverse the positive idea that Europeans are civilized – and we have already seen the symbolic importance of clothing and hats. On other occasions animal metaphors refer to countries rather than people, and are motivated by the conceptual metaphor, COUNTRIES ARE ANIMALS, that we also found in the previous chapter; for example, verb choices are from the domain of animal behaviour:

> Is our country independent? America dictates to us from one direction and the Soviet Union from the other. *America digs its claws deep* into the depths of our oil wells while the Soviet Union *does the same* to our gas supplies.[34]

We should first consider the potency of particular animal metaphors because of cultural factors; in Islamic cultures the dog is an animal with largely negative associations (though there is little basis for this in the Koran). In October 1964 Khomeini gave a speech that led directly to his arrest and exile; this was in opposition to legislation known as the Capitulation Bill that would grant Americans legal indemnity from prosecution. He communicates a powerful political evaluation by an analogy between Iranians and dogs:

> They have reduced the Iranian people to a level lower than that of an American dog. If someone runs over a dog belonging to an American, he will be prosecuted. Even if the Shah himself were to run over a dog belonging to an American, he would be prosecuted. But if an American cook runs over the Shah, or the *marja'* of Iran, or the highest official, no one will have the right to object.

His choice of 'dog' was intended to maximize the sense of outrage his followers might experience on finding out about the legislation because it implies the concept IRANIANS ARE ANIMALS.

Animal metaphors may be intensified either through elaborating the semantic tensions between the two elements in the metaphor or by blending one element with a metaphor from another source. For example, the rhetorical force of the following metaphor is intensified by blending an animal domain with a death domain:

> With marches and demonstrations all across the country, our great people must bury once and for all this *stinking carrion of monarchy*.[35]

In the following passage Khomeini explores the rhetorical potential of the conceptual metaphor PEOPLE ARE ANIMALS by elaborating the metaphor through contrasting outer and inner aspects of the person: appearance and substance:

> In other words, someone whose appearance is now one of a human being but whose nature, whose natural disposition, is so bad it resembles not that of a human being but of a fierce animal will take this form when he leaves this world. For the time being he resembles a human being, but when he passes on and appearances are pushed into the background and his true nature is made manifest, he will look like a savage beast. His face will become that of a ferocious animal. But we have to wait and see which one of these savage beasts he will resemble most. Is he a leopard, so will he resemble a leopard? Is he a wolf, so will he resemble a wolf? Or is he worse than these and will consequently resemble something much worse?[36]

The metaphor becomes more resonant because it implies a state of spiritual metamorphosis in which what starts materially as a man is transformed by spiritual forces into an animal – but there is an uncertainty as to exactly into which external form the inner nature will resolve itself. However, there is an implication that the metamorphosis will not stop at the boundaries of known animals, but may shift into something beyond what is known – a mythological monstrous creature in which human and animal are blended. He explores the dramatic potential of the conceptual metaphor HUMAN BEHAVIOUR IS ANIMAL BEHAVIOUR to describe extremes of spiritual and moral states by considering its limitations:

> The ferocity of animals has a limit. Their savagery has its limits. Wolves are a case in point. A wolf attacks another animal, feeds on it then rests. It is not the nature of a wolf to devour just any animal! One may find an exception, but generally there is a limit. Other animals too are limited in their ferociousness. Man, however, differs from other animals because he has no limits.[37]

Therefore, the metaphor becomes more potent by analysing not only what aspects of animal appearance and behaviour *can* be used to describe humans, but also those aspects of human behaviour that *defy* analogy with animals: here the unlimited nature of man's moral and spiritual condition:

> That is to say the side of man's nature which pertains to blessedness and moral excellence knows no bounds: he can reach the stage where all his attributes are God-like . . . Man can attain such perfection that his hand is the hand of God, he becomes the eyes and ears of God. Man is unlimited in the perfection he can attain. At the same time that defective side of his nature, the side that pertains to nastiness, also knows no bounds.[38]

Explaining how people are not like animals – as well how they are – heightens the argumentative potential of the metaphor because it leads him to argue that man has the potential to become a devilish monster incorporating various savage attributes:

> You will see some people who have ten personality traits which are made manifest in ten faces. He's only one person, but his animal nature is so dominant, his carnal appetite so strong, that his face resembles that of a greedy animal like a pig. His ferociousness too predominates – as it does in animals like leopards – and devilishness and deceitfulness fill his face. In the hereafter, when this page is turned, he will be the devil of all devils. And at the same time as he has a devilish face he will also have a ferocious face, the last level of ferocity; he will have the face of a lustful animal too, the last level of sensuality. He will appear with these different faces.[39]

These transformations correspond with the Great Chain of Being metaphor. Lakoff and Turner describe this as a 'cultural model that concerns kinds of beings and their properties and places them in a vertical scale with "higher" beings and properties above "lower" beings and properties'.[40] It is a model that pervades western culture; though it has classical origins in Plato's thought, it was developed in medieval times to account for man's relationship with other beings, with his natural environment and with God.

The model is based on a hierarchy with different levels; each level is distinguished from the one below through the possession of all the attributes found at this level and, in addition, by one or more attributes that are not found there. These attributes could be taken as the defining ones of the species in question. For example, insects have senses that distinguish them from plants, but animals also have instincts and emotions that distinguish them from insects. In addition to senses, instincts and emotions, human beings also have attributes such as morality and verbal communication that distinguish them from animals. Those entities found at the upper levels are always positively evaluated while those at the lower are always negatively evaluated. The expressive potential of the model for the communication of ideology is that, when combined with metaphor, it facilitates representation of a higher-level creature as a lower-level one.

Although primarily a western model, there is clear evidence of it in Khomeini's rhetoric; for example, the use of metaphor to compare the way Iranians were treated by Americans (and the Shah) and the way Iranians treat dogs implies a chain of being in which some categories of human are evaluated more highly than others. We can find further evidence of the Great Chain of Being by considering the lowest level on the animal hierarchy, that of insects; here Khomeini's favoured metaphor is 'parasite' and can be represented conceptually as OPPONENTS ARE PARASITES.

The universities were centres of political activity in the years prior to the revolution and a number of political groups were active there – in particular Islamic socialists known as the *Mojahedin* who were a guerrilla organization of young religious middle class students who were inspired partly by the thought of Shari'ati. There was the also the Marxist *Fada'iyan Khalq* and the *Tudeh* or communist party. Khomeini dismissed these political opponents as 'parasites' who were in alliance with external forces of oppression:

> But when the culture is corrupt, our youth, who form the foundations of our society, are lost to us, *they are trained to become parasites*, to become infatuated with the West.[41]

Of course, the schema that is activated by the parasite metaphor (used frequently both in left and right wing political discourse – for example by Castro and by Hitler) is the notion of a social group that does not contribute anything to the health of society but, to the contrary, drains it of its vital energies represented symbolically by its 'blood'. The foremost amongst the social groups represented by Khomeini as 'parasites' was the Pahlavi dynasty itself:

> As for what would happen once these have gone, once we have driven out these parasites and these gluttons for oil – the 'superpowers' *being both parasites* and gluttons for oil, and this Pahlavi family along with all those who have had dealings with this family over the past fifty years, *being the parasites* who are benefiting from the wealth of our very own country whilst our youngsters are paying the price with their lives.[42]

To heighten the political spectacle and create clear boundaries between his allies and his opponents, Khomeini's rhetoric is dramatically persuasive because it combines the metaphor of parasites with the figures of contrast (or antithesis), rhetorical question and cumulative repetition:

> Now these students of the religious sciences who spend the best and most active part of their lives in these narrow cells, and whose monthly

income is somewhere between 40 and 100 tumans – *are they parasites?* And those to whom one course of income alone brings hundreds of millions of tumans *are not parasites?* Are the *'ulama parasites?* And those who have filled foreign banks with the wealth produced by the topic of our poverty-stricken people, who have erected towering palaces but still will not leave the people in peace, wishing to fill their own pockets and those of Israel with our resources – *they are not parasites?* Let the world judge, let the nation judge *who the parasites are!*[43]

The logic of the Great Chain of Being metaphor is that below the lowest level of natural being (insect or worm) is the demonic level of monsters and devils. As we saw in the description of man as a ferocious monster, animal metaphors are at their most hyperbolic when they are based on satanic associations:

And now, during your own lifetime, you too are afflicted with misfortunes inflicted upon you by another *injudicious horned beast.* For do not be mistaken in thinking that even one bullet is fired without the Shah's permission ... All these incidents are reported to him and clearly *this evil man* has to give the orders to shoot.[44]

It is the Shah himself (rather than his government) who is the 'horned beast' implying a conceptual metaphor: THE SHAH IS THE DEVIL; this illustrates again the personalization of political issues as a persuasive and rhetorical strategy. Once the revolutionary movement had gained momentum and the Islamic republic was being established, Iran was represented as being delivered from alien satanic forces. This implies the parallel conceptual metaphor, FOREIGNERS ARE DEVILS, that is evident in the following:

You all, the nation of Iran and the nation of Islam are currently confronting a *satanic power* which for years has determined your destiny. Gradually, the Muslim lands have begun to think about freeing themselves from this power, and this includes Iran, which for some time now has been thinking about liberating itself from the hands of foreigners and *from the grasp of this satanic power.*[45]

Extremes of good and bad are communicated by contrasting Allah and Satan, that are placed at the top of the moral and ideological level of values shown in Figure 7.1. Once we move to the moral and ideological level of evaluation that contrasts Islam and infidels (Christians, Jews etc.), there is also the potential to draw on the metaphor system of the Koran. In a study I undertook of metaphors in the Koran, light and fire metaphors were the most frequently used. These are based on the concepts SPIRITUAL KNOWLEDGE IS LIGHT and IGNORANCE IS DARKNESS and ALLAH IS LIGHT.[46] This is evident in passages such as the following:

With it Allah guides him who will follow His pleasure into the ways of safety and brings them out of utter *darkness into light* by His will and guides them to the right path.[47]

Khomeini explores intertextual reference to the Koran through analysis and explanation of this metaphor system:

God is the Protector of those who have faith, from the depths of darkness He will lead them forth into light. Of those who reject faith the patrons are the evil ones, from light they will lead them forth into the depths of darkness. 'Into the depths of darkness' not simply into darkness, but into all the degrees of darkness.[48]

These metaphors probably evoke the earlier Zorastrian belief system that predated Islam in which all creation was interpreted as a fundamental struggle between light and darkness. Most significantly, Khomeini also uses light metaphors to communicate the legitimacy for Islamic government and the rule of imams by speaking of those who intend to base government in Islamic principles as being the 'shadow of God':

Those 'holders of authority' who are mentioned immediately after God and His Messenger in the Koran must also be close to God and His Messenger in their practice. *They must be the shadow of God* and his Messenger. Yes, the Islamic ruler is the *shadow of God*, but that which is meant by shadow is something which of itself has no motion. Your shadow does not move by itself, it moves only when you move. Islam recognizes that person as the *'shadow of God'* who abandons all individual volition in the sense that he acts only in accordance with the ordinances of Islam, his motion therefore being dependent and not independent.

Here we see how metaphor describes how followers become leaders through a process of divinely-inspired transcendence; Khomeini's design of leadership was to communicate that he was the shadow of God. Conversely, as we have seen elsewhere in his communication of a value system, this vision of the holy leader is contrasted with one in which leaders are unholy when they are not motivated by Islamic principles:

The Messenger of God (peace and blessings be upon him) was indeed *a true shadow of God*. But can the same be said for this vile man, the Shah?[49]

In his rhetorical representation of values and vision there is a contrast between inherently good and inherently evil forces. This contrast operates at the levels of ideology, history and social and political agency, but becomes most persuasive when individuals are classified accordingly. A rhetoric in which a good, Islamic nation is delivered from an evil intrusive invading force – assisted by the corrupt Shah and his government – gives a powerful persuasive momentum to his arguments.

Communication of legitimacy

We have seen in the preceding sections how metaphors and slogans were used to create positive representations of political supporters and negative representations of political opponents through positioning various social agents, ideologies and historical actors on the extreme ends of a moral scale. Legitimization of self and followers and de-legitimization of opponents was therefore central to the design of Khomeini's leadership communication. We have also seen that the inseparability of politics and religion is central to his formal explanations of legitimacy.

His views on Islamic government are fully expounded in a series of 12 lectures he gave in the early part of 1970. The main leadership theme is that there is a duty on religious scholars to bring about the governance of the *faqih* (or *vilayat-i-faqih*). From this perspective, legitimacy originates in God as communicated to man by the Prophet Muhammad through the revelation of the Koran. Subsequently, Islam offers the necessary legal basis for every aspect of life:

> The entire system of government and administration, together with the necessary laws, lies ready for you. If the administration of the country calls for taxes, Islam has made the necessary provision; and if laws are needed, Islam has established them all. There is no need for you, after establishing a government, to sit down and draw up laws, or, like rulers who worship foreigners and are infatuated with the West, run after others to borrow their laws. Everything is ready and waiting, all that remains is to draw up ministerial programs, and that can be accomplished with the help and cooperation of consultants and advisers who are experts in different fields, gathered together in a consultative assembly.[50]

The legitimacy of a government depends on the extent to which it is in keeping with the social system of Islam and the legitimacy of a leader depends on the extent to which his morality and beliefs are consistent with Islam:

> If the ruler adheres to Islam, he must necessarily submit to the *faqih* themselves ... The ruler must also posses excellence in morals and belief; he must be just and untainted by major sin.[51]

In Shi'ism – pending the arrival of the hidden imam – leadership is transferred to theologians (or *faqih*) who have the authority to interpret religious laws and duty for followers. At times, a single all powerful *faqih* can become a Supreme Jurisprudent who is treated as if they were they were the hidden twelfth imam; as we have seen, everything in Khomeini's leadership style was designed to encourage self-identification with the twelfth imam. As Martin explains, the very use of the term 'imam' to refer to Khomeini had important connotations for his legitimacy:

> The huge demonstrations were mobilized at the exhortation of Khomeini as leader, a frequent slogan being *'Allah Akbar, Khomeini Rahbar'* ('God is great, Khomeini is the leader'). Khomeini, however, was most often referred to as the Imam. The word 'Imam' derives from the Arabic for 'leader' and thus originally had a straightforward meaning. It is also a word full of connotations. It suggests the absent Imam, the last of the 12 infallibles, and although Khomeini did not claim authority such as theirs, both he and his followers were aware of the charismatic and immaculate power it suggested to the ordinary people in a Shi'ite culture. The term linked to Khomeini's natural piety, which in press interviews, for example, together with an emphasis on the modesty of his abodes, was used to suggest his saintly attributes – very important for winning respect and authority among the pious poor.[52]

Khomeini's legitimacy as a leader was designed so that everything in his appearance, use of language and behaviour evoked the powerful cultural resonance of Shi'ism by symbolizing his status as the imam. His overriding claim to legitimacy was in the moral authority underlying his actions and behaviour; as he explained in *Islamic Government*:

> The believers, men and women, are friends and protectors to each other; they enjoin the good and forbid the evil. (Koran 9:71) . . . If the duty of enjoining the good and forbidding the evil is properly performed, all other duties will automatically fall into place.[53]

Just as the leader inherited his authority from God, the Prophet and the Imams, so his behaviour should become the model that would empower followers:

> Act so that your deeds, conduct, character and aversion to worldly ambition will have an uplifting effect on the people. They will imitate your example, and you will become models for them and soldiers of God. Only thus can you make Islam and Islamic government known to the people.[54]

We have seen in Chapter 1 that such an effect on followers is very much the defining characteristic of transformational leaders. Martin argues that because Khomeini's views on legitimacy rely on the moral virtue, wisdom and knowledge of the leader, this shows evidence of the influence of Plato's Republic since his philosopher-king necessarily demonstrates virtue and knowledge.

In addition to personal behaviour, Khomeini also argued for legal knowledge as the basis for a leader's legitimacy:

> The qualifications essential for the ruler derive directly from the nature and form of Islamic government. In addition to general qualifications like intelligence and administrative ability, there are two other essential qualifications: knowledge of the law and justice.[55]

Possession of these two qualifications implied that the leader emulated the Prophet Muhammad:

> If a worthy individual possessing these two qualities (knowledge of the law and justice) arises and establishes a government, he will possess the same authority as the Most Noble Messenger (upon whom be peace and blessings) in the administration of society, and it will be the duty of all people to obey him.[56]

Khomeini's legitimacy claims were designed by contrasting the legitimate with the illegitimate: he did everything possible to represent himself and his supporters as the former and the Shah and his opponents as the latter. This complies with general theories of charismatic communication:

> The charismatic's verbal messages construct reality such that only the positive features of the future vision and only the negative features of the status quo are emphasized.[57]

Legitimate government is systematically contrasted with illegitimate government:

> Tyrannical governments ... comprise what is meant by *taghut*, for they have rebelled against divine command by instituting evil laws, implementing them, and then making them the basis of judicial practice. God has commanded us to disbelieve in them; that is to revolt against them and their commands and ordinances.[58]

Just as Islam was the basis of legitimacy, so foreign sources of authority were illegitimate precisely because they were not Islamic:

> This is our situation then – created for us by foreigners through their propaganda and their agents. They have removed from operation all the judicial processes and political laws of Islam and replaced them with European importations, thus diminishing the scope of Islam and

ousting it from Islamic society. For the sake of exploitation they have installed their agents in power.[59]

Imperialism was an especially illegitimate source of authority because it was motivated by greed for economic power:

> The British imperialists penetrated the countries of the East more than three hundred years ago. Being knowledgeable about all aspects of these countries, they drew up elaborate plans for assuming control of them. Then came the new imperialists, the Americans and others. They allied themselves with the British and took part in the execution of their plans ... Foreign experts have studied our country and have discovered all our mineral reserves – gold, copper, petroleum, and so on. They have also made an assessment of our people's intelligence and come to the conclusion that the only barriers blocking their way are Islam and the religious leadership.[60]

The knowledge and wisdom of a legitimate leader are contrasted with the ignorance of an illegitimate source of authority:

> What are the qualifications of those who now rule the Muslim countries? What gives them the ability to rule that we allegedly lack? Who among them has any more ability than the average man? Many of them have never studied anything! Where did the ruler of the Hijaz ever go to study? As for Riza Khan, he was totally illiterate, an illiterate soldier, no more![61]

Indeed, Khomeini's design of illegitimacy is central to his rhetoric of self-legitimacy. For example, a group that attracted his wrath was the 'false saints', who – though they were less illegitimate and deserving of punishment than tyrannical rulers or foreigners – were nevertheless to be chastised:

> The state of Muslim society today is such that these false saints prevent Islam from exerting its proper influence; acting in the name of Islam, they are inflicting damage upon Islam.[62]

He referred to these false saints as *akhunds* and argued that they were not to be confused with genuine *fuqaha* and should be symbolically punished by removal of their turbans:

> Our youth must strip them of their turbans. The turbans of these *akhunds*, who cause corruption in Muslim society while claiming to be *fuqaha* and *'ulama* must be removed. They do not need to be beaten much; just take off their turbans, and do not permit them to appear in public wearing turbans. The turban is a noble garment; not everyone is fit to wear it.[63]

The reason why the design of illegitimate authority is so important is because it obliges true believers to rebel against tyranny. This style of illegitimacy design evoked Shi'ite myths grounded in the rebellion of Hossein against the oppressions of the Umayyid rule. The incorruptible rule of the *faqih* and himself was contrasted with the corrupt rule of the Pahlavi dynasty and imperialism. This required followers of legitimate rule to take up arms against illegitimate rulers:

> In the Koran, God Almighty has forbidden men to obey the *taghut* – illegitimate regimes – and even encouraged them to rise against kings, just as he commanded Moses to rebel, there are a number of traditions encouraging people to fight against the oppressors and those who wish to pervert religion . . . Tyrannical rulers, for their part, stood in terror of the Imams.[64]

Khomeini needed to create a body of active political followers who would become legitimate agents of change to bring about Islamic government and to resist the oppressors in true Shi'ite style; for this purpose he looked to religious youth:

> Grant that the younger generation studying in the religious colleges and the universities may struggle to reach the sacred aims of Islam and strive together, with ranks united, first, to deliver the Islamic countries from the clutches of imperialism and its vile agents, and then to defend them.[65]

The universities in particular were seen as reservoirs of potential political support and students were often victims – and even martyrs – of illegitimate sources of authority; his rhetoric therefore dramatized their victim status:

> If our universities were proper universities then when the students there try to speak a word of truth, the police would not suppress them so. The things they do to them! They beat the girls, they beat the boys, they beat our youth and imprison them.

Young followers had the opportunity to participate in a cycle of redemption that followed the Shi'ite tradition of self-sacrifice and implied that the more they suffered, the stronger they would become – indeed the extent of their suffering would correspond with their degree of legitimacy:

> In Iran our young men were imprisoned and banished and now they are subject to the same measures again. But when these courageous youths return from prison or exile they recommence their struggle, returning to the themes of their earlier preaching. Again they are sent into exile. But even if they were to be banished or imprisoned and then released ten

times over they would still be the same people that they were in the beginning. This is because they have received true Islamic training.[66]

Given the importance that Islam places on law and the persuasive potential of the myth of the twelfth imam, Khomeini's rhetoric was highly effective in the performance of leadership. The contrast between legitimate and the illegitimate sources of authority placed an ethical obligation on religiously minded people – especially young people – to oppose, physically, the rule of the Shah. The extent to which he was successful was seen when the Shah departed from Iran in January 1979 and then in the referendum of March 1979 when 98.2 per cent voted in favour of the Islamic Republic. As his biographer summarizes, legitimacy ultimately originates in creating a belief in a state of unity with God:

> As a mystic, Khomeini was an elitist, but as a theological he was expedient and as a politician a calculating popularist to the point of being opportunistic. He believed in the use of force and, if need be, violence. He felt entitled to order the execution of thousands of infidels without shedding a tear. For Khomeini the mystic, Man reaches a state of unity with God, his anger becomes the wrath of God.[67]

Leadership and the media

For a political leader who based his appeal in the sacred texts of the past Khomeini was surprisingly contemporary in his use of modern media for the distribution of his message. He was personally very interested in the media and dedicated much of his time to reading the daily press and listening to international radio services, especially in times of heightened political tension. He needed to keep well-informed on the consequences of his actions, and those of his opponents, on followers as this could be highly influential in determining his next political move; this use of the media was certainly opportunist. This was because he understood the importance of the media in bringing about an Islamic Revolution and then in maintaining an Islamic government once it had been established. He also saw the media as playing a vital role in the subsequent export of the Islamic Revolution. It was for him a crucial material means to an ideological end:

As Wright summarizes:

> Through mimeographed and photocopies texts and, later on, tape cassettes and videos, he provided his former *talbabehs* with regular pronouncements on events in Iran for clandestine distribution. He also used technology to keep current ... During his final four months in Paris, Khomeini also made extensive us of a sophisticated telephone system, which had been installed by an American company to maintain links with the simmering revolution.[68]

Although he was perhaps most impressive when his speeches were heard live, his sermons were deliberately designed to inspire his followers and he was aware of the wider audience that he could potentially reach. In this respect he was especially aware of the potential of visual media – photographs, posters and videos – in leadership performance. He also used technology in developing an external demand for cassette recordings of his speeches, and while in exile in Turkey he tried to prevent photographs of him wearing the western clothing he was required to wear. However, in spite of the religious constraints that Islam places on representations of the human form, he made no effort to prevent followers from using images of him, often on a very large-scale in the posters that have become icons of the Iranian Revolution.

Summary

Khomeini's status as a powerful national leader has been summarized as follows:

> Khomeini represented the strong and charismatic leadership that Iranians have looked to since the day of Cyrus the Great and Darius in the 6th century B.C. . . . his mass appeal stemmed from his impassioned eloquence an absolute sense of righteousness . . . in public addresses and taped messages, he could speak as one of the people, not above them, and he used the familiar and comforting idiom of a religion that offered answers to questions of theology as well as of daily life.[69]

We have seen how he designed his leadership by rhetorical representation of values on the extreme ends of a scale that contrasted inherently good and evil forces. This contrast operated at the levels of ideology and history as well as social and individual agency. The primary contrast is between the valued indigenous cultural forces – such as Shi'ism – and the devalued external cultural agents of imperialism. A rhetoric in which a good, Islamic nation is dramatically contrasted with an evil intrusive invading force – assisted by the Shah and his supporters – provides the persuasive momentum of his arguments. They are communicated by antithesis, hyperbole and metaphor; metaphors may be represented as conceptually motivated by the following ideas: COUNTRIES ARE ANIMALS, OPPONENTS ARE PARASITES, THE SHAH IS THE DEVIL, FOREIGNERS ARE DEVILS, and these may be inter-related through the Great Chain of Being metaphor. I have also explained the connection with conceptual metaphors originating in the Koran such as: SPIRITUAL KNOWLEDGE IS LIGHT and IGNORANCE IS DARKNESS.

I have explained how his design of leadership style involves legitimization of self and followers and de-legitimization of the Shah and his supporters. Above all, I have argued that Khomeini's legitimacy as a leader was designed so that everything in his appearance, use of language and behaviour evoked the powerful cultural resonance of Shi'ism by symbolizing his mythic status as the hidden, twelfth imam. Consider this eyewitness account:

> At the start of the revolution, a rumor had taken root that Khomeini's image could be seen in the moon. Many people, even perfectly modern and educated individuals, came to believe this. They had seen him in the moon. He has been a conscious mythmaker, and he had turned himself into a myth.[70]

Khomeini's leadership performance transformed followers into warriors, and provided visions that appealed to the needs, desires and beliefs of a large section of the Iranian population. As a charismatic leader, he communicated a symbolically consistent message, both as regards the non-verbal semiotics of appearance, dress and symbolic action, and as regards the verbal semiotics of rhetorical figures such as metaphor and slogan. Above all, his highly personalized legitimacy assaults on opponents were central to his leadership performance. He was media-savvy and his rhetoric targeted the social groups to whom it was most designed to appeal. Khomeini can therefore be considered as the prototype of a charismatic Islamic leader precisely because he was highly successful in the design and performance of leadership style; the effect of his leadership style continues and has powerfully influenced all subsequent charismatic Islamic leaders.

8 Mahathir Muhammad

Modernizer or traditionalist?

Introduction

Unlike the leaders discussed in earlier chapters, it could be argued that Mahathir of Malaysia and Lee Kuan Yew of Singapore are leaders whose significance is limited to their own country, or at most to the region of southeast Asia – rather than having truly global influence. However, for purposes of comparison it is vital to consider leaders who have successfully challenged western global dominance in the pursuit of modernity. The emergence of countries such as Singapore and Malaysia, Japan and Korea is not because of their association with particular ideologies – capitalist, communist or Islamic – but because of their success in adapting to, and creating, modernity without sacrificing traditions. In many 'Asian' societies the 'western' version of modernity – with its emphasis on individual self-expression, human rights and freedom of the press – is perceived as culturally restricted. Many belonging to Malaysia and Singapore's three distinct ethnic groups – the Malay, Chinese and Indian – share a religious view on life and a close attachment to the family. They typically follow traditional values – returning home during religious festivals for 'open house' and showing respect to the elders; the religious festivals of each group are also public holidays. There is a collectivist orientation, a preference for compromise and negotiation over competition and conflict, a concern with maintaining face and an importance on age.[1] I will consider the design of leadership style in these Asian cultural settings by analysing Mahathir in this chapter and Lee Kuan Yew in the following one.

It is probably because of the apparent contrariness of his views that there is a lack of an established consensus on Mahathir – he is seen as, at best, mercurial and, at worst, as a maverick – without any consistent views other than Malaysian nationalism and a postcolonial antagonism towards Anglo-Saxon hegemony. When we examine his leadership performance in more detail we find that his success as a leader is because he successfully challenges some existing beliefs and attitudes regarding cultural and political identity by confirming others and, in doing so, redefines what it means to be Malay, Muslim and a member of the fast-track developing world. It is only by *reinforcing* some dimensions of existing identities that he is able to *challenge* others, therefore the rhetorical style of his leadership has been characterized by paradox and ambiguity.

The element of paradox extends to the personality of the Malaysian leader: 'He is a politician whose blunt, no-nonsense style clashes oddly with a political culture that is essentially consensual. More than anything else, according to his friends, he is a shy, reticent individual and yet his combative public image barely hints at this'.[2] In many Asian cultures interpersonal communication is designed to save the face of in-group members – loss of standing within the community is considered tantamount to social exclusion – and communication is organized to demonstrate awareness of social position. This manifests itself linguistically in a range of phenomena such as honorifics and address terms that are governed by the social relationship between speaker and hearer. In the polemic that defined his early political philosophy, *The Malay Dilemma*, Mahathir notes the traditional style for showing deference:

> The Malay is courteous and self-effacing. His work is full of nobility and he is never far from his rajas and chiefs. He gives way and he shows deference. It is good manners to do so. It is not degrading. It is in fact a mark of breeding.[3]

He goes on to explain how the Malay style has often been misinterpreted by the out-group; for example, body language and verbal habits were misinterpreted as evidence of weakness and inferiority by the British. The Malay habit of addressing the British using the deferential form *tuan*, literally 'master', was misinterpreted as evidence that the Malays thought of the British as their masters and Mahathir rejected a style that symbolized a master-servant relationship.

Mahathir's main leadership objective was to ensure the survival of the Malays by transforming the way that they interacted with outsiders and by urging them to *struggle* for their rights in a competitive world in which the devil takes the hindmost. He appealed to the consensual values of the in-group in order to create awareness of the challenges of survival in the modern world:

> One of his definitive characteristics is his constant concern to keep ahead of a constantly changing world. In the life of a nation, as in that of an individual, to be forewarned is to be forearmed; Mahathir considers it the duty of a leader to forearm his people and his nation continuously ... Not for nothing are 'dilemmas', 'obstacles', and 'challenges' some of the key words in the Mahathirist lexicon.[4]

Mahathir's leadership style in the international arena has usually been competitive and confrontational; his claim to leadership lay in articulating the nature of *challenges* and in identifying opponents – often in terms that were not specific. Initially, it was British colonialism, then Chinese economic practice; later it was 'The West' in general – either as symbolized by human rights activists, environmentalists such as Bruno Manser[5] or representatives of the international banking system such as the World Trade Organization. Politically, the strategy was to unite followers by creating awareness of the threats and dangers of alien forces. As his political success increased, so did his definition of his followership: at first it was defined *ethnically* as a member of the Malay race – symbolized by being a party member of UMNO,[6] then *nationally* as Malaysian, then it broadened further through pan-national appeals to *Islamic* or *regional* loyalty. He sought to create a regional identity among followers as belonging to 'the south' and 'the east' – in opposition to 'the north' and 'the west'. By constantly redefining his followership, Mahathir has broadened his domestic and international power bases and has designed a successful style of leadership.

He admires modernizing leaders such as Peter the Great but his models are primarily social rather than individual: in particular the Asian societies that embraced postwar capitalism and turned the Protestant work ethic into an Asian phenomenon. His awareness of the need for effort and struggle can be traced to his father – Muhammad Iskandar – a caring but strict man who imposed a strong domestic discipline. As a Malaysian schoolmaster typical of the emerging urban lower middle class, he also imposed on his family the 'English' public school ethic of a balanced regime of work and play. The values of diligence, thrift, self-improvement and attainment were readily adopted by his son and fitted well with the new Asian models of self-reliance based on hard work.

Mahathir experienced personal poverty as a 16-year-old student when his secondary education was interrupted by the Japanese occupation and he was forced to make a living from a small food and drink stall. In 1947, at the age of 22, he travelled from rural Kedah to study medicine in Singapore where he became aware of the economic success of the urban Chinese as compared with rural Malays. As a young man in Singapore (which was part of Malaysia until its expulsion in 1965) he supplemented his income by writing articles for the *Sunday Times* under the pseudonym of C.H.E. Det. In 1957 he set up a medical practice in Alor Star and was elected to parliament in 1964 under the nickname 'Dr UMNO'. He allied himself with the ruling Alliance in opposition to the People's Action Party of Singapore and became identified with the Malay 'ultras' who reacted to the 'threat' of Chinese encroachment on the 'special position' of Malays. The emotional intensity of his debates with Lee Kuan Yew contributed to the expulsion of Singapore from Malaysia on 9 August 1965; but, in fact, the two shared a similar vision of a national self-sufficiency based on enterprise and the work ethic that was oriented towards capitalism and free market neo-liberalism. Ultimately, this was to prove more important than the personal rivalry that has at times characterized their political positions.

In fact, Mahathir's dual career as a doctor–politician gave him both a natural constituency amongst his local community in Alor Star as well as providing him with the financial independence that allowed him to survive during such a period of exile. He is fondly remembered for offering lifts to patients in his own car, and accepting chickens or farm produce in lieu of payment for his medical services. As we will see in the analysis of his rhetorical style, it also gave him a plentiful supply of metaphors with which he could develop and exploit his social position as a doctor–politician. Of course, if he failed in politics he could resume medical practice, but as he admitted: 'the study of medicine was at least partly in order to further my career as a politician' and so 'it was not too difficult to give up medicine for my other and more abiding love, politics'.[7]

Mahathir has also been noted as having a ruthless streak and not taking lightly any opposition to his leadership. In April 1987 there was a struggle for leadership of UMNO between Mahathir and Musa, who formed Team A, and Team B; the victory of the former led to the instant purging of the latter from the Cabinet. His major biographer, Khoo Boo Teik asks the question: 'Was the apparent novelty of Mahathir's approach merely a matter of his "style" as he claimed when he insisted that he was retaining the policies of his predecessors?'.[8] However, I suggest that it is misguided to see leadership as *merely* a matter of 'style' – since the successful design of style is essential to leadership and Mahathir's style has been to create ambiguity through rejecting stereotypes.

Non-linguistic communication of charisma

Appearance and leadership style

Mahathir's appearance is conducive to acceptance as a leader; he is conventionally good-looking in a way that fits the norms and tastes of a largely conservative society such as Malaysia. His appearance is that of a trusted member of the professional classes: he could be an urbane lawyer, a well-presented doctor or even a schoolmaster of the type students idolize. He is usually photographed – either smiling benevolently in a way that shows concern for followers or with a serious expression of concentration and reflection that befits a statesman. At UMNO General Assemblies there is a picture of him laughing uproariously at the speaker on the podium. In wider arenas the benevolence and social acceptability of his appearance contrasts with his often confrontational and unconventional communication style; by showing outward conformity to general societal norms as regards appearance, he was able to create rhetorical tension with an argumentative rhetorical style that could be considered novel in Malay leadership.

Dress

Mahathir's dress choice shows an awareness of how style messages vary according to the setting; the message can either look towards the future or back to the past according to rhetorical intention. He wears either the white shirt, collar, tie and suit of a western corporate executive – just as would, say, a Japanese director of a large company – or the traditional clothing of a Malay that would be worn, say, on Friday (the Muslim holy day), or at the UMNO General Assembly. The most common form of Malay traditional clothing is a loose-fitting bright coloured shirt (*baju*) and trousers (*seluar*) with a cloth worn around the waist known as *samping* and a dark velvet cylindrical hat known as the *songkok*; together this is known as '*Baju Melayu*' or Malay dress.

In a survey I undertook of 200 images of Mahathir (using Google 'images'), 58.5 per cent showed him wearing a suit, collar and tie; 29.5 per cent showed him wearing Malay traditional clothing and the remaining 12 per cent showed him wearing western informal clothing (shirt with no tie, slacks etc.). The most common type of Malay costume was the formal Malay dress, but on other occasions he wears more stylish semi-traditional clothes such as the Nehru jacket – a high-collared jacket that is buttoned right up to a closed collar. Sometimes he wears the batik shirt that is commonly part of Malay formal wear at evening social occasions. A few images show him wearing a 'bush jacket': a high-waisted loose jacket practical for visits to villages where the more formal suit and tie would not be practical.

The switching of clothes to specific settings reflects the various audiences he is performing to: either national, indigenous audiences that place high value on *adat* or custom and adherence to traditional Malay values, or audiences that place value on a modernizing corporate strategy and managerialism. Choice of dress is therefore something on which Mahathir places high importance and demonstrates some skill – showing awareness of both what is appropriate to the occasion but also, where feasible, adding dimensions of personal taste and style that enhance the uniqueness of his leadership image.

Artefacts

The symbol of the new Malaysia was the design of a new range of Proton cars; the first model, released in 1985, was the Proton Saga. Though the technology and parts were imported from Mitsubishi there has been a gradual transference of skills and technological knowledge; the car symbolizes the presence of heavy industry in Malaysia and has created a mass market: the Proton currently holds over 60 per cent of the market share in Malaysia. It was a project initiated by Mahathir and the car has become a symbol of his leadership vision of Malaysia as a fully industrialized country. This is symbolically represented by changes in the Proton logo; originally it featured a crescent and a 14-pointed star but now it has a stylized tiger's head symbolizing Malaysia's status as a 'Tiger economy'. An important feature of the product development of the Proton range is that they are pitched at market segments that correspond with Malaysian social hierarchies. The social message has been reinforced by providing all civil servants above a certain rank with the top of the range Proton Perdana that was first produced in 1994. This is Mahathir's own choice and his registration number 2020 refers to 'Vision 2020' (discussed later in this chapter). Evidently, the Proton project is a salient example of how leaders use artefacts to create symbolic meanings that blend together economic, social and political objectives, by creating an object that integrates a personal style choice with a range of social choices made by the leader.

The use of other artefacts such as tie-pins, shields, sports trophies and other artefacts that communicate the integration of national icons with success and social status is very much a hallmark of the Malaysian leadership style. This reflects even in social habits that are not otherwise socially approved; the sales slogan of Dunhill cigarettes (for which advertising in Malaysia has been unrestricted) is 'Style, Quality, Excellence' – these attributes associate a particular commodity with a positive social image that corresponds with leadership objectives.

On the larger scale, another symbol of the Mahathir's vision of a new Malaysia is the Petronas Twin Towers which – at least for a period – were the highest building in the world. The important thing about this and other building projects initiated by Mahathir, such as the Menara Kuala Lumpur, is that they were symbols of a national vision that combined positive images of success with aesthetic statements of Islamic cultural identity.

Symbolic action

Traditional Malay culture attaches great symbolic importance to physical positioning and gesture; a study of Malay idioms shows the importance attached to particular parts of the human body when combined with a verb of action; for example, consider the phrase *campur tangan* this literally means 'mix + hand/arm' (in Malay *tangan* refers to 'hand' and 'arm'); however, its figurative meaning is 'to interfere in a way that is somewhat intrusive'. A thief or pickpocket is known as *tangan panjang* or 'arm/hand long'. Gestures, including very subtle ones such as the movement of the eyes, are heavily endowed with symbolic signification; for example, in Malay *bermain mata* – 'play eye' – may be translated as 'to flirt with sidelong glances' and *angkat mata* – 'raise eye' – means 'to invite someone to a fight'. Cultural perspectives on the symbolism of body language are evident, then, from linguistic features.

However, in contrast to the subtle communication of such coded signs that reflect traditional cultural values, Mahathir preferred actual physical contact with followers:

> I feel good about making contact (with crowds). My training as a doctor
> helps me to communicate. The touch of the hand, that is important. It
> is like the healing concept of the 'laying of hands'. That is why I try to
> shake the hands of as many people as I can.[9]

While the handshake itself is likely to be a light one, the importance
attached to actual contact is all the more important in a culture that is typically reserved in its manifestations of emotion. This is part of the restraint
that typifies Malay culture – one that is associated with politeness, courtesy
to others, and modesty; at times, Mahathir is keen to emphasize his accommodation to these norms – as when he informs his interviewer of his reluctance to walk on the traditional red carpet laid out for VIPs:

> Initially, when I used to go with Tun Razak, I would not walk on the
> red carpet. I would walk off it. He would tell me, 'This is laid for you.' I
> learnt then to gingerly walk on it . . . I don't deserve that much respect.
> I'm nobody. I'm just one of them.[10]

In many respects Mahathir's most symbolic actions relate to his foreign
policy. He developed a policy that was often aggressive and belied both his
personal reticence, and the deference that he described in *The Malay
Dilemma* as characterizing Malays. His early acts of charismatic leadership
sought to dispense with any evidence of a colonial heritage – such as economic dependency on Britain – through the 'Buy British Last' policy. A
particular event which riled him was the decision by the British government
in 1981 to increase tuition fees for overseas students; this affected 13,000
Malaysian students in Britain and came on top of other irritations such as
unfavourable terms of trade for Malaysia's primary exports; the reaction was
to take over the Guthrie Corporation, one of Britain's largest plantation
companies. By cocking a snook at the colonial power he raised national self-
confidence. As part of the same rejection of postcolonial accommodation,
Mahathir absented himself from the Commonwealth Heads of Government
Meeting in Melbourne in 1981, although his friendship with Margaret
Thatcher helped overcome this rift.

Mahathir also developed a 'Look East' policy that aimed to model
Malaysia's development on that of Japan and other successful eastern
economies. His discourse contrasted an industrialized, colonizing and
exploiting west/north with a formerly colonized and exploited east/south.
This ignored Japan and Korea's close reliance on the west to build up their
economies in the postwar period and the fact that some emerging eastern
nations such as Thailand had not been colonized. However, Mahathir positioned himself as a leader of a group of emerging southern nations rather
than as a follower of western hegemony. This symbolism served to conceal
the fact that in political and economical terms the policies of these nations
were based on the capitalist principles of entrepreneurship, the work ethic,

open markets and free trade. The symbolic actions of a nationalist leader who embraced Asian values was an effective leadership style because it led to international recognition of Malaysia.[11]

However, these bold nationally symbolic actions may be contrasted with dramatic performances, for example at the televised UMNO party conference in 2002 Mahathir broke down in tears while expressing the belief that his struggle to re-position the Malays economically had not succeeded. This intimation of resignation caused passionate emotions among followers and an outbreak of grief on a national scale. Though naturally reserved, crying, in Malay culture, is considered an acceptable part of growing old; however, I suggest that the desire to break with social and cultural norms regarding the display of emotion in public communicated a subliminal message that was in keeping with Mahathir's style of leadership. Here was a leader who desired that his nation modernized successfully, but whose care for followers evoked feelings that were reminiscent of the ideal traditional Malay leader-follower relationship based on personal trust and loyalty. Symbolic action through the display of powerful emotion contributed to the development of a charismatic image because it evoked feelings of loss among followers as the boundaries between leader and follower dissolved. However, it was also an indication that he had reached an age when there was a need for a transition of leadership to those more physically and emotionally able to bear its burdens.

Stylistic features of verbal communication

Mahathir's communication style created the image of a strong leader with unique and well-articulated ideas. His greatest fear was of appearing as weak or lacking in ideas and he sought to create an image that differentiated him from rivals. This explains why he adopts a polemical tone, even when arguing a point that actually complies with dominant ideologies such as neo-liberalism. Having rejected communism and adopted a free market model, he embraced the robust nationalism that had earlier characterized the discourse of western powers when they embarked on colonization. He wanted to come over as confident, determined to uphold the national interest and keenly independent – a style of discourse that evoked another politician with whom he got on very well: Margaret Thatcher. I have summarized her thinking with metaphors such as POLITICAL OPPONENTS ARE ENEMIES and traced them generically to the conceptual metaphor POLITICS IS CONFLICT:[12] I would suggest that Mahathir's communication of leadership is stylistically very similar. We see this in the following description of globalization where I have italicized the metaphors:

> The effect is the same as a military invasion. In fact, it is worse than that. Every aspect of our lives *will be invaded*. Our minds *will be invaded*. Even our religion *will be invaded*.[13]

> We now know that the *weapons to be used against us* are not just military forces but also *economic forces. The assaults* through economic forces are more subtle but are no less damaging and effective compared to military assaults. We need to know about the *economic forces* that may be used and how *we may defend ourselves*.[14]

Here the cognitive framework of war metaphors communicates the abstract process of globalization and this creates a strong, belligerent style of communication.

In fact, the most characteristic rhetorical myth of Mahathir's leadership is the identification of what Edelman refers to as a Conspiratorial Enemy;[15] this is a myth in which an out-group that is not identified with the leader is plotting to harm an in-group that is identified with the leader. Initially the enemy was the colonizing power of Britain, then it was the Chinese who threatened to take over the economy by excluding Malays from trade and commerce, and then it became generalized to a decadent 'west' – associated with social ills such as drugs, pornography, obscenity and anything related to the decline of 'traditional' values. As we have seen above, since the crash of the tiger economies in 1997, the enemy has become the invisible forces of globalization. In each case the loyalty of followers was appealed to on the basis of their fear that alien, external cultural and economic practices would corrupt pure, Islamic, indigenous Malay values.

A major stylistic feature of Mahathir's style of political argumentation is that it integrates the language of medicine with the language of politics. His discourse is concerned with the 'diagnosis' of a problem, through observation of its 'symptoms' and the recommendation of a 'cure'; he once explained this underlying metaphor THE POLITICIAN IS A DOCTOR:

> The first lesson is the methodical way that doctors approach medical problems, observance, history taking, physical examinations, special examinations, narrowing the diagnosis and then deciding on the most likely diagnosis and the treatment required. These are most useful in any problem in life, and they serve me well in attending top political problems.[16]

Since Mahathir's early political success was based on his medical practice, it is not surprising that his style seeks to transfer the human qualities of the patient-doctor relationship – such as trust, reliance and dependency – to the follower-leader relationship. Above all, patients rarely challenge a diagnosis, especially when it fits a description of the symptoms, and they therefore acquiesce in the cure – no matter how bitter the medicines may be.

Mahathir's first book *The Malay Dilemma* was primarily an extended 'diagnosis' of the social and economic problems of the Malays; 'symptoms' are identified, their causes elaborated and a 'cure' is proposed.[17] The book itself was a response to the major symptom of Malaysia's social disharmony:

the 1969 riots in Kuala Lumpur and the sensitivity surrounding these events is one reason why it was banned from publication in Singapore until after he became Prime Minister in 1981. He attributes the origins of social disharmony to the influx of Chinese and Indians under British rule and their physical separateness from the largely rural Malays. Following a broadly Darwinian diagnosis, he identifies a range of environmental and socio-cultural reasons why the Chinese were better equipped for survival.[18] Gradually this is used to develop an argument that they represent an even greater threat to national 'health' than had the British:

> In fact Chinese monopoly is even greater than the monopoly practiced by the British during the colonial period. The British confined themselves to big business and left retail trade to the Chinese. With the Chinese, every form of business from hawking fruits to multi-million dollar construction work is monopolized by them. Not even the crumbs are left to others.[19]

Another part of the 'diagnosis' is the reluctance of Malays to be frank about their problems:

> But as usual, politeness and a genuine desire to be accommodating have prevented the Malays from openly voicing their thoughts.[20]

> The whole idea seems to be that the less they talk about it the more the country will benefit from the economic stability built on Chinese economic domination.[21]

His status as doctor–politician makes it acceptable for him to be frank about the nation's problems – just as it would be unprofessional for a doctor *not* to make a diagnosis because the causes of the illness were too embarrassing to discuss. Cultural studies of Asian societies emphasize the importance of avoiding face loss by maintaining the communication forms that distinguish a social group:

> memberships in particular groups tend to take on a permanent in-group character along with special forms of discourse which carefully preserve the boundaries between those who are inside members of the groups and all others who are not members of the group.[22]

Mahathir identified the special forms of discourse that made it difficult for Malays to articulate their beliefs about their threatened status. By adopting the discourse pattern of the doctor-patient relationship he was able to develop a leadership style in which being open about the relations between ethnic groups was an acceptable style of political communication between Malay leaders and followers. The social distancing provided by the doctor's persona enabled him to offer apparently 'objective' professional assessments of the social attributes of Malaysia's two major ethnic groups. His ethnic 'diagnosis' is summarized in Table 8.1 below:

Because of the tensions caused by these ethnic incompatibilities, he identifies the Malay dilemma as:

> whether they should stop trying to help themselves in order that they should be proud to be the poor citizens of a prosperous country or whether they should try to get at some of the riches that this country boasts of, even if it blurs the economic picture of Malaysia a little.[23]

He represents the Malays as essentially patients who are in need of long-term care in the form of 'preferential treatment'; as a doctor he is especially aware of the negative impact of their economic situation on their health:

> From these inequalities of opportunities spring other inequalities, such as the miserable houses of the Malays compared to the houses of the non-Malays, the poor health of the Malays against the vigour of the non-Malays, the high death and infant mortality rates of the Malays compared to the non-Malays, the lack of savings and capital of the Malays when compared to the non-Malays.[24]

Doctors are aware of the variations of posture, and another dimension of the diagnosis concerns bodily performance:

> It is typical of the Malay to stand aside and let someone else pass. Not only does he stand aside, but he inclines himself in seeming obeisance. And the Malay who avails himself of this courtesy shows his breeding by not completely taking the path preferred. He too gives way and inclines himself ... It is bad manners to embarrass your guest and the non-Malay is always a guest to the Malay, a guest in his country.[25]

Table 8.1 Ethnic traits as described in *The Malay Dilemma*

	Positive	Negative
Malays	Tolerant, polite, courteous, restrained, deferent, self-effacing, practicing moderation, good mannered, well-bred.	Fatalistic, failing to value time, failing to value money and property, lacking frankness.
Chinese	Good at business, hard-working.	Unsympathetic, predatory, economically dominant, preferring other Chinese in business, undercutting competition.

What is interesting here is that the characteristic body language that communicates deference and politeness is then used as the basis for a particular metaphor that conceptualizes the Malay as the 'host' and the Chinese as the 'guest'. This concept was at the heart of crucial issues of ownership and identity that were to dominate southeast Asian politics – with its history of migrations across relatively loose political frontiers. He goes on to explain how the British misinterpreted deferential body language as evidence of weakness and inferiority. This misapprehension was aggravated by the Malay linguistic practice of addressing the British as *tuan*, meaning literally 'master'; in fact *tuan* is used as a polite form of address to anyone who is not known to the speaker and he argues that the British misinterpreted this as evidence that the Malays thought of them as their masters.

Mahathir's style of discourse based on the conceptual metaphor THE POLITICIAN IS A DOCTOR is sustained through particular medical metaphors:

How much can the Malay problem be *blown up before it bursts*?[26]

The Malaysian nation cannot expect to thrive and prosper *with this cancer* (i.e. the Malaysian dilemma) eating away at its heart.[27]

But the deluge of immigrants which the British encouraged, and the segregation which followed, arrested this *healthy, natural process* and precipitated the problems which have *plagued* the Malays ever since, and which have undermined their rights as the definitive people of the peninsula.[28]

Related then to THE POLITICIAN IS A DOCTOR I suggest another conceptual representation: POLITICAL PRACTICE IS MEDICAL PRACTICE. Since at times there is a degree of brutality and force necessary in the practice of medicine, this is also necessary in politics; for example, in a speech made on the merger of Nanyang University with the University of Singapore, Mahathir argued that: 'When the indications are irrefutable, amputations, however painful, must be undertaken'[29] and at the 1987 UMNO General Assembly a delegate observed that Mahathir was choosing a 'medical solution ... to cut out the cancer'. We see here how metaphors contain their own covert political arguments. However, the brutality of his 'surgical' approach could be used as a criticism of his leadership style as when one commentator complained that 'the problem with Dr. Mahathir is he crass, rough and hard. This man pushes things down your throat'.[30]

There is evidence that metaphors from the domain of health and medicine are more than a passing characteristic of Mahathir's communication of leadership. If we consider a more recent collection of speeches given after the Asian currency crisis of 1997, there are numerous metaphors that create associations between the process of globalization and the cause of illness:

The kind of globalisation promoted by the rich western countries has not convinced Asia that it is the answer to *economics ills* or the *vitamin for economic growth*.[31]

We had thought that since our economy was strong the ringgit would be not be attacked. But then we were told that *the disease affecting* the currencies of our neighbours are *contagious*. Although our ringgit was *healthy*, *the sickness* of the Thai baht *had sickened* the ringgit.[32]

He then contrasts the responses offered by institutions associated with globalization – in particular the IMF – with his own responses in terms of alternative cures or treatments:

Malaysia's rejection of the IMF formula and the decisions to regain exchange control ... have now been accepted by the international community as a viable alternative to the *IMF prescription*. By their own admission a *'cure-all'* for *economic ills* of the world simply does not exist.[33]

In terms of political argument, he contrasts the incompetence of IMF diagnoses with his own correct diagnoses:

The reasons why the IMF policy failed in Asia are now well known. The basic problem, of course, was that the IMF *misdiagnosed* the problems in Asia and applied the same *remedies* that were used in Latin America before.[34]

Mahathir was not only concerned with physical health; he had already begun to develop further the metaphor POLITICAL PRACTICE IS MEDICAL PRACTICE when he moved on to consider the type of mental states that could arise from a dilemma:

The impression given is one of continuous restraint which taxes the will. It seems to lead to an inner conflict, and at time the restraining bonds *seems to burst* and suddenly the polite formality disappears to be replaced by a *violent outburst* that is frightening in its intensity.[35]

He had already noted the phenomenon of the *amok*, or frenzy, as the direct physical manifestation of cumulative and pathological psychological repression and towards the end of *The Malay Dilemma* he makes a significant shift to the question of the psychological health of the Malays:

In modern psychology seeking out and identifying causes serves not only to facilitate treatment but is also part of the treatment.[36]

He begins to speak of a therapy rather than medicine as a cure:

To cure, it is imperative that the painful process of identifying the causes of the ailment be examined. A *therapy* based on the successful experience and methods of others will have minimal or not effect. There is no other way but to face boldly the pain of self-examination, the admission that one is wrong, and the acceptance that the *cure* lies in the rejection of some ideas and concepts no matter how dear to the heart they may be.[37]

It would seem worthwhile trying some of the ways of the West in order to get at the root of the failure of the Malays to compete with others. This examination of the value system and ethical codes of the Malays is therefore an attempt at a *therapeutic diagnosis*.[38]

He even moves on to make quite clear that psychiatry is the basis for his thinking:

By and large, the Malay value system and code of ethics are impediments to their progress. If they admit this, and if the need for change is realized, then there is hope; for as in *psychiatry*, success in isolating the root cause is in itself part of the *treatment*. From then on *planning a cure* would be relatively simple.[39]

The representation of political problems as issues of mental health also occurs in more recent speeches:

Too many believe that utter selfishness is a voter, that greed is great, that enlightened caring and compassion is a weakness. That selflessness and sacrifice for the common good is *a mental illness*.[40]

Crucial to Mahathir's performance of leadership is not only his self-representation as a concerned and frank doctor but also, perhaps more influentially, as a psychotherapist who is able to identify more deep-rooted conditions whose causes may be concealed from followers until revealed by 'therapy'. Effectively, Mahathir again creates a relationship of expectancy *and* dependency among followers, the more they *expect* him to provide a solution to their problems, the more *dependent* they become upon his insights into their true nature, their hidden desires, repressions and aspirations: their cultural condition. However, the relationship of dependency does not pave the way for an easy succession.

The leadership situation reached a crisis point at the 2002 UMNO General Assembly, when the 77-year-old leader gave an intimation of what was to follow by apologizing several times, expressing despair at having reached the limit of his efforts, before breaking down in tears. He told his followers that from now on they could no longer use him as a 'crutch'. At this cathartic moment the diagnosis of a national malaise was now expressed as a self-diagnosis so that his personal depression caused a national outpouring of grief. His use of medical and psychiatric metaphors is crucial in his design of leadership style because they serve to create a relationship of trust between follower and leader by drawing on the frames of other dependency relationships: those of the patient and doctor or psychotherapist; the child and the father – and when the pressures are too great the father can become a child again. These stylistic features also serve to counterbalance the belligerent political communication based on the concept POLITICS IS CONFLICT. Like the good-cop, bad-cop routine of interrogators, such tensions and variation of emotional mood are essential in the development of leadership style.

Communication of visions and values

Visions and values form a central element in Mahathir's leadership communication and there is a very close relationship between them because his vision of the future is based on a criticism of the values of the past. A belief in the importance of values is clearly articulated in his understanding of leadership:

> If the indications are that there should be a change in the value system and ethical code, then the leaders can lead the way with the certainty that they will be followed by the masses.[41]

Indeed the main argument of *The Malay Dilemma* is based on a critical evaluation of the traditional values of the Malays and the proposal that they should be replaced by modern 'western' values:

> The invasion of the Malay system of values by the Western system has been taking place since the first contact between the Malay States and the West. The results of the invasion have not all been bad. Some outdated Malay values have been replaced by rather positive Western ones. But many undesirable values have seeped into the Malay system.[42]

Chapter 9 of *The Malay Dilemma* is entitled 'Code of ethics and value systems of the Malays'; he starts by explaining that values are closely related to religious beliefs; for Malays there are both Islamic values and those determined by *adat* or custom. He then goes on to examine Malay attitudes and values towards life in general – death, time, money and property – before outlining the influence of the social code on the value system. What is interesting is a thematic progression from the ethical to the economic. His main claim is that Malay ethical values impede their economic position in society, and therefore in order to be more competitive, the Malays need to change their value system – as he puts it: 'Without a radical change in their code of ethics and value concepts, the efforts to effect a mass cure of the ills affecting the Malays will merely increase the general frustration of all concerned'.[43]

They should do this by placing more value on time, money and property – that is, on an economic notion of 'value'.

The criticism is that Malay values are backward and not in keeping with the demands of the modern world; for example, in relation to the fatalism that characterizes the Malay attitude to life: 'The effect of this fatalism is to relegate the struggle for worldly good to a low priority';[44] in relation to time: 'A community which is not conscious of time must be regarded as a very backward society . . . There is no doubt that the Malay failure to value time is one of the most important handicaps to their progress'.[45] Then in relation to money:

> This inability to understand the potential capacity of money is what makes the Malays poor businessmen. Beyond selling what they produce in work or in kind, the Malays appear unable to devise ways of acquiring money.[46]

He refers to Malay attitudes to time and money as 'underdeveloped' and rooted in traditional feudal organization of society. However his leadership aim is not to change the hierarchical nature of society but simply to replace the role of ruler with his own leadership:

> In itself the feudalist inclination of the Malays is not damaging. It makes for an orderly law-abiding society . . . A revolution in such a society is unusual unless led from above. A feudal society . . . can be a dynamic society if there is dynamism at the top. When the top fails, or is preoccupied with its own well-being, the masses become devoid of incentive for progress.[47]

Mahathir's diagnosis, then, primarily concerns the value system of the Malays and he concludes:

> This analysis of the value systems of the Malays clearly shows that it hinders the progress and competitive abilities of the Malays in a multiracial society . . . the Malay value system and code of ethics are impediments to their progress. If they admit this, and if the need for change is realized, then there is hope.[48]

What direction, then, should the change in values take? It was certainly not towards the ethics of a declining west – a west of 'many undesirable values';[49] indicators of western decadence included nudity in public, smoking marijuana, male prostitution, homosexual marriage, unisex attire, obscene films etc. He makes reference to a 'perversion of values',[50] so western nations could 'no longer stand tall as models for the world to emulate'.[51] In this respect Mahathir is articulating the values of the traditional Malay in-group that are in turn rooted in the ethical values of Islam, in contrast to those of a colonial, western and non-Muslim out-group. He draws on stereo-types of 'The West' – themselves generated by the western media – such as the dominance of sexual promiscuity and trade unions and advocates the values of 'The East' as an alternative model for development:

> Mahathir decided that the truly indispensable elements of the Japanese and South Korean 'economic miracles' were the moral and cultural pillars: a strong work ethic, worthy Eastern values, a capacity for learn-ing, courage to compete, self-reliance, and national pride.[52]

Education formed a central part of this vision of a new Malaysia, and after a brief flirtation with a fully Malay curriculum, English was introduced back into the education system as the language of Science and Mathematics. He also developed a new university (*Universiti Utara Malaysia*) that would con-centrate on business and management courses as part of the goal of training business leaders. Above all, the values that Mahathir sought to instil were concerned with modernity and the dignity of work; he seeks to emulate the 'East Asian' work ethic:

> One can, therefore view the world with Mahathir's eyes and see that it can be divided into the workaholic and the idle: races and groups which progress on the basis of hard work and those which stagnate out of an aversion to hard work.[53]

However, it has been argued that by perpetrating myths such as the laziness of the Malays, Mahathir was inheriting a colonial perspective which preju-dices against the natives for 'their refusal to supply plantation labour' and their 'non-involvement in the colonially-controlled urban capitalist eco-nomic activity'.[54] From this point of view Mahathir's vision of a state mod-ernized by privatization into 'Malaysia Incorporated' was in fact a postcolonial, capitalist vision; this is perhaps not surprising given that when he rose to power the main ideological alternative was communism.

Mahathir is exceptional among leaders as having made a formal mission statement known as 'Vision 2020'; this was the year by which Malaysia would be a fully developed society; it originated in a publication in 1991 and was restated in a keynote address in April 1997.[55] There were economic and social objectives in the vision. Economically, GDP would increase by eight times in the period 1990–2020, realization of the vision would require the transfer of knowledge, skills and technology; moreover such a transfer would also ensure the success of Islam as Islam has failed when it has taken an outmoded attitude towards scientific knowledge. Socially, the prime objective was to replace ethnically determined identities with a new Malaysian social identity. Focusing on broader regionally defined concepts such as 'Eastern', or 'Asian' values – rather than specifically 'Malay' values – was vital to realizing this aspect of the vision. A philosophy based on hard work, self-dependence, learning and other components of the 'Look East' policy reduced the importance of ethnicity in the creation of national identity – without removing altogether the importance of religion in the creation of a new hard-working Malaysian. As he put it: 'Allah does not help those who do not help themselves. Tie the camel and then leave it to Him. We have indeed to help ourselves, to tie our camels'.[56]

Mahathir's incorporation of religious aspects in his vision is in contrast to a vision of modernity and globalization that is dissociated from genuine religious values; this is perhaps to conceal the extent to which his own rhetoric replaced *ethical values* with *economic values* by making a 'religion' out of the market:

> The new *economic religion* of our time sincerely believes that it is only right and proper, indeed it is a religious duty to believe, that the market mechanism should be allowed, in the word of an observer, to 'be the sole director of the fate of human beings'.[57]

He continues – albeit ironically:

> As you all know, the neo-liberal *religion has many prominent temples*. The IMF, the World Bank, the WTO, the most powerful amongst them, work closely with those who walk the corridors of power in the great capitals of the world, and who have such spectacular views from the skyscrapers of money on Wall Street. This once lunatic fringe who now inhabit the citadels of wealth, power and orthodoxy has huge sums of money and vast reservoirs of intellectual resources. And each year, tens of thousands . . . *swell the ranks of priesthood*.[58]

Some may find this hypocritical coming from the essentially business leader of 'Malaysia Incorporated', as when he accused George Soros of causing the downfall of the tiger economies through currency speculation that brought about the economic crash in 1997. Mahathir's communication of a vision faces a tension between the materialism of modernity (implied by the economic goals of 'Vision 2020') and the fact that alternative spiritual value systems are described in terms of a religion associated with only *one* of the ethnic groupings. This therefore makes the social dimension of the vision more difficult to attain; however, Mahathir is forever discussing and embracing challenges!

Communication of legitimacy

Mahathir's communication of legitimacy evolved over time according to the requirements of the political situation and we can identify four stages in this evolution. Initially, he was concerned with establishing the legitimacy of the Malays as the source of political power in an independent Malaya, then with establishing himself as the legitimate leader of Malaya, then with becoming the leader of a multi-ethnic Malaysia and finally with resisting the rival legitimacy claims of his Deputy Prime Minister Ibrahim Anwar. In this progression we can see a shift from socially-based legitimacy claims towards more personalized ones.

Establishing the legitimacy of the Malays was crucial initially because the British Malayan Union plan to grant equal citizenship to all (irrespective of ethnic background) threatened the legitimacy of the Malays. His main argument in *The Malay Dilemma* is that the Malays are the definitive people of Malaya:

> The definitive people are those who set up the first government and these governments were the ones with which other countries did official business and had diplomatic relations.[59]

He argues that when they had granted independence in 1957 the British had recognized Malay legitimacy because they had negotiated independence with Malay political representatives.[60] He goes on to argue that they have inalienable rights because they have a single loyalty and are therefore the definitive race to which other races should assimilate. The most definitive characteristic of citizenship is language: 'In Malaya, Malay is the language of the original people who set up the first effective government'.[61] He contrasts this with the status of language in Indonesia where it served as a lingua franca and was a second language for the majority.

Rhetorically, the communication of Malay legitimacy is combined with delegitimizing the rival claims of other immigrant groups: the Chinese and Indians. While the Chinese and Indians had assisted in the development of Malaya, they had been allowed in by the Malays and retained alternative loyalties to the countries of origin – as he asked rhetorically: 'Where can the Malays go if they should be banished from Malaya?'[62] He suggests that those who arrived as a result of British rule have not fully severed their loyalties to their countries of origin and contrasts these immigrants with the more gradual immigrants to Malacca where Chinese and Indians had assimilated to Malay culture in terms of language and dress.

He criticizes those who demand to use 'immigrant' languages claiming concessions have been made to them only because of the courteous and gentle nature of the Malays. He argues that once the Malays had lost control of Malacca, Penang and Singapore 'these colonies became staging posts for Chinese and Indian invasion of the hinterland'.[63] His language is emotive; for example: 'The fear they (the Malays) were beginning to feel over the greatly increased Chinese and Indian immigration was stilled for a time, and the move to close the floodgates was put off'.[64] A particular example of undermining native rights was the British policy of allowing separate schools: English, Chinese, Tamil etc. in addition to Malay: both language and educational policy should be formed around the defining features of the definitive people.

He draws a number of comparisons with the way that the definitive people protect their rights against immigrants in other countries such as America, Australia, and other southeast Asian countries – again in the emotive terms of the POLITICS IS CONFLICT conceptual metaphor: 'The laws are designed to prevent conquest, for when immigrants retain their own cultures and also assume political and economic control of a country, they would in fact have conquered the original people'.[65] He argues that immigrants under the British had not wanted to become permanent citizens and should identify with the definitive people by assimilating to a homogeneous community before they could be given equal citizenship rights in the way proposed by the Malayan Union plan – as he put it: 'citizenship must carry obligations as well as privileges'. The primary obligation, it seems, is to accept the hegemony of the Malay ethnic group.

Mahathir's rhetorical claims for his legitimacy as a leader of the Malays were based on challenging alternative sources of power: the royalty and a Prime Minister from a royal family. Paradoxically, this entailed a highly critical analysis of the feudal characteristics of traditional Malay leadership. Legitimacy in a feudal society is established by birth rather than by merit because individuals become leaders through their hereditary position. The legitimacy of a traditional leader is established through the non-verbal and verbal behaviours that become the social rituals of followers:

> The highest rank is that of the ruling princes, the hereditary rajas of the Malay states ... It is a mark of breeding how to know how to behave towards rajas. This code of behaviour includes the use of a whole range of special words regarding the person of the raja and his family. Indeed as the title of *Tunku*, or prince, is lavishly used by the descendents of every raja, past and present, contact between the *ra'ayat*[66] and royalty is common and few Malays remain unfamiliar with the tabooed language, the special privileges and accepted codes of behaviour towards the rajas.[67]

Mahathir's bid for leadership was based on breaking with the 'tabooed language' that had traditionally been used towards leaders on the grounds that it was no longer in the interests of the Malays. He challenged the party leadership by writing an open letter requesting the Tunku's[68] resignation because his lack of firmness in dealing with the problems of Malaysia's multi-ethnic population had caused a loss of confidence in the institutions of the state. Although the letter led to his temporary expulsion from UMNO, it was a successful legitimacy challenge because:

> It transformed him from being a failed electoral candidate into a living symbol of Malay Nationalism. Before the confrontation, Mahathir was only one of several 'Ultras'. After his expulsion – seen as a personal sacrifice – he became something of a martyr for the Malay cause.[69]

Allegations of corruption were made in *The Malay Dilemma* and 'He immediately became a cult figure in exile, with prominent Malays beating a path
to his door'.[70] Mahathir argued that by appeasing the Chinese, UMNO
leaders were repeating the mistakes of the British colonial rulers. Mahathir's
claim to leadership again used disease metaphors to represent 'patronage' as
corruption and argued that leaders had lost touch with followers:

> A feeling of power normally grips those who wield patronage, a feeling
> that they can mould and shape people and opinion any way they please.
> The leaders of UMNO, the senior partners of the Alliance Government,
> succumbed to this *disease*. Believing that they no longer needed to heed
> to the opinions of their supporters, they disregarded them at very turn.[71]

Mahathir's claim to legitimacy was based in articulating the unspoken fears,
beliefs and aspirations of Malays who were potential supporters of UMNO.
His core beliefs regarding nationalism, capitalism, Islam, populism and
authoritarianism were all directed to appealing to the Malay community.

Once he had established his legitimacy as leader of the Malays, Mahathir
sought to redefine his followership by making it more inclusive and extending his legitimacy as leader of *Malaya* to leader of *Malaysia*. This motivated
his 'Buy British Last' policy of 1981 – which aimed to unite all Malaysians
since they shared the economic damage caused by Britain's increase in overseas tuition fees – and his 'Look East' policy. Whereas it was *Chinese* economic dominance that had threatened the Malays, it was *western* economic
dominance that threatened Malaysia. His potential followers extended to *all*
poorer nations of the 'East' and 'South' as his rhetoric contrasted their interests with those of the colonizing nations of the 'West' and the 'North'. Geographical poles served to simplify the argument and to create legitimacy
based on general humanitarian principles of equality of wealth distribution.
Inevitably this simplification overlooked the fact that eastern countries, such
as Japan and Korea, had expanded partly because of the impact of American
military bases and associated injections of capital. By focusing on moral
values such as the work ethic and the 'Vision 2020' he aimed to create legitimacy based on the strength of a successful and united Malaysia.

A crucial feature of Mahathir's performance of leadership was to break
with verbal taboos by challenging what were generally perceived as 'good
causes' in the west. He argued that western environmentalist groups: 'have
come to instigate our people's thinking on the preservation of the environmental beauty of our tropical forests' – but in reality meant to trap developing countries in a 'condition where our rural people live and remain in
poverty'.[72] His communication of legitimacy was based on a mixture of rea-
soned argument, using, for example, historical analogies and emotive language that polarized social groups. By developing a confrontational style
assumed by the POLITICS IS CONFLICT metaphor, he was effectively
testing the loyalty of followers; as Milne and Mauzy argue:

A more appropriate and sterner test is whether a follower trusts a leader enough to follow him if he embarks on an unusual course of action. This is a necessary qualification for a leader. As Mahathir remarked 'You have to lead, You should be sensitive to what your followers think. But if you do exactly what they want, you're not a leader'. In the long run, it must be supplemented by the leader evoking sufficient feelings of loyalty, and providing enough material benefits, to establish legitimacy.

Mahathir evoked feelings of loyalty by attacking conspiratorial enemies; these could be internal social groups – disloyal immigrants – or broadly defined external ones – 'Britain', 'environmentalists', 'the west' etc. – but his most ruthless attacks were reserved for individual internal conspirators.

The legitimacy of alternative leaders was vigorously challenged and removed. The legitimacy of the royalty was effectively challenged and terminated by his Amendment Bill of 1983; this removed the need for royal assent to legislation and effectively terminated the royal veto. He argued that traditional rulers had lost their legitimacy by making huge concessions both to colonialists and to immigrants. He organized a series of rallies to communicate the same arguments as the anti-Malayan Union campaign: royalty has lost its legitimacy by accepting threats to Malay leadership. By making appeals to the sovereignty of the Malays, legitimacy now shifted to 'the people' or *rakyat* – and, by implication, leaders who articulated their hopes and beliefs. The success of creating equivalence between the needs of the Malays and needs of the people, partly through making education more democratic, lead to a huge electoral victory of August 1986 where the *Barisan Nasional* won 148 out of 177 seats.

The major individual whom he identified as an opponent was the Deputy Prime Minister Anwar Ibrahim, who was arrested, removed from office in September 1998 and subsequently tried for sodomy and imprisoned. The major reason was because he was a more idealistic leader who threatened the interests of that powerful elites that had benefited from Mahathir's failure to tackle corruption. For all his earlier criticisms of the corruption of the Tunku's Alliance government, Mahathir had been unsuccessful in tackling corruption in the form of the 'money politics' of UMNO that had increased with his New Economic Policy. During an absence from Malaysia in 1997 Mahathir left Anwar as Acting Prime Minister to launch an attack on corruption and it seems that he was ready to listen to Anwar's rivals because his value-based vision rivalled his own legitimacy claims.

Leadership and the media

The rally has been Mahathir's preferred means of political communication and morale-raising rallies have become an opportunity for him to perform as leader of the Malays:

The typical Mahathir rally wore at least a semi-official atmosphere no matter how overtly political the occasion for the rally might be. It was organized and staged by his UMNO lieutenants ... Its programme would incorporate elaborate gestures of welcome, official ceremonies, emotional speech-making and even oath-taking. Free transport, food and drinks, and sometimes, it was rumored, an 'attendance fee' ... There would be ample press, radio, and television coverage of the rally to ensure its transmission to the rest of the nation.[73]

Mahathir's rallies resemble the social rituals that are popular throughout traditional Malay society on occasions such as marriages and the celebration of *Hari Raya* at the end of the fasting month.[74] These invariably centre on generous provision of food and soft drinks – with formal activities such as speech-making providing a ritualistic backdrop. Their significance as a form of in-group bonding through the exchange of news and membership is established and reinforced through social interaction. In this respect their communicative meaning is symbolic rather than verbal:

By way of the symbolic power of the political rally, Mahathir, as it were, kept faith with the crowds from whose midst he must have perceived himself from time to time as 'a man of the people', each time blessed with a reaffirmed mandate, and reassured that his services as a leader were still required.[75]

Rather like party political conferences the role of the rally recreates the emotional and charismatic links between leader(s) and followers; it is a fully interactive event that provides the opportunity for displays of mutual trust and affection. It allows the feelings of security and emotional belonging that arise from membership of a group to form the basis for political action. The choreographed rally as a vehicle of mass mobilization culminated in Mahathir's SEMARAK ('glow', 'lustre', 'shine') campaign. His style was to exploit the emotional and trust-forging nature of the rally by making frequent offers to resign at such occasions; made in this climate of mutual support the offer is theatrically rejected by followers and the leader responds by dramatically breaking into tears.

Summary

Mahathir displayed most of Stogdil's characteristics attributes of great leaders: intelligence, alertness, insight, responsibility, initiative, persistence, self-confidence and sociability.[76] Other qualities have been identified, for example:

The key to comprehending his mercurial and, at times, frighteningly aggressive personality lies in recognizing the forces that drive him.

There are two aspects to his political persona – the intensity of his passion and his surprising ability to compromise.[77]

In addition, his self-conscious awareness of leadership enabled him to design a unique leadership style. In 1983 he launched a 'leadership by example' campaign,[78] in which 'leaders of developing countries must influence the selection of systems of values of the people'.[79] There is no doubt that Mahathir saw leadership as something that depended on exceptional traits, as he said: 'The ability to provide guidance . . . something superior to what your people can do by themselves' and 'A leader must have initiative and ideas that are not common'.[80] Evidence that Mahathir sees his views as remarkable and exceptional is the fact that while researching this book it was found much more difficult to find versions of his speeches and writings than for the other leaders studied. This is probably because of the attention he has paid to protecting the copyright of his many published works. Unlike other leaders, there was no web site on which his speeches or writings were readily available. From this it may be inferred that Mahathir places a high value on his opinions – seeing them as highly original; again there is a paradox between his demands that the west should open up their resources, ensuring easy access to information, while he maintains a close control over his own intellectual property.

It might be thought that the reduced status of the individual in a collectivist culture such as Malaysia would change the nature of leadership from that found in individualist cultures; however, when a leader expresses the *shared* wants, needs and desires of followers by creating loyalty to the social group, the effect is just as potent in collectivist cultures as it is in individualist ones. The difference is that in these cultures the only individual who has the right to *full* self-expression is the leader who takes on the authority of the collective. Successful leadership is often a question of finding the right combination between *confirming* existing beliefs and attitudes and *challenging* them; to some extent this explains a range of ambiguities associated with Mahathir. He sought to secure the survival of the Malays through dramatic performances that conflicted with many aspects of traditional culture[81] – such as its collectivist nature; he sought to emulate the west by modernizing, while rejecting western values.[82] The concept underlying his rhetorical style that POLITICAL PRACTICE IS MEDICAL PRACTICE has dramatic contrast with the other main concepts: POLITICS IS CONFLICT and POLITICAL OPPONENTS ARE ENEMIES. Inherent ambiguity – but with consistent dramaturgical appeal – are the defining characteristics of his performance of leadership.

While ultimately successful as a modernizer who has created a genuine sense of inter-ethnic national identity, Mahathir has proved much less successful in maintaining his charisma because of his inability to plan effectively for a succession to his leadership. He has been successful in establishing the legitimacy of the Malays and himself as their legitimate leader. However, his status as leader of Malaysia has often been tainted by his tendency to revert to earlier legitimacy claims based on an ethnic appeal and rejection of the Chinese; ethnicity has impeded his vision of a highly modernized state and has been reinforced by the accusations of cronyism from which he has never fully escaped. His fear of a rival leader with a more vibrant vision has challenged his status as a morally pure leader – and raised doubts as to the authenticity of his performance.

9 Lee Kuan Yew

Surviving insecurity

Introduction

It is somewhat ironic that an Asian leader who has achieved a widely-reputed global stature in the contemporary period has been the leader of one of its smallest nations: Lee Kuan Yew has become a leader – like Castro in Cuba – whose reputation has outgrown that of his country, to the extent that it is unquestioned and unchallenged. It is almost impossible to think of Cuba without Castro, or Singapore without Lee Kuan Yew, because the two diametrically opposed ideologies of these nations are represented by their leaders' beliefs and values so that both countries appear to be manifestations of their complex psychologies. Existing alongside much larger and potentially threatening neighbours, the size difference of Cuba and Singapore was used by both leaders as an excuse for autocratic rule. Both leaders experienced similar personal and historical circumstances: they were born into upper middle class families, educated in the most prestigious schools and colleges,[1] studied law and were politically inspired by a rejection of colonialism. Both were so successful in dominating their national political culture, and extinguishing any effective opposition that, paradoxically, as with Mahathir, their major failing was in ensuring their succession.

Communism contributed enormously to the emergence of both leaders; for Castro it provided an alternative power base from which to resist the external threat of the USA, while for Lee Kuan Yew it was the opposite: the threat of communism had permitted the British to accept an independent Singapore, as he put it: 'It was the disagreeable alternative the Communists posed that made the constitutional methods of gentle erosion of colonial authority effective for the nationalists and acceptable to the colonialists'.[2] Another fundamental characteristic that defined both leaders is that they understood the extent to which political power originated in military power. This can be directly attributed to the influence of Mao – both had witnessed at firsthand the truth of his dictum 'power is at the barrel of a gun'; he held an attraction for both because of his understanding of the interconnectedness of power, leadership and action. Lee often quoted Mao and referred to him as the 'great Chinese theoretician'.[3]

For Harry Lee, as he was brought up, the experience of the Japanese invasion at the age of 18 was a profoundly unsettling experience that was both a watershed in his personal psychological development and in the evolution of Singapore. Prior to the invasion, as a member of the 'King's Chinese'[4] there was the comfortable paternalism of British colonial rule; he admired British organization (without liking the English) but was quick to learn how easily the comfortable life could collapse in the face of ruthless opposition:

> I saw a whole social system crumble suddenly before an occupying army that was absolutely merciless. The Japanese demanded total obedience and got it from nearly all ... I had not yet read Mao's dictum 'power grows out of the barrel of a gun' but I knew that Japanese brutality, Japanese guns, Japanese bayonets and swords, and Japanese terror and torture settled the argument as to who was in charge.[5]

An approach to power that also based its legitimacy on beliefs about ethnic superiority and group loyalty left an indelible mark on his thinking; as he noted 'We had to praise their gods, extol their culture and emulate their behaviour'. His views on the genetic superiority of the Chinese may have been because they were the only people who resisted the Japanese invaders. Above all, he learnt from the Japanese occupation the need for adaptability and change:

> They were hated by almost everyone but everyone knew their power to do harm and so everyone adjusted. Those who were slow or reluctant to change and to accept the new masters suffered ... Those who were quick off the mark in assessing the new situation, and swift to take advantage of the new opportunities by making themselves useful to the new masters, made fortunes out of the terrible misfortune that had befallen all in Singapore.[6]

Identifying and responding quickly to new opportunities was the hallmark of the Singapore that he created in his image. Communication skills were a crucial part of this adaptability; he learnt Japanese while working for the Japanese propaganda department and later learnt Mandarin and Hokkien. The Japanese invasion effectively created a ground zero situation in which a self-made individual could emerge as a leader by understanding the dynamics of power and attaining the skills necessary for political success. He understood that there was a distinction between the leadership strategies necessary to *attain* power, and those required to *retain* it. Like Mahathir, Castro and Khomeini, Lee has always had very keen instincts of political survival and shown a ruthless streak when necessary.

Crucial to his survival were his powers of observation and speed of learning – he was prepared to learn as much from his opponents as from his allies. His first lessons were from the British: the value of education, self-discipline, social cohesion and professionalism in the conduct of diplomacy. As he said after his African tour in January–February 1964:

> I had received an unforgettable lesson in decolonisation, on how crucial it was to have social cohesion and capable, effective government to take power from the colonial authority, especially in Africa. When the leader did not preserve the unity of the country by sharing power with the chiefs of the minority tribes, but excluded them, the system soon broke down.[7]

A prime motivation for his own considerable efforts to embark on the challenging task of adult language learning was to enable him to communicate social cohesion by appealing to the various 'minority tribes' of Singapore. From the Japanese he learnt that courage and determination arising from a strong group identity were necessary for attaining power and from the communists he learnt the methods necessary for retaining it:

> Communists followed an unscrupulous book of rules which, once they attained power, knocked opponents once and for all and it was only appropriate that non-Communist governments should also play for keeps.[8]

It is little wonder – given the importance that learning has played in his understanding of leadership – that he placed a high value on education. It also reflects the importance of traditional Confucian values in forming his views on citizenship:

> In looking back over the past 30 years, I believe we were fortunate that 77% of our people had strong Chinese traditional values which put emphasis on the strength of the family, the bringing up of children to be modest, hardworking, thrifty, filial, loyal and law abiding. Their behaviour had an influence on the non-Chinese Singaporeans.[9]

However, in some respects his later espousal of Confucian values was a rediscovered identity that originated in political expediency: it was his personal war and immediate postwar experiences that had greater psychological influence on his leadership style. For example, they left him with a fear of dirt and an obsession with hygiene; he describes graphically in his memoirs the broken-down shophouses in Narcis Street:

> They had not been repaired for years, and the drains were clogged with rubbish left by roadside hawkers, so that there was always a stink of decaying food. Enormous rats ran fearlessly in and out of these drains, ignoring the cats around. Again I retched, When I got home, washing my hands was not good enough. Before I could sit down to dinner, I had to bath and have a complete change of clothes.[10]

This shows little evidence of any idealization of Confucian values. He has always had a regime of morning exercises, been careful about his weight, avoided hard liquor and adopted the habits of a 'clean' lifestyle – indeed, cleanliness and hygiene are central components of both his leadership style and his political policy. Part of his vision of Singapore has been to turn it into a clean, hygienic, Garden City. Soon after he became Prime Minister of Singapore in June 1959 he organized a series of high profile cleaning campaigns in which he led by example, personally getting involved with clearing debris; a popular leadership slogan was 'Clean and Green'. Singapore became widely publicized in the west for its fines on littering, chewing gum[11] and not flushing public toilets; the attack on dirt has been metaphorically extended to the associated habits of drug-taking and other fashions associated with 'The West' – such as long hair, ragged jeans and jukeboxes.

Ironically, all the advantages of a tiger economy – based on developing Singapore as a major international port with Asia's largest oil refining and distribution centre, and subsequently as a high-tech, financial and tourist centre – have only enhanced Lee's sense of the fragility of the enterprise. Dependent on its water supply from peninsular Malaysia, Singapore has always invested heavily in military defence in spite of the absence of enemies on anything like the scale of the Japanese in the 1940s or the communists in the 1950s. The emphasis on defence seems to originate in his early experiences and insecurities and has provided a warrant for an authoritarian style of leadership.

His leadership style received intellectual respectability through Toynbee's 'Challenge and Response' theory of political style to which Lee came across while at Cambridge. This entailed interpreting new situations as challenges, or crises, adapting to these challenges and responding to them by stimulating economic development.[12] This has meant that essential to Lee's design of leadership style has been the manufacture of the *illusion of crisis* – even though, in reality, life in Singapore is like living in a large well-maintained house where everything works efficiently and provision is made for every contingency. This yearning for security may be traced to the loss of the early security he had felt under British colonial rule and the fear that what had happened to the British could happen to any other power; consider this recollection of Government House in Lusaka that he visited in 1964:

> It is well-furnished and well-maintained, but not luxurious. The toiletries, soap, towels, cutlery and china were similar to those I had found in British government houses in Singapore, Sarawak, and North Borneo. They were all part of one well-run system.

Then he contrasts this with later visits:

> I remember the flowers, shrubs and trees and greenery at the side of the roads and at the roundabouts when I was driven from the airport in

1964. Roses grew in abundance, six years later, the roses had gone and weeds had taken over. Nine years after that even the weeds had given up; the roundabouts were covered in tarmac. And there seemed to be fewer animals and birds in the grounds of Government House, now the President's Lodge. I wondered why.[13]

However, when the desire for control becomes obsessive it risks creating an unnatural environment that stifles feelings of creativity and self-expression. Some exposure to dirt is necessary for the human body to strengthen its immune system and, in social terms, some non-conformity can be the basis for developing innovation and creativity. Excessively clean houses have been proposed as a possible cause of the vast increase in conditions such as asthma and eczema. The danger of creating a sterile environment for a biological organism is that it can inhibit the diversity that is necessary for further adaptation and change – this is somewhat ironic as we have seen that the strength of Lee's early social-political experiences taught him the need for such flexibility. After all, how can one respond if there are no challenges? One of the difficulties he has faced has been sustaining the impression of crisis when the success of his policies and leadership has meant that the 'crises' that inform his rhetoric are largely the creations of it.

In summary, what characterizes Lee Kuan Yew's leadership style is his profound understanding of the nature of power and his leadership provides security for followers who feel that, while they may prefer others, they are ultimately dependent upon him.

Non-linguistic communication of charisma

Appearance and leadership style

Lee is handsome in a conventional way – he has high cheekbones, high arched eyebrows, a broad face and a hairline that started to recede fairly early in life (see Plate 6, p. 110). His appearance is trim and well proportioned as one might expect of someone who places importance on health and diet. At times he has suffered self-doubt about his appearance: when he first saw himself on television, he was appalled by what he called his 'gangersterlike look' and asked aides to soften his image. The combination of high cheekbones and sternly brushed back hair probably gave an impression of severity and the inflexibility of someone who is used to being obeyed rather than to making himself pleasing to others.

There is a piercing quality to his eyes, which, though small, always contain an intensity of the type associated with charismatic leaders. He was also aware of the importance of the human dimension in his communication of leadership – particularly when overcoming the differences of a multi-ethnic society:

But it is important that there should be in place of facility of communication a belief in the magic of leadership, faith confidence. Why, how? It is in the human eye.[14]

Without doubt Lee is aware of the importance of appearance in creating positive first impressions – just as any businessman would be.

Dress

Dress style played an important part in communicating a new democratic and postcolonial image. After their success in the 1959 election, the members of the People's Action Party who formed the new government presented themselves for the swearing-in ceremony at Government House wearing open-necked white shirts and trousers; the Governor wore only a light fawn suit and tie. This contrasted with the previous practice of new ministers wearing lounge suits to be sworn in by a governor who would be wearing a white ceremonial dress uniform with a white plumed hat. White symbolized that the new government would also be free of corruption but the rejection of ties and suits symbolized a rejection of western colonial style.

After the referendum supporting the merger with Malaysia, Lee embarked on regular visits to the 51 constituencies because he understood the need to maintain popular support through regular contact with followers. He describes the importance he placed on ensuring a freshness of appearance by regular changes of clothes:

> Sometimes I made as many as ten speeches in a day, each in Malay, English, and Hokkien or Mandarin. I would sweat profusely. I brought three or four singlets and shirts with me and would nip quietly into somebody's toilet or behind the partition inside a shop from time to time to change into dry clothes, and I carried a small towel to wipe the sweat off my face.[15]

The effect of clean clothes was to communicate the image of a dynamic and energetic leader and, according to this own record, he was successful in this:

> News of how each tour had been more successful than the last spread rapidly by word of mouth in the coffee shops and through the press and television. It generated a groundswell of enthusiasm among the people, especially the shopkeepers and community leaders. I became kind of political pop star.[16]

As a young, reasonably good-looking man, Lee ensured that his dress corresponded with the style of a young, charismatic leader.

Artefacts

Like most of the leaders described in this work, Lee Kuan Yew was not interested in artefacts as ends in themselves but because of their symbolic meaning. His own preference for simplicity and stoicism was strongly influenced by experience of the hardships of the war and Japanese occupation; according to those who have met him the style of his office is spartan:

> no paneling, no historical regalia, no priceless paintings on the walls. No seal of office – and no ashtrays. Its only luxury is air-conditioning. The large table at which the premier sits is polished, shining.[17]

The simplicity of his artefacts was designed to communicate a highly disciplined personal lifestyle, and a sacrifice of personal need for social gain; his concern has been with creating a clean social environment rather than private luxury. It is perhaps in keeping with this simplicity that the artefact with which he became most closely associated was a thermos flask containing Chinese tea; he carried this around with him to meetings – preferring a warm drink as he was afraid of catching a chill. His desire for maintaining a constant temperature through air conditioning is no doubt enforced by traditional Chinese medical views on the need to balance hot and cold, but may also be a reaction to the heat and perspiration associated with his energetic campaigning style.

The initiative for purchasing more luxurious artefacts came from his wife who was concerned with designing the image that would be crucial to his success:

> And now I traveled in style because once we decided in February 1959 to fight to win, Choo has bought a Mercedes Benz 220 to replace the ageing Studebaker. She wanted to be seen in it so nobody would doubt that I could afford a Mercedes without becoming Prime Minister, and she would accompany me to meetings, sometimes driving me herself.[18]

Other kinds of symbolic artefact on which he placed a high personal value were the gifts he received as symbolic tokens of loyalty from followers:

> One memorable gift was an exquisite ivory carving of an imperial Chinese sailing ship resting on a dark acquired based under a glass case. It was the owner's most precious *object d'art*. He was a shopkeeper, about 50 years old, graying at the temples, and he wished me happiness and long life in Hokkien. It still sits proudly in my sitting room, a gift I treasure, reminding me of that great monument when I could feel the people warming to me and accepting me as their leader.[19]

For Lee, gifts were important to the design of leadership because they embodied the personal expressions of feeling and gratitude of followers towards their leader.

Symbolic action

In considering symbolic action it is sometimes important to distinguish between the symbolic action of followers and leaders. An important form of symbolic, or subliminal, communication with followers is through ritual. The ritual greeting of a leader by performers who symbolize a cultural group of followers has a powerful meaning for that group when the leader is visiting a venue associated with their identity. In the case of Indian and Chinese communities this would typically be the temple and for the Malays it would be the mosque: Lee describes such ritual greetings:

> The Chinese would also bring me to their temples and greet me at the entrance with lion dancers and the sound of gongs and drums to herald my arrival. It was good for their devotees to see the Prime Minister honoring their places of worship. I would burn joss-sticks in front of the altars, some Buddhist, others Taoist. The Malays would greet me with their *kompang* bands, 12 or 14 young men with tambourines and hand-held drums, and their elders would place on my head a *tanjak*, the brocade cloth folded into a cap worn by chieftains.[20]

Here we see that the multimedia effect was enhanced by the addition of sound in the form of traditional instruments and also by smell through the burning of joss sticks. The subliminal effect of communicating through all the senses simultaneously is highly effective in blending cognition with emotion and is likely to lead to acceptance of the leader to whom tribute is being paid through such symbolism.

We should not underestimate the importance of organized and *ritualistic* follower response behaviour because its antithesis was probably the most potent political action of disaffected followers in Singapore and Malaysia in the 1960s. The riots in Kuala Lumpur in 1969 – causing 196 deaths – sent shockwaves through the peninsular and there were also racially motivated riots in Singapore in July and September 1964. In his biography, Lee blames these on a propaganda campaign by the Malay leader Ja'afar Albar and his mouthpiece, the newspaper *Utusan Melayu*, which reported speeches in which he argued that the Malays were discriminated against by the largely Chinese People's Action Party.

I would suggest that Lee was assisted by observing an important form of symbolic action of the Malaysian leader – the Tunku: like Mahathir later, he responded to the 1964 riots by dramatically breaking down in tears in public. The abandonment of Asian social norms that require tight restraint on emotional expression by *losing* emotional control is a type of symbolic action that seems to characterize Asian leaders and makes crying an effective communication technique. At the end of the merger between Singapore and Malaysia, Lee gave a televised press conference:

And I would like to add one ... You see, this is a moment of ... every time we look back on this moment when we signed this agreement which severed Singapore from Malaysia, it will be a moment of anguish. For me it is a moment of anguish because all my life ... you see, the whole of my adult life ... I have believed in Merger and the unity of these two territories. You know, it's a people, connected by geography, economics, and ties of kinship ... Would you mind if we stop for a while?[21]

At this point: 'As if to prove his anguish, he broke down and wept before the cameras, and the press conference had to be postponed for 15 minutes to let him recover his composure. The Tunku later expressed surprise at the TV tears and remarked: "I don't know why Mr Lee acted like that ... He was quite pleased about it"'.[22] Evidently, then, there was some questioning as to the authenticity of these tears and although taken as a genuine instance of being overwhelmed by emotion, it may have been Lee's awareness of the powerful symbolic effect that led him to emulate the act of breaking with cultural constraints on the display of emotion. I will discuss the role of metaphor in the breakdown of the merger in the section on legitimacy.

Another form of symbolic action that I have identified in relation to Gandhi and Khomeini is undertaking actual journeys; after independence Lee aimed to legitimize the new state of Singapore by going on an extensive tour of recently independent African countries to rally support. He visited 17 capitals and met leaders including Nasser in Egypt, Bourguiba in Tunisia, Nkrumah in Ghana, Kenyatta in Kenya, and Haille Selassie in Ethiopia. The act of arriving as *head of state* is an important form of symbolism in communicating leadership.

At home, the performance of leadership took the form of Cleaning Campaigns. These were significant because they symbolized taking control of the environment; apparently they originated in observing how communist followers were engaged by the leadership:

> We mounted a series of well-publicized campaigns to clean the streets of the city, clear the beaches of debris and cut the weeds on unkempt vacant land. It as a copycat exercise borrowed from the Communists – ostentatious mobilization of everyone including ministers to toil with their hands and soil their clothes in order to serve the people.[23]

There are many photographs of Lee clearing debris (and later planting trees). These are symbolic actions for overcoming the divide between leaders and followers – subliminally, if leaders behave like followers by *doing* the actions they advocate it implies that followers are themselves agents of social action; it is therefore performing an act of empowerment in which leader and follower take joint control of the material world.

Symbols themselves were also very important for communication to the multilingual audiences of Singapore; Lee shows his awareness of the semiotic power of symbols when describing the origin of the People's Action Party logo:

> In a semi-literate, multilingual country, the candidate's symbol is crucial; it is like the logo of a designer product, and the PAP's blue circle with a red lightning flash across it had already won brand recognition.[24]

The circle implied social cohesion and the flash of lightning could be interpreted as the catalytic effect of the leader on the people. However, the lightning flash was also an important semiotic of European fascist movements – representing violence as a creative force when it was in the pursuit of social transformation. There were also extensive discussions over the symbolism of the flag for an independent Singapore: the Chinese wanted red for good fortune while the Malays desired red to symbolize courage and white to symbolize purity. The Chinese wanted stars because of the yellow stars on the flag of communist China, while the Malays wanted a crescent moon because of its significance for Muslims. The eventual design of the flag incorporated a crescent moon with five white stars (as opposed to the traditional one star for Islam) and therefore managed to integrate the preferred symbols of each group. The five stars represented the ideals of the new country: democracy, peace, progress, justice and equality. The solution indicates an awareness of the potential for symbolism to ensure social cohesion and to overcome divisions among followers by recognizing their different symbolic needs.[25]

Language choice and political communication

Multilingualism is a significant fact that is easily overlooked when considering political communication in Singapore. Those from monolingual societies often forget that simply being understood is the primary communication need of leaders in such societies. During the colonial period the British had continued to organize education in Singapore along ethnic lines (as in Malaysia) so that there were separate schools for Chinese, Malays and Indians. English was the language of Singapore's government and the ruling elite; most Indians and some Malays would be familiar with it – along with the English-educated Chinese. However, English was totally foreign to most of the Chinese-educated who were the core followers of the communist-backed opposition party, *Barison Sosialis* (Socialist Front).[26] While English was needed for advance in the professions and among the social elite, a democratic politician also needed to communicate with the Chinese-educated.

While some were bilingual through exposure to English in their education, their level might not be adequate to comprehend abstract ideas and the second language may not activate the same positive attitudinal responses as the 'mother tongue'. Lee identified with Nehru's view that: 'I cry when I think that I cannot speak my mother tongue as well as I can speak the English language'[27] and also shared the same sentiments of frustration and inadequacy at being a second-language speaker that were felt by Gandhi. As he put it: 'The English-educated is somewhat uncertain and hesitant, speaking and thinking in a language he has learnt all his waiting (*sic*) life but which is not part of his own being'.[28]

The range of varieties of Chinese further complicated the linguistic situation, and Lee admired the emotional appeal of orators who used the native dialect:

> This time, Chinese orators tool off. Speaking in their own dialects – Hokkien, Cantonese, Teochew – they were superlative crowd-rousers, they could wax eloquent, quote proverbs, use metaphors and allegories or traditional legends to illustrate contemporary situations. They spoke with a passion that filled their listeners with emotion and exhilaration at the prospect of Chinese greatness held out to them.[29]

It is not surprising that he described bilingualism using the metaphor of 3-D vision: 'I believe that the bilingual capacity of our Chinese-educated has given them binocular vision and a 3-D vision of the world. As long as he was monolingual, he saw only a 2-D picture of the world'.[30] His native variety was Hakka, however he also embarked on learning Mandarin and put this to use in the 1959 election campaign and he describes the value of this effort of self-control:

> my Mandarin had improved; although it was not good enough for a flight of rhetoric, it was not adequate to express my thoughts without any script. I might be repeating what I had said in English or Malay in a less elegant way in Mandarin, but I won the respect of the Chinese-speaking for working hard at their language.[31]

Just speaking the language of his audience sent the message that he identified with them and with their needs. However he realized that Mandarin could only reach those under 35 who had been to Chinese schools and therefore that he also needed to learn Hokkien; this was especially the case since, being in the lower social levels, many Hokkien speakers were likely to be tempted to support the growing communist movement. Moreover, the PAP had lost its only effective speaker of Hokkien after Lim Chin Siong switched to the communist party. He describes in his autobiography the effort he put into learning it:

> So I started to learn the dialect, snatching an hour either at lunchtime or in the evening, three, often five times a week. I had two good tutors,

both from our radio station, who first had to teach me a whole new romanized script to capture the Hokkein pronunciation of Chinese characters.

He then goes on to describe the difficulties that he had in actually putting his learning to use in a leadership role during an election campaign and his eventual success:

The first time I made a Hokkien speech in Long Li, the children in the crowd laughed at my mistakes – wrong sounds, wrong tones, wrong sentence structure, wrong almost everything. But I could not afford to be shy or embarrassed, it was a matter of life and death . . . I was preparing for the inevitable showdown with Lim Chion Siong and the Communists. I would lose by default if I could not speak the dialect well enough to get my views across to the uneducated and poorly educated Chinese who were then the majority but whom I could not reach with Mandarin. By the end of the campaign and after innumerable speeches, I spoke understandable Hokkein.[32]

His knowledge of Hokkein portrayed him as a man of the people rather than a distant member of the elite – as he put it: 'my command of the dialect had become an asset that protected me from *Barison* charges that I was betraying the people'.[33]

Lee was also aware of the potential for cross-cultural communication problems with the Malays: 'You know this is the Malay way. If they hesitate . . . They will not say "no" to it. They will say "I'll think about it" '.[34] Barr is probably right in his view that he never fully understood the subtleties of Malay conversation. However, he did seek to appeal to the Malays and to resist the perception that the PAP was an exclusively Chinese party – this was particularly important after the merger between Malaysia and Singapore. Even after the end of the merger he still needed to appeal to the Malays in order to guard against their feelings of isolation and to eliminate the threat of a potential fifth column.

He was always aware of the importance of language within multicultural communities in which it was fundamental to group identity and introduced a bilingual policy in which all students were required to study English and their mother tongue. He believed that bilingualism was central to national identity as a Singaporean and practiced what he preached; he once humorously argued that the Malaysian Prime Minister was envious of the level he had reached in the language quoted him as saying: 'He (Lee) would think himself as legitimate as I was to be the leader of Malays because he speaks Malay better than I do'.[35] Language policy an essential means to social cohesion:

Our policy of bilingualism, encouraging each community to preserve its own language and culture, and emphasizing shared national values, has been the right formula for building our multi-racial, multilingual and multi-religious society. So long as we keep this formula, Singaporeans will remain distinct from the countries where our ancestors came from, whether it be China, India, Indonesia or Malaysia.

He saw bilingualism as providing a social identity for the English-educated Chinese: 'Therefore, there is the necessity for preserving for each child that cultural ballast and appreciation of his origin and his background in order to give him that confidence to face the problems of society'.[36]

Stylistic features of verbal communication

Lee's style of verbal communication projects his own psychological state onto the nation state of Singapore. He sees himself as the leader of a small, progressive nation state that has arisen phoenix-like out the ashes of the Second World War, and is surrounded by large potentially aggressive states and has been threatened by the ideologies of British and American colonialism and communism. Its insecurity is enhanced by a lack of natural resources and reinforced by the physical proximity of political and ideological 'others' as well as by the internal danger of inter-ethnic division. The combination of external and internal threats – supported by Toynbee's Challenge and Response theory – has led to a style of leadership discourse designed to emphasize the need to respond to insecurity through control, innovation and action to ensure unity, purpose and success. This is to be attained through a nation-building programme that emphasizes economic progress – through education, technology and hard work – and political progress – through the prioritization of national identity over allegiance to ethnic group, social class or religion. A commitment to the English language plays an important part in all these goals. Like the self-made man who pulled himself up against rivals through his own efforts, Singapore is constructed through the language of its leader as an independent but insecure nation whose survival depends on control, dynamism and teamwork.

The style of communication adopted by Lee is highly practical because it is simple and comprehensible; it includes rather than excludes; he is a man who speaks the language of his followers. An example of this is the communication of political arguments through slogans; The Malaysian Solidarity Convention that came to stand for rejection of the special position of the Malays within Malaysia used the slogan '40-40-20' to refer to the ratio of population between Malays, Chinese and others. His own vision of transforming Singapore into a Garden City was summarized in the slogan: 'Clean and Green'. Political ideas are often communicated by analogy with other international contexts and comparison and competition with other countries is a central element in this rhetoric. After the invasion of Egypt in 1967 he chose Israel as a model because of the importance placed on internal social discipline in the face of a powerful external enemy:

We made a study of what smaller countries surrounded by large neighbours with big populations do for their own survival ... In the end, Singapore opted for the Israeli pattern, for in our situation it appears necessary not only to train every boy but also every girl to be a disciplined and effective digit in the defence of their country.[37]

By choosing Israel he saw the opportunity of attracting subconscious sympathy from the powerful Jewish lobby around the world (especially in the United States). As with Israel, the possibility of a pre-emptive strike against a large threatening neighbour was part of his strategy and it has been noted that he selected tanks light enough to roll over the causeway into Malaysia. This idea of the beleaguered state – the small but energetic fighter that could control its destiny by pulling a punch above its weight – is central to his communication of leadership. We should also note that the choice of 'digit' implies that individuals were only important so long as they contributed to social survival.

It is possible to gain some insight into the communication style of Lee's using a corpus of 2,014 speeches, interviews and press releases that is available from the Singapore government web site.[38] A search of this corpus of political communication permits us to identify words that occur with a high frequency and therefore as communicating core leadership concepts. Initially, I read a sample of the transcripts and then searched for keywords that occurred there to establish their frequency in the whole corpus. Table 9.1 shows the findings for words that appeared from the reading to be keywords and that occurred more than 100 times (or at least 5 per cent) in the whole corpus. In the table I have grouped them into five separate, though related, ideas: competition and sport; energy; control; survival; and success:

This simple analysis of word frequency takes us to the central ideas that characterize his leadership communication. The words given above are only a sample of words that could be related to these five central ideas, for example, if we look at the lexical field of 'competition and sport' we find the following occurrences of particular sports terms: football (13); lap (10); baton (9); basketball (5); wrestle (4); cricket (4). Of course, without checking individually we do not know whether they are used metaphorically or literally. However, the overall total indicates that a word from one of these five domains occurs nearly three times (on average) in each of the Lee speeches. Singapore is represented as an insecure nation whose survival depends on success through its energy, discipline and efficiency, so that it is able to compete with other nations as if they were sporting opponents. In this section I will consider the notions of 'sports and competition' and 'energy', I will discuss 'control' in the section on 'vision and values' and 'survival and success' in the section on 'legitimacy'. I will argue that survival is the predominant concept because there is evidence of it in nearly all his use of metaphor.

Competition and sports metaphors are related to ideas of survival because it is necessary to be healthy in order to compete in sports and increase the

Table 9.1 Lee Kuan Yew's core leadership concepts

Concept	Number of related words
Competition and sport	490 – compete/competition/competitive/ competitiveness
	225 – race
	131 – team
	110 – speed
Total	956
Energy	458 – power
	210 – charge
	136 – energy
	121 – dynamo/dynamic/dynamism
Total	925
Control	447 – force
	262 – technology
	248 – control
	192 – discipline
	113 – efficient/efficiency
	104 – machine/mechanical
Total	1,366
Survival	287 – danger/dangerous
	341 – survive/survival
	321 – threat/threatening/threatened
	128 – protect
Total	1,077
Success	801 – success/successful/succeed
	253 – fail/failure
Total	1,054

chances of survival. He employs sports metaphors to represent his view of nation states engaged in competitive struggles for economic survival:

> It is a constant struggle to stay fit, strong and alive. Economic competition is a harsh fact of life. It is like sumo wrestlers jousting for top place. You throw one sumo wrestler out of the ring, there is another sumo wrestler waiting to get in. The only way to avoid both competition and defeat is to retire from wrestling, and give up the prizes of victory. I don't think Singaporeans want to do that.[39]

Sports metaphors are persuasive because they imply simultaneously the existence of competitors (opponents) and the need for unity among leaders and between leaders and followers; hence the notion of a leadership team is very central to this. In the following speech he contrasts the older and the younger teams:

> And the government is Singapore. The core group of men who have led the PAP are not indestructible ... Here, in the heat, we burn ourselves up. It is our recognition of the mortality of men and their declining capacity that makes us want to *get a younger team in place*. I am not saying that the old guard is washed-out and drained. They will be around until *the younger team* is ready to take over. *The younger team* does not have to take over, not for a few years ... Do not forget that the process of injecting new blood has been going on since 1965.[40]

Medical imagery combines here with the sports concept of teamwork. The younger team requires a suitably 'fit' opposition in order to develop its leadership skills:

> I have come to the conclusion that we have to ensure that several better and more intelligent opposition members are in Parliament. Without opposition members, the *younger team has no sparring partners. They need real sparring partners to keep fit and agile*.[41]

Team spirit is necessary to ensure success in competition:

> Now Singapore is independent on its own. For 16 years we have maximized the use of our only resource, ourselves. We have created conditions of political and social stability to enable economic development *to speed up*. We have invested heavily in education and training. We must learn to increase productivity through *greater team spirit*. We shall learn the lessons from other countries *who have been successful*, like Japan and Germany.[42]

The use of sports metaphors in relation to national and political affairs implies a concept: SURVIVAL IS SPORTING SUCCESS.[43] Sports success also requires energy and the concept of energy contributes to his rhetoric. We will remember that the flash of red lightning is part of the symbol of the PAP and Lee's use of words such as 'power', 'charging', 'dynamos' etc. is intended to highlight both the literal truth of Singapore's reliance on energy (initially it developed itself as a major centre for oil refining and export) but also the metaphorical truth of reliance on an energetic leader. It is the ambiguity of literal and metaphorical senses that he exploits with 'energy' images in his design of leadership rhetoric; consider a phrase he uses metaphorically a number of times: 'plugging into a grid':

> For us, the easier way is just *plug it into the grid*. We stand other risks, of course, because the grid is already there. You tap Western science,

Western technology, trade with the West. But when they have a depression, recession and unemployment, we get the rigor.[44]

But the industrial countries of the West face increasing animosity and resentment from the developing countries, aggravated because there is no alternative better *economic grid for the developing countries to plug themselves into.*[45]

She wants to get the same economic uplift that Japan, South Korea, Taiwan, Hongkong and ASEAN have had from the free market economies of the West by *plugging into their trading and investments power grid.*[46]

The metaphor here is one where the west is conceptualized as a source of energy – a huge power grid – that can be drawn on as circumstances dictate to stimulate trade and the economy. The value of the metaphor is that it implies that access is effectively free – like a squatter who draws on the mains without paying any bills; it also implies that one does not need to take anything more from the west other than its economic resources – because an electrical current can be 'switched off' at will. Lee uses similarly mechanistic metaphors to compare the values of Chinese and Malay cultures:

Now these two societies really move at two different speeds. It's like the difference between a high-revolution engine and low-revolution engine.[47]

The use of such metaphors in relation to national efforts implies a conceptual metaphor SURVIVAL IS ENERGY.

Another important part of the discourse of nation-building is the creation of a sense of historical identity, and he perhaps aims to counterbalance the mechanistic nature of his rhetoric by recollecting of formative social events that were significant in his own life:

I remember the numerous strikes, the Hock Lee Bus riots, the Chinese Middle School students' examination boycott, the bomb that went off at MacDonald House during Sukarno's campaign of Confrontation, killing two innocent office workers, the 1964 racial riots, the tension, the curfews, the announcement of Separation from Malaysia on 9 August 1965.

He then goes onto to highlight the personal dimension of these experiences:

My generation also enjoyed the fruits of growth under a good government. We appreciated them all the more after the dangers and uncertainties we had gone through. When my mother bought a 3-room HDB flat in Queenstown in 1963, my family was extremely grateful to the Government. Before that, we had lived in a house without electricity and modern sanitation.[48]

The technique of shifting from social to personal experience reinforces the underlying metonym LEADER FOR NATION, so that whatever happens to the people is also the experience of the leader. We saw similar creations of equivalence in the discourse of Castro in which the experiences of the nation and the people are equated with those of the leader.

Communication of vision and values

Lee's vision is a progressive one in which – given the right leadership, government and education – society can continue to improve indefinitely. This vision became symbolized by the notion of a 'rugged society':

> It depends on the education we give them; the training they receive; the values that they are taught – what is good, what is bad; what should be done; what should not be done; whether you should have a soft society, fun-loving, pleasure-loving, weak, effete or whether you should have *a rugged, robust, disciplined effective society, a hard society, a tough, rugged society*.[49]

The vision was, then, fundamentally founded in values and these were collectivist rather than individualist in so far as they guaranteed the overarching goal of survival: 'And I say it is a tough, a rugged society like this thrown into an area of great turbulence which can survive'.[50] However, in the pursuit of a collectivist vision there would inevitably be sacrifices: one aspect of Lee's ruggedness was that the individual members of society should not object to becoming social 'digits'. Analysis of his language indicates that his vision of a successful nation is one that considers the individual as an abstraction. It is the ruggedness of the collective, rather than the ruggedness of the individual that is valued: the fact that a rugged society is one that survives therefore justifies control:

> But you may find some solace and encouragement from what we mean when we talk about a lean and rugged society. We have been stressing this for two years, with a purpose: to create that mood in our people to be prepared to sacrifice, to make the effort to respond to a harsher situation.[51]

In order to realize the vision of the rugged society it is essential to have discipline:

> With each year of nation building, we approach closer to the ideal of one people, one nation, one Singapore. We have no strikes, no political

upheavals, no communal discord. We can reach national consensus and act quickly, even in areas which require some restraint on personal freedom, like road traffic management and no smoking in enclosed public areas. Maintaining social cohesion has been our key competitive edge over both developed and developing countries.[52]

The prerequisite of success was that there are rules clearly laid out for control and discipline in every aspect of life – and especially working life:

> Good housekeeping also means that machines have to be properly oiled and greased before they are left to stand idle until the following day. Accessories and tools have to be properly kept so as not to expose them to rust and pilferage. Other responsibilities and duties refer to the personal discipline; reporting to work on time, refraining from malingering, slow and sloppy work, receiving and taking orders well and generally contributing to the productivity and efficiency of the enterprise.[53]

His utopia is an environment in which all physical dirt will be removed – by, say, regular cleaning campaigns – but also one in which everything that was associated in his mind with dirt is removed because it implies lack of self-discipline and loss of control. This may be summarized conceptually as SURVIVAL IS CONTROL. Famously, laws were brought in against all forms of absence of control: not flushing public toilets, smoking, and chewing gum – all types of self-indulgence that threatened a fully controlled environment. His vision of control includes his own physical environment and his concern with the ardors of a tropical climate has led to his adoration of air conditioning as he likes to live his entire waking life at 22 degrees C (reduced to 19 degrees C at night while sleeping).[54] Ironically, the idea of control does not stretch to the free market as this would conflict with another fundamental vision – that effort and hard work are rewarded – the rugged society is a highly competitive one.

Lee has subsequently 'discovered' a strong belief in the concept of Asian values; the core values were summarized in 1989 as: 'placing society above self, upholding the family as the basic building block of society, resolving major issues through consensus instead of contention, and stressing religious tolerance and harmony'.[55] He traces these values back to Confucian and Chinese culture:

> The Japanese have the right attributes for high group performance. They are hardworking, business oriented, highly competitive and pragmatic. But the other East Asians, Koreans, Chinese, Vietnamese, are not inferior in these qualities, as their histories bear out. They share many characteristics derived from a common cultural base, Chinese in origin. Some observers have attributed this emphasis on hard work and thrift to the

'Confucian ethic' . . . The habits of hard work, thrift and group solidarity propelled these countries beyond fighting for survival on to creating wealth, through producing for export. The history of these countries has also resulted in strong social cohesion within their societies.[56]

Although this was a somewhat retrospective interpretation by Lee, Confucian values had previously been identified by others as important in establishing the political legitimacy of the People's Action Party:

The PAP leadership may be said to have 'Confucianized' itself by prescribing a code of ethic, that of the *junzi* or honourable individual. They have set themselves up as the model of a moral leadership which governs in the interests of the people rather than through self-interest.[57]

Lee's leadership – while not democratic in a western way – has not been characterized by the type of corruption that is usually associated with authoritarian systems. Western perspectives have criticized his underlying Social Darwinism that interprets the core values of 'hard work, thrift and group solidarity' as the product of environment and race. In a series of speeches in the 1960s he displayed his admiration for the energy and drive displayed by those of 'migrant stock', who have inherited their 'good glands' from their parents, and his peculiar notion of acclimatization as genetically passed down through generations. The speeches also reveal a fear that the ethnic Chinese of Singapore will lose the drive which has made them successful because they have left the 'hard environment' of their forebears and are now living in the tropics and living in a more prosperous, but 'softer' culture.[58] A highly symbolic campaign that was the first major sign of Lee's 'conversion' to Confucian values was his 'Speak Mandarin' campaign, commencing in 1978; this called for the teaching of Chinese proverbs, sayings, fables and folk tales in English medium schools and set up special schools for gifted Chinese-educated that had the same status as English medium schools. In this respect language was primarily important as the embodiment of the cultural values of the largest of Singapore's communities: Mandarin was significant because it symbolized culturally determined Chinese and Confucian beliefs and values.

Communication of legitimacy

The basis for Lee's legitimacy was that he claimed to symbolize the survival of a Singapore (as implied by the metonym LEADER FOR NATION) that was continually faced by strategic threats:

One day, I don't know when – 10, 15, 20 years – one of these three countries will overtake us in terms of material wealth and power; either Indonesia or China, or India. And if before then, we have not yet welded the three communities into a new national identity, then I say it must come unscrambled ... time is not on our side, as far as this critical issue is concerned.[59]

Since survival was the overriding basis for legitimacy, the difficulty Lee faced – along with many independence leaders – was in shifting his vision from that of an anti-colonialism that *challenged* existing authority to a new nationalism that *reinforced* authority. This entailed a fundamental switch in his legitimacy claims from the period before and after independence.

Prior to independence the legitimacy claims of the People's Action Party were based on delegitimizing alternative sources of authority; their aims were:

> To destroy the colonial system by methods of non-violence, we abjure violence ... we are not prepared to fight, perpetuate or prolong the colonial system. But give us our rights and we will fight the Communists or any others who threaten the existence of an independent and democratic non-Communist Malaya.[60]

In fact the legitimacy of the PAP was enhanced by the combined 'threat' of colonialism and communism because it was able to play one off against the other. The basis for the legitimacy claims of an aspiring nationalist movement was through evidence of popular support and this entailed struggle with rivals. He reserved his main attacks for the communists because they were the main rivals for popular support; for example, he used disease metaphors to represent communism as a threat:[61]

> But this is a lesson we must learn – that the Communists are an endemic threat. *You are not going to cure it by having a jab of penicillin or taking a dose of atremyacin.* It is something endemic. The moment *your health goes down*, your resistance goes down. *They come up, but if you keep fit,* the country sound, employment is full, houses, schools, homes, clinics, hope of a better life and immediate tangible results, then we can fight them openly and win.[62]

Such metaphors can be traced to the earliest days of the Cold War[63] and it may be that Lee was influenced by exposure to this discourse. However, he extends their political range further to social democracy by criticizing state-based welfare systems:

> All the Western countries that have gone in for state welfare are now caught in bind ... the West Germans are the latest *victims of this malaise.* It is an *interesting political disease* which the Japanese have managed to escape because they do not go in for state welfare. They go in for company welfare.[64]

In some cases his use of extended medical metaphors is reminiscent of Mahathir:

> The French President, in his wisdom, has proclaimed neutralism as the *panacea for all the ills* of South East Asia. Whether *this simple pill will work* in such an *advanced state of cancer* in South East Asia is dubious. Nevertheless it illustrates differing assessments of *what is wrong with the patient*, and whether he *needs medical or surgical treatment*.[65]

Health metaphors relate closely to other metaphors for competition, sport, survival and control that I have shown are the core concepts that dominate his communication. However, they are also highly typical of right wing political discourse since they create a framework of thinking that places power in a single individual: the politician-doctor, who diagnoses and advocates remedies. 'Follower-patients' – made insecure by illness – are invited to put their trust in a 'leader-doctor' who gains legitimacy in their eyes.

Once independence was achieved – and the threat from the 'disease' of communism had abated – survival became central to Lee's design of leadership style: survival of the leader and of the nation – as implied by the LEADER FOR NATION concept. A discourse of threat and response took over in which any challenge to *his own authority* was represented as an issue of *life and death survival for Singapore*. Survival was the key theme at Lee's press conference at broadcasting house on the day of Singapore's separation from Malaysia:

> We would like to settle any difficulties and differences with Indonesia. *But we must survive. We have a right to survive. And, to survive*, we must be sure that we cannot be just over-run. You know, *invaded by armies or knocked out by rockets*, if they have rockets – which they have, ground-to-air.[66]

From now on every political issue was construed as a crisis that threatened the survival of Singapore; first there was the crisis of the end of the merger; then the premature closure of British bases in 1968; then the ongoing threat of Communist infiltration. In 1974 there was the oil crisis; the fall of Vietnam in 1975; the bilingual education policy was deemed a failure in 1978. There was the threat of trade unions and of western values in general. There was the eugenics problem of the poorly educated having more children than well-educated. As Lee summarized: 'We are responsible for our own survival, if that survival is jeopardized, we can expect no Santa Claus, no Lone Ranger, to come to the rescue'.[67] In fact, so long as Lee is alive there was no need for any of these.

A particular metaphor for crisis survival that Lee exploited in the breakdown of the merger with Singapore is the survival of a marriage. As Wee explains,[68] when the metaphor was used by Malaysian politicians (and it was not used prior to the merger) it always mapped Malaysia as the husband (because of its greater size) and Singapore as the wife; however, each side sought to represent the other as primarily responsible for the breakdown. The Tunku represented the divorce as being forced on Malaysia while Lee manipulated the metaphor to imply that it was Malaysia that was 'divorcing' Singapore who became a passive victim. This is clear from Lee's use of the passive 'Singapore was cast out'. Their union had been marred by failure to agree over whether the new Federation should be a truly multi-racial society, or one dominated by the Malays. Lee employed the more intense hyperbolic metaphor 'marred by conjugal strife' as compared with the Tunku's 'don't get on well'. Lee elaborated on Singapore's lack of control by treating the separation not just as a divorce, but as a Malay–Muslim divorce. The choice of a specifically Malay–Muslim divorce source domain was motivated by the number of parliamentary readings that took place (three) – which is the same as the number of times 'Talak' that needs to be uttered for a Malay–Muslim divorce to be absolutely final.[69]

The deliberate evocation of a Muslim cultural schema for divorce is significant as it represents Singapore as in an equivalent crisis to that of a Muslim woman – who, once divorced, is vulnerable and insecure because she no longer has the right to protection, nor is a virgin – which significantly reduces her chances of re-marriage. The representation of a situation as a crisis is important because it implies that in order to survive there is a need for a leader who symbolizes the social cohesion necessary to overcome insecurity.

Ultimately, Lee establishes himself as the reference point in establishing the identity of Singapore: he adopts the leadership style of a Confucian paternalist who is always strong and authoritarian because he knows the vulnerability of his society-family. This symbolizes a complete rejection (at the level of discourse) of the female role in which Singapore had been cast by Malaysia during the period of the merger. He is keen to arouse the type of emotional responses that are associated with the need of a father to protect his family and, in the case of Singapore, it is a family containing both natural and adopted children.

As well as being successful in becoming a prototype 'tiger' economy, Singapore has overcome the inter-ethnic tensions that had characterized the politics of the 1960s, it has developed the most efficient transport and communications infrastructure in southeast Asia and provided low-cost public housing. It has the lowest crime rate and the best health and education systems. Many of the core notions I have discussed – competition, fitness, good health, energy, sporting success – are integrally related to the argument that success *creates* legitimacy. Lee's leadership style was alternatively to raise the spectre of annihilation to arouse insecurities that were then assuaged with images of success; in this way his leadership style was to design a mass psychological dependency among followers.

Leadership and the media

Lee understood the social psychology of crowd behaviour; he was particularly aware of how the communists had developed methods for influencing and controlling crowds. The main opponents of the People's Action Party was the Malaysian Communist party and he describes how they were 'superb stage managers, and their cheerleaders had orchestrated prolonged applause for all speakers who attacked the Emergency Regulations'.[70] What is significant here is that political influence does not reside in the symbolic actions of the leader alone – but in followers' responses. He goes onto describe in detail how stooges were employed to initiate follower responses:

> But as I attended rally after rally over the next to years, I gradually became aware that these cheerleaders were scattered among the audience. Furthermore, they would always be led by a master cheerleader, from whom they took their cue, and each in turn would have his own clique of 30–40 who would begin to applaud when he did, triggering off a response from the audience around him.[71]

When describing a visit to St Peter's in Rome he noticed the similarity of crowd control methods: 'After my experience with Communist rallies I instinctively looked for cheerleaders. I found them above me, choirboys on circular balconies up the pillars. The Roman Catholic Church had used such methods of mass mobilization long before the Communists'.[72] Lee understood the social dynamics involved in mass face-to-face communication and that rallies provided an opportunity for symbolic displays in which followers are subliminally controlled by a leader. Some have viewed charismatic leadership as a socially constructed phenomenon in which interaction between followers leads to the attribution of charisma occurring through a process referred to as 'social contagion'.[73] Meindl refers to a 'charismatic syndrome' characterized by emotional involvement, heightened self-esteem and identification with a leader's beliefs and values. 'Contagion' refers to the process by which initially passive members of an audience become active by responding to the behaviour of followers. In neuro-cognitive terms it is those who witness the pleasure obtained by others who are emotionally involved leads them to obtain a similar pleasure through imitation. Applauding, cheering, and other physical manifestations of involvement, enables spectators to become participants.

There is certainly evidence of considerable stage management of the symbolic actions of followers in the rallies of 1959 election campaign; they provided opportunities for the performance of rituals of followership that simultaneously encouraged a social contagion effect:

> The Chinese showed support for their candidates by presenting them personally with silk banners with elegant four- or eight-character apho-

risms stitched onto them. A banner could measure up to three or four yards across and require as many people to come on stage to help the donor unfold and show to an admiring audience. After the candidate had received it with a ceremonial bow, there would be the souvenir photograph. A popular candidate could collect 50 to 100 Chinese banners, which, when hung up between strings of colored bulbs lent a rally a festive air. Each banner would display the name of the donor or donors, perhaps a class society or a trade association that identified itself with the candidate and, having thus committed its members, would work to help him win.[74]

There is clearly an important theatrical dimension to these staged performances that integrated some of the multimedia effects of traditional Chinese opera.[75] The power of banners is significant in political communication because of the size, texture and simplicity of the message; the aesthetic effect of the script; the colour – enhanced by lighting. The combined sensual effect produced a powerful semiotic that was vital to communicating group identity of the ethnic Chinese among followers.

Lee's basic communication mode has been through face-to-face contacts, but he also took the opportunity offered by each innovation in media to get his message across. In the critical political issue of whether Singapore should merge with Malaysia he made a series of 12 radio broadcasts. He was aware of the need to integrate into the new media the dramaturgical skills he had developed at rallies:

> I had told a story that was part of their own recent experience – of riots, strikes, boycotts, all of them fresh reference points in their minds – and I had given them the explanation for mysteries that had puzzled them. It was as if I had gone up on the stage where a magician had been performing and exposed his props and accessories by lighting up the darkened areas they had not noticed before.[76]

He showed the same energy and desire to learn the skills of communication by television broadcasting that he shown in relation to language learning by getting expert feedback on his performance:

> When I was in London in September 1962, Alex Josey, my press secretary, arranged for Hugh Burnett of the BBC to run a mock interview with me and then review my performance on screen. I had seen an earlier programme in which I had appeared, and had been astounded at how fierce I looked. Burnett assured me that I was a natural. All I needed were a few tips: always look into the camera, never cover your mouth or nose with your hand as you speak, always lean forward in your chair – to lean backwards would make you look slovenly. His main advice: 'Be natural, be direct, be yourself'. I was reassured.[77]

He goes on to explain that when television was introduced in Singapore in February 1963 it was a very effective weapon against the communists. In the lead up to independence he had also employed the new visual media for the surveillance purpose of identifying opposition supporters:

> We also decided to install powerful spotlights ready to run on any section of the crowd that started trouble, especially those in the front row who could most effectively disrupt the meeting. When these spot-lights focused on them, the photographers and TV cameramen would dash up to take close-up pictures so that the police could later identify the ringleaders.[78]

By treating the media as a communication resource Lee was able to control the message that he put over and influence the effect it had on his audience. His enthusiasm for technological innovation can be seen in the fact that much of the data employed in this chapter was drawn from a Singapore government web site. While not perhaps naturally media-friendly he has always been aware of the huge potential of media management for the control and influence of followers.

Summary

In a more recent speech Lee combines a perspective that is formed through historical experience into a forward looking, positive and optimistic vision of the future:

> My vision of Singapore in the twenty-first century is: a cohesive, vibrant, and prosperous country, founded on justice and equality, excel-lence and social mobility, discipline and graciousness. Citizens care for one another. The ablest commit themselves to lead. People of all races, from all walks of life, work together to make this our best home. History and geography made us a small island, in a strategic location, with three million people of different races, languages and religions. These are our material for building a nation. They will always make our survival a challenge. If we don't understand these basic facts, we will perish.

But it is above all this threat of extinction that legitimizes his role as leader of a united and cohesive nation, and he argues the case with conviction and passion:

> Building such a nation will not be easy. We need strong attitudes of self-sacrifice and service. We must involve ourselves in the life of our community, to create a cohesive society with strong bonds between us. We must uphold sound values, and transmit them from generation to

generation. We are fellow citizens, fellow owners of Singapore. I say to all Singaporeans: You have to feel passionately about Singapore. Being Singaporean should resonate in our hearts and minds. We built this country. We live, work and raise our children here. We will fight and, if we must, we will die to defend our way of life and our home. Here we will realize our hopes and aspirations. Here our children will have a bright future. Singapore becomes our home of choice. Let us work together to make Singapore our best home.[79]

The preoccupation with fear – as evidenced by defining the nature of 'dirt' and his desire to control and eliminate it – reflects an underlying psychological insecurity that may be traced to early social influences of the collapse of the British under Japanese invasion; the desire for cleanliness signifies a fear of loss of control and above all it seems to be the vision of creating a highly controlled environment that has motivated Lee. There is evidence throughout his leadership style of the conceptual metaphors SURVIVAL IS SPORTING SUCCESS, SURVIVAL IS ENERGY and SURVIVAL IS CONTROL. The value of a controlled environment shows in the achievements of Singapore: its extensive public housing; its education, health systems and transport and communication infrastructure. His communication of leadership has been based on the underlying concept of LEADER FOR NATION – later incorporating Confucian paternalism – through which he created the impression that national survival depended entirely on his own survival. Above all, Lee has been the proof of his own theories of leadership – that in order to survive and overcome insecurities you have to be hugely competitive, hugely energetic, and have a will to govern that allows you to perform as a leader.

10 The design of leadership style

I have examined a range of leaders from different cultural and political settings spanning an extended period of time from the earlier part of the last
century until the present. I have found similarities and differences in how
they have communicated leadership and have intended to represent a range
of patterns of commonality and difference in the notions of 'the design of
leadership style' and 'performance'. 'Style' implies that there is no single
formula for charismatic leadership and the 'design'/'performance' distinction
implies that there is a separation between a *planning* phase in which leadership strategies are formulated and a *doing* phase in which they are enacted.
The concept of 'the design of leadership style' places equal importance on
the full range of communication resources – including the verbal and the
non-verbal. Following Goffman's comment that: 'Performers can stop giving
expressions but cannot stop giving them off',[1] I have argued that successful
leaders rely as much on unspoken communication in the performance of
leadership as they do on language.

For this reason, I have argued for the essential multi-modal nature of
leadership communication, as Goffman noted, individuals want to 'discover
the facts of a situation' – and since full information is rarely available as to
the actual outcomes, or end product of a social activity:

> the individual tends to employ substitutes – cues, tests, hints, expres-
> sive gestures, status symbols, etc. as predictive devices. In short, since
> the reality that the individual is concerned with is unperceivable at the
> moment, appearances must be relied upon in its stead.[2]

We may readily substitute 'followers' for 'individual' since they rely on the
evidence from how communication resources are deployed in the performance of leadership to infer the validity of a leader's legitimacy claims.
Goffman's quotation has been modified as follows: 'The performer who
learns to control expressions he is apparently only giving off has achieved a
higher level of social control over performance'.[3] All the leaders described in
this work can be considered to have mastered this higher level of social
control through their presence.

A summary of the model for leadership communication is presented in Figure 10.1.

I have first distinguished between verbal and non-verbal communication and then in each of these primary modes I have identified four component elements that contribute to the design of a leadership style that is realized in

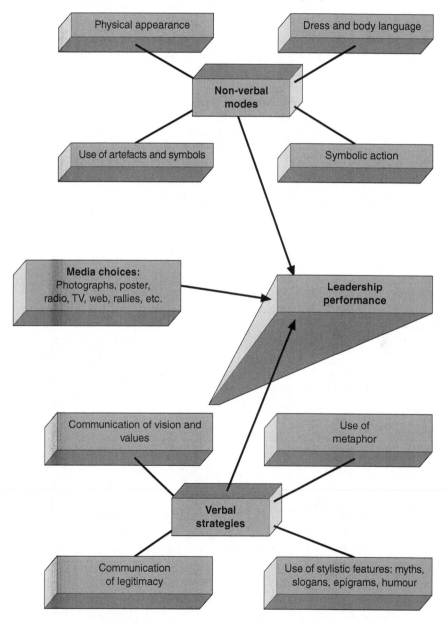

Figure 10.1 A model for leadership communication.

performance. The choice of effective media for integrating verbal and non-verbal modes also constitutes the performance of leadership. I propose, therefore, that successful leaders both 'give' and 'give off' expressions.

The model that I have presented describes the potential communication resources that are available to leaders; however, *how* these criteria are actually deployed in specific instances depends on the nature of the performance. The design of leadership style implies that being different and 'doing it your way' is itself a criterion for successful leadership communication. There is no such thing as an ideal performance and as Goffman puts it: 'details of the expression and movements do not come from a script but from the command of an idiom'.[4] There is inevitably variation in how leadership is performed because individuals have their own genetic characteristics, appearance, physique, personality, social and environmental influences, personal histories etc. that give rise to different communication potentialities in different social and cultural settings. Successful leaders are able to exploit effectively their leadership potentialities by adapting them to these specific performance settings.

I also propose that in performance the components outlined in the figure above have a *cumulative* interactive effect. It is the performance fit between the appearance, behaviour etc., and language that communicates integrity, or style, and permits followers to invest leaders with significance. It is their fit that accounts for their irresistible symbolic power. Their symbolic meaning sustains followers' general struggle of life by providing an exemplar:

> we resolve the conflict between our self-image and what we want and think it should be by making the leader the embodiment of our ego ideal. By accepting a leader with transcendental objectives, followers can fulfil their desires to go beyond their own self-interests and to become more noble and worthy.[5]

This realization of the ego ideal is something that only occurs through holistic messages in which the effect of the whole is greater than the sum of the parts. Indeed when the parts become conspicuous, followers may doubt whether the leader is genuine – or has simply learnt techniques of impression management. Successful performance resists analysis when the leader *believes* in his performance. In order to do this, leaders need to improvise naturally to produce an inimitable leadership style – like the bards:

> These 'singers of tales' do not possess the fabulous powers of memorization sometimes attributed to 'primitive' peoples. They do not memorize much at all. Instead, they combine stock phrases, formulas, and narrative segments in patterns improvised according to the response of their audience. Recordings of the same epic by the same singer demonstrate that each performance is unique ... In each case, the singer proceeds as

if he were walking down a well-known path . . . he creates his text as he goes, picking new routes through old themes.[6]

While the combined operation of all the components in Figure 10.1 contribute to successful leadership communication, the balance between them varies according to the individual leader's style. Consider, for example, the basic distinction between verbal and non-verbal communication: follower testimonies refer more frequently to the appearance of Mandela and Gandhi than they do to that of Mahathir or Lee Kuan Yew who relied more on language to enhance followers' self-esteem. While all these leaders gave their followers a sense of national pride, political independence and self-reliance, they did so in their own unique way. This variability of style is well summarized as follows:

> The specificities and combinations of modes vary not only in different cultural conditions but up to a point within and during each personal enactment: the detailed balance between different channels, say, or the use or avoidance of touch or smell; the patterning of visible gesture, facial expression, posture, orientation, spacing, personal adornment; of the processes of audible interaction through manipulation of volume, tone, speed, vocabulary or mood.[7]

Nelson Mandela's performance created an intimacy with anyone in his proximity – not just those in authority – through personalized contact by facial expression and speech style, he often undermined the potential formality of a situation. In this respect he even at times subverted the script designed for his style – but subversion is always a powerful instrument for those who are oppressed, and he is drawing on skills that had worked so well when he was a victim of authority. Leaders may deliberately and playfully satirize their image in actual performances that show them to be human rather than mythological beings. With these qualifications in mind, then, concerning the different ways in which the components of the model in Figure 10.1 are put into practice, I will consider the balance of similarities and differences in non-verbal and verbal communication that together constitute the design and performance of leadership style.

Non-verbal communication

Within each of the non-verbal modes of communication some aspects may be more significant than others for particular leaders. For example, dress may be a more or less salient aspect of physical appearance and differ according to whether it has a social or an individual meaning: Khomeini's dress is significant because of its complete absence of variation – always the black robes and black turban of the twelfth imam. His dress had a powerful symbolic meaning in defining the ideological struggle between the fundamentalist values of Islam and the values of the Pahlavis. Similarly, Castro has given dress a powerful social meaning by retaining the dress of a revolutionary guerrilla leader. The appeal of both leaders is that they hardly ever changed their dress style because it appealed to the shared norms that underlay their appeal: followers are looking to make consistent inferences from a range of appearance-related information. This is unlike Mandela who frequently changed his dress and appearance – particularly when on the run from the government – and for whom dress was a powerful expression of individual style. However, the ability to transform appearance fitted well with his leadership objective of transforming South African social norms, and part of his style as an agent of change was to change himself.

Appearance can be normative or non-normative and reflect the norms of leaders or followers; effective design of leadership style requires finding a stylistic balance for particular social and cultural settings – according to whether the leader is representing himself as an innovative modernizer or as an upholder of traditional values. Looks and dress make the individual stand out from, or blend in with, followers and in some cases even the same aspect of physical appearance can have different effects according to cultural norms. For example, beards are normative for leaders operating in Islamic settings but may be individual expressions of identity for revolutionary leaders where social norms encourage shaving. Such leaders prefer beards because they make them look more exotic and individual rather than because they make them blend in with potential followers; similarly, followers may imitate unusual appearance as an expression of loyalty and change in values. Even when leaders seek to replace one set of appearance norms with another, this may still be influenced by awareness of the symbolic meaning of such a substitution: when Gandhi adopted the clothes of an Indian peasant he was rejecting the norms of dress for metropolitan 'westernized' leaders but embracing those of his intended followers – the Indian rural peasantry.

I have argued that symbolic action contributes significantly to performance – in some cases actions were symbolic precisely because they were normative – for example, Khomeini's performance of the daily routine of ablutions and prayer inspired followers because of its consistency with a religious tradition. Even when he performed symbolic actions – such as declaring the *fatwa* on Salmon Rushdi and supporting the hostage seizure from the US embassy – he was effectively condoning actions that symbolized the new revolutionary norms of followers. Similarly, Gandhi's fasts communicated the message that followers could become leaders in their own right, by a performance that symbolized this. This contrasts with other types of symbolic actions that were non-normative performances. These include displaying powerful emotions at significant moments – Mahathir and Lee Kuan Yew – or Castro's reluctance to terminate a TV interview on hearing that his son had been injured in a car accident, or Mandela taking de Klerk's hand at the end of a TV debate. The symbolic meaning of these actions was precisely because they were unexpected – they were not part of the script, though they gave off expression. The effect of symbolic actions depends on how they contribute to performance – and this will be influenced by seemingly spontaneous and instinctive response to performance conditions.

Verbal communication

Similarly, within verbal communication strategies there is also significant variation that is partly determined by socio-historical setting – for example, independence leaders such as Gandhi, Mahathir and Lee Kuan Yew all raised the issue of the actual language employed to communicate with followers' because the use of native languages itself gave off a powerful leadership message. However, for Castro and Khomeini language choice was not a significant factor in the design of leadership style.

In the communication of visions and values all leaders are concerned with morality; however, the design of leadership style leads to variation: Gandhi and Khomeini relied more extensively on the traditional religious value systems than Mandela or Castro – although the latter based their vision of the future on an underlying moral vision, this was not as the result of a previously codified or formalized body of doctrine as it was for Gandhi and Khomeini. Mandela's underlying ideas – such as the THE ANC IS A MORAL FORCE – and Castro's claim that THE REVOLUTION IS ETHI- CALLY PURE reflected a humanist vision of a morally improved world. This differs from Khomeini's communication that depended on a fundamental contrast between inherently good and bad ideological, historical and socio-political agents. Gandhi's communication espouses moral values that reflect core ideas rooted in a transcendental religious outlook, such as NON- VIOLENCE IS WAR/A SCIENCE/A PHYSICAL FORCE etc. However, while there are subtle differences in the shade of emphasis placed on values and visions, *any* successful leadership communication will exhibit attention to visions and values. As Goffman wrote in relation to the social individual: 'The impressions that the others give tend to be treated as claims and promises they have implicitly made, and claims and promises tend to have a moral character'[8] – this is all the more so for leaders.

In some cases there are cultural factors that influence the design and performance of leadership style. As one writer argues:

> For the charismatic leader to resort to particular psychological mechanisms in his appeals, the followers must have shared norms. Since sinfulness is a shared norm in the Judeo-Christian world, the Western charismatic leader can stimulate guilt among followers. The importance of 'face' is a shared norm in the Orient; if it were possible to do so, the Oriental charismatic leader would have to focus on shame.[9]

It is certainly true that – while hardly a model Christian – Castro frequently argues that the United States is essentially a *guilty* party through ideas such as IMPERIALISM IS A RAPACIOUS ANIMAL and SMALL COUNTRIES ARE RIPE FRUIT and through the use of the David and Goliath metaphor for US–Cuba relations. This is rather different from Mahathir's rejection of 'western values': the basis for his claims that nudity in public, smoking marijuana, male prostitution etc. are a 'perversion of values'[10] is because they are *shameful* to those from an Islamic cultural background. In this respect, while 'values' are vital to the communication of all leaders, a particular leader will only appeal to the values of the cultural group to which they or their followers belong. By appealing to culturally governed notions of guilt and shame, leaders' claims inhere in sharing followers' value norms. It seems that it would be a very unusual communication strategy for leaders to challenge their followers' existing value systems, and – while their visions may be prospective in some cases seeking to create new or utopian societies – their values are always retrospectively anchoring such changes in the familiar and the known.

As regards the communication of legitimacy there are perhaps more similarities than variations. All leaders base their claims in appeals to the values, beliefs and history of followers; however, rhetorical claims vary in the extent to which, and how, an appeal is made to 'history'. Mandela saw the end of apartheid as part of the natural process of history, Castro argued that history would absolve him and Khomeini saw his messianic role as the hidden imam who would fulfil the prophecies of Moses and Muhammad. So all leaders argue either that their own actions were to reverse problems created by 'history', or that 'history' is 'on their side'. All the leaders analysed here also claimed to represent and embody the beliefs of particular social groups – typically 'the nation' following the conceptual metaphor THE LEADER IS THE NATION. They all (to varying degrees) enhance their own legitimacy by delegitimizing opponents. Typically, this is by using metaphor domains such as health and disease to contrast the social health arising from their own leadership with the potential for disease arising from that of their opponents – whether this was the 'disease' of communism, of capitalism or of colonialism.

In this respect, there is perhaps less variation in the communication of legitimacy in the design of leadership style than in the communication of visions and values. However, only some leaders – for example Mandela, Gandhi and Lee Kuan Yew – represent their opponents as *also* 'victims' of history; this was not the case with Castro or Khomeini – whose mutual hatred of the United States seems to inhibit any understanding of the United States as also motivated by its own history – as a land where people came to free themselves from the social problems, poverty and oppression of the 'old' world: it is not always the role of leaders to take a broader view – especially when their followers are suffering from immediate oppression.

Similarly, all the leaders show awareness of the importance of the media; the use of print by Gandhi and Mandela (both of whose autobiographies are powerful leadership testimonies); the use of television and/or radio in the cases of Castro, Lee Kuan Yew and Khomeini; the use of photographs and posters by Mandela and Khomeini and the carefully stage-managed rallies by Mahathir and Lee Kuan Yew. What unites all these leaders is an awareness that their leadership will be more effective by disseminating their message to as wide an audience as possible. The media – irrespective of cultural or historical settings – enhances the power of leadership, and technological advance has accelerated the range of media available. In this respect impression management in which followers infer certain characteristics about leaders from all their communication resources – physical appearance, facial expressions, tone of voice as well as what is said – is vital to the communication of leadership. Therefore, knowledge of the media available, effective command of media skills, and, at times, control of the media itself, are essential components in the successful design of leadership style.

The danger of the recent emphasis on impression management – through guidance on physical appearance and dress as well as on the delivery and content of verbal messages – the 'spin' – is that it implies that leadership can be manufactured. My view is that while it has the potential to be manufactured or engineered, there is no sure way of predicting the expressive effect of the particular range of communicative resources that are employed by a leader. Goffman has advised of the need to be aware of the inherently dramaturgical nature of *all* human social interaction:

> In their basic capacity as performers, individuals will be concerned with maintaining the impression that they are living up to the many standards by which they are their products are judged . . . the very obligation and profitability of appearing always in a steady moral light, of being a socialized character, forces one to be the sort of person who is practised in the ways of the stage.[11]

If this is the case for individuals, the concern is magnified for leaders. Their need to communicate leadership necessarily entails skill in the art of representation and deception; their *intentions* may be moral, but in order to perform them they will need to *act the role* of a moral being. The role of legitimacy creation is easier for leaders who believe themselves to be moral than it is for those who do not, but the requirement to *perform* always creates an opportunity for a successful impostor, for a moral chameleon whose ethical front is a cover for self-preservation, self-promotion and self-adulation. For this reason, if for no other, it is helpful for those concerned with leadership and communication, whether from the perspective of potential leaders or followers, to understand the design and performance of leadership style.

Notes

1 The magic of leadership

1 J. Charteris-Black, *Politicians and Rhetoric: The Persuasive Power of Metaphor*, Basingstoke and New York: Palgrave-Macmillan, 2005, investigates the verbal strategies for leadership of three British and three American leaders.
2 P.G. Northouse, *Leadership Theory & Practice* (3rd edition), London: Sage, 2004, p. 3.
3 For example, the ayatollahs of the Iranian theocracies.
4 Northouse, 2004.
5 R.M. Stogdill, 'Personal factors associated with leadership: A survey of the literature', *Journal of Psychology*, 25, 1948, pp. 35–71.
6 J.M. Burns, *Leadership*, New York: Harper Row, 1978, p. 18.
7 T.E. Cronin, 'Thinking and learning about leadership'. In W.E. Rosenbach and R.L. Taylor, *Contemporary Issues in Leadership*, Boulder, San Francisco and London: Westview Press, 1989, p. 48.
8 Burns, 1978, p. 19.
9 Ibid., p. 19.
10 Ibid., p. 20.
11 R.J. House and J.V. Singh, 'Organizational behavior. Some new directions for I/O psychology', *Annual Review of Psychology*, 38, 1987, pp. 669–718.
12 Conceptual metaphors are discussed in Chapter 3.
13 B.M. Bass, *Leadership and Performance Expectations*, London and New York: The Free Press, 1985, p. 16.
14 H.L. Tosi, J.R. Rizzo and S.J. Carroll, *Managing Organizational Behaviour*, New York: Harper Row, 1990, p. 616.
15 W.E. Rosenbach and R.L. Taylor, *Contemporary Issues in Leadership*, Boulder, San Francisco and London: Westview Press, 1989, p. 152.
16 Cf. A. Maslow, *Motivation and Personality*, New York: Harper & Row, 1954.
17 Cronin, 1989, p. 53.
18 House 1977 quoted in B.M. Bass, *Bass and Stogdill's Handbook of Leadership: A Survey of Theory and Research*, New York: Free Press, 1990, pp. 189–90.
19 A. Bryman, *Charisma & Leadership in Organizations*, London: Sage, 1992, p. 146.
20 Bass, 1985, p. 18.
21 W. Bennis and B. Nanus, *Leaders: The Strategies for Taking Charge*, New York: Harper Row, 1985, p. 90.
22 J.A. Conger, 'Charismatic and transformational leadership in organizations: an insider's perspective on these developing streams of research', *The Leadership Quarterly*, 10, 2, 1999, p. 36.
23 Bennis and Nanus, 1985, p. 92.
24 C. Handy, 'The language of leadership'. In Rosenbach and Taylor, 1989, p. 238.

25 J.W. Gardner 'The tasks of leadership'. In Rosenbach and Taylor, 1989, pp. 25–6.
26 A. Zaleznik 'Charismatic and consensus leaders: a psychological comparison'. In Rosenbach and Taylor, 1989, p. 38.
27 M. Weber, in Bryman, 1992, p. 24.
28 Bass, 1985, p. 40.
29 Bass, 1990, p. 205.
30 Bass, 1985, p. 40.
31 W.L. Gardner and B.J. Avolio, 'The charismatic relationship: a dramaturgical perspective', *Academy of Management Review*, 23, 1998, p. 143.
32 L. Fischer, *The Life of Mahatma Gandhi*, London: HarperCollins, 1997, p. 397.
33 K.D. Miller, *Voice of Deliverance: the Language of Martin Luther King Jr. and its Sources*, New York: Free Press, 1992, p. 173.
34 Ibid., p. 172.
35 Cf. J. Charteris-Black, *Corpus Approaches to Critical Metaphor Analysis*, Basingstoke and New York: Palgrave-Macmillan, 2004, p. 38.
36 Burns, 1978, p. 246.
37 In A. Sampson, *Mandela*, London: HarperCollins, 2000, pp. 191–2.
38 Kathrada *Star*, 17 July 1998.
39 M. Weber, quoted in Bryman, 1992, p. 25.
40 A political myth is 'An ideologically marked narrative which purports to give a true account of a set of past, present or predicted political events and which is accepted as valid in its essential by a social group' C.G. Flood, *Political Myth: A Theoretical Introduction*, New York and London: Garland 1996, p. 44.
41 In Bryman, 1992, p. 24.
42 Gardner and Avolio, 1998, p. 3.
43 Bass, 1985, p. 37.
44 Though some later research has challenged this view (cf. Bryman op. cit., p. 28).
45 Sampson, 2000, p. 180.
46 The success of New Labour in the 1997 election in Britain was probably largely because of a period of 18 years of Conservative rule. New Labour seemed to gain a double powerful charismatic effect by appearing to overturn both the values of 'Old' Labour and those of the Conservative Party, while in fact many of its policies were highly centrist social democratic ones of full employment, social provision of health and education etc. The very use of the adjective 'New' by New Labour was a very transparent, though successful, attempt to occupy this position as the 'new' centre. In western democratic traditions challenging existing values is therefore very central to a western definition of charisma.
47 Cf. Charteris-Black, 2005, pp. 207–9.
48 Fischer, 1997, p. 134.
49 Cronin, 1989, p. 51.
50 Quoted in Cronin, 1989, p. 62.
51 Bass, 1990, p. 92.
52 Stohl 'The role of memorable messages in the process of organizational socialization', *Communication Quarterly*, 34, 1986, pp. 231–49.
53 Bass, 1990, Chapter 8.
54 R.T. Stein and T. Heller, 'An empirical analysis of the correlations between leadership status and participation rates reported in the literature', *Journal of Personality and Social Psychology*, 37, 1979, pp. 1993–2002.
55 Cf. Conger, 1999, pp. 145–79.

2 Non-verbal communication and leadership

1 R. Finnegan, *Communicating: the Multiple Modes of Human Interconnection*, London and New York: Routledge, 2002.
2 E. Goffman, *The Presentation of Self in Everyday Life*, London: Allen House, 1969, p. 19.
3 Ibid., p. 26.
4 W.L. Gardner and B.J. Avolio, 'The charismatic relationship: a dramaturgical perspective', *Academy of Management Review*, 23, 1998.
5 Schlenker in Gardner and Avolio, 1998, p. 68.
6 T.E. Cronin, 'Thinking and learning about leadership'. In W.E. Rosenbach and R.L. Taylor, *Contemporary Issues in Leadership*, Boulder, San Francisco and London: Westview Press, 1989, p. 48.
7 Cf. J. Charteris-Black, *Corpus Approaches to Critical Metaphor Analysis*, Basingstoke and New York: Palgrave-Macmillan, 2004, p. 21 for a detailed definition.
8 W. Bennis and B. Nanus, *Leaders: The Strategies for Taking Charge*, New York: Harper Row, 1985, pp. 107–8.
9 M. Bass, *Leadership and Performance Expectations*, London and New York: The Free Press, 1985, pp. 109 ff.
10 W. Bennis, 'Leadership transforms vision into action', *Industry Week*, 31 May 1982, pp. 54–6.
11 C. Jung, *Man and His Symbols*, London: Pan Books, 1964, p. 83.
12 Bass, 1985, p. 40.
13 J.A. Conger and R.N. Kanungo, 'Toward a behavioural theory of charismatic leadership in organizational settings', *Academy of Management*, 12, 1988, p. 317.
14 A. Bryman, *Charisma & Leadership in Organizations*, London: Sage, 1992, p. 44.
15 R.L. Applbaum, K.W.E. Anatol, E.R. Hays, O.O. Jenson, R.E. Porter and J.E. Mandel, *Fundamental Concepts in Human Communication*, New York: Canfield Press, 1973, p. 117.
16 Finnegan, 2002, p. 98.
17 J.M. Atkinson, *Our Masters' Voices: The Language and Body Language of Politics*, London: Methuen, 1984.
18 Freud describes this process in 'Mass Psychology and Analysis of the "I"'. In *Mass Psychology & Other Writings*, London, Penguin, 2004, pp. 79–81.
19 Finnegan, 2002, p. 133.
20 A. Sampson, *Mandela*, London: HarperCollins, 2000, p. 487.
21 L. Coltman, *The Real Fidel Castro*, New Haven and London: Yale University Press, 2003, p. 140.
22 Jung, 1964, p. 93.
23 Ibid., p. 4.
24 E.G. Bormann, *Communication Theory*, New York: Holt, Rinehart and Winston, 1980.
25 T.L. Mitchell, in C. De Landtsheer and O. Feldman (eds) *Beyond Public Speech and Symbols: Explorations in the Rhetoric of Politicians and the Media*, Westport and London: Praeger, 2000.
26 Cf. M.A. Ball, 'Political language and the search for an honourable peace'. In De Landtsheer and Feldman, ibid., p. 38.
27 R.J. House, 'Theory of charismatic leadership'. In J.G. Hunt and L.L. Larson (eds) *Leadership: The Cutting Edge*, Carbondale: Southern Illinois University Press, 1977, pp. 189–207.
28 Gardner and Avolio, 1998.

29 F. Schnell, N. Terkildsen and K. Callagan, 'Symbolism and social movements'. In De Landtsheer and Feldman, 2000, p. 226.
30 Ibid., p. 237.
31 This became likened by his followers to the flight of the Prophet Muhammad from Mecca to Medina.
32 G. Milton, *White Gold: The Extraordinary Story of Thomas Pellow*, London: Hodder & Stoughton, 2004, p. 78.
33 Goffman, 1969, p. 213.
34 M. Mauss, 'Une categories de l'esprit humaine', *Journal of the Royal Anthropological Institute*, 67, 1938, p. 256ff.
35 Wang Renzhong. In Zhisui Li, *The Private Life of Chairman Mao*, London: Arrow Books, 1996.
36 Goffman, 1969, pp. 58–61.
37 A. Zaleznik, 'Charismatic and consensus leaders: a psychological comparison'. In Rosenbach and Taylor, 1989, p. 98.

3 Verbal communication, leadership and the media

1 See J.M. Atkinson, *Our Masters' Voices: The Language and Body Language of Politics*, London: Methuen, 1984; J. Charteris-Black, *Politicians and Rhetoric: The Persuasive Power of Metaphor*, Basingstoke: Palgrave-Macmillan, 2005.
2 The rhetorical features of Martin Luther King are analysed in Charteris-Black, 2005, Chapter 3.
3 J. Charteris-Black, *Corpus Approaches to Critical Metaphor Analysis*, Basingstoke and New York: Palgrave-Macmillan, 2004, p. 21.
4 Charteris-Black, 2005, pp. 198–202.
5 A. Bryman, *Charisma & Leadership in Organizations*, London: Sage, 1992, p. 61.
6 Charteris-Black, 2005, Chapter 4.
7 J. Charteris-Black and A. Musolff, 'Battered hero or innocent victim? A comparative study of metaphor in describing Euro trading in British and German financial reporting', *English for Specific Purposes*, 22, 2003, pp. 153–76.
8 W.L. Gardner and B.J. Avolio, 'The charismatic relationship: a dramaturgical perspective', *Academy of Management Review*, 23, 1998, p. 1.
9 A. Musolff, *Metaphor and Political Discourse*, Basingstoke: Palgrave-Macmillan, 2004, pp. 32–3.
10 See Charteris-Black, 2004, p. 34.
11 For example, G. Lakoff and M. Johnson, *Philosophy in the Flesh: Embodied Mind and its Challenge to Western Thought*, New York: Basic Books, 1999.
12 Charteris-Black, 2004, p. 84.
13 *Oxford Concise Dictionary of English Etymology*, my italics.
14 The five pledges related to youth unemployment, primary school class sizes, economic stability, NHS waiting lists and waiting times for young offenders and can be found in the 1997 election manifesto.
15 Cf. p. Chilton, *Analysing Political Discourse: Theory & Practice*, New York and London: Routledge, 2004, p. 23.
16 J.A. Conger, 'Charismatic and transformational leadership in organizations: an insider's perspective on these developing streams of research', *The Leadership Quarterly*, 1999, 10, 2: 145–79.
17 See Charteris-Black, 2005, Chapters 5 and 6.
18 S. Taran, 'Mythical thinking, Aristotelian logic, and metaphors in the Parliament of Ukraine'. In C. De Landtsheer and O. Feldman (eds) *Beyond Public Speech and Symbols: Explorations in the Rhetoric of Politicians and the Media*, Westport and London: Praeger, 2000.

19 See Atkinson, 1984.
20 Bryman, 1922, p. 31.
21 Atkinson, 1984, p. 180.
22 N. Jones, *Soundbites and Spin Doctors: How Politicians Manipulate the Media – and Visa Versa*, Guernsey: Indigo, 1996, p. 27.
23 P. Bull, 'New Labour, new rhetoric? An analysis of the rhetoric of Tony Blair'. In De Landtsheer and Feldman (eds), 2000.
24 Charteris-Black, 2005, p. 60.

4 Mahatma Gandhi

1 Said by Gokhala, President of the Servants of India Society, during his visit to South Africa, L. Fischer, *The Life of Mahatma Gandhi*. London: HarperCollins, 1997, p. 140.
2 L. Fischer, 1997, p. 22.
3 Gandhi in R. Attenborough, *Words of Gandhi*, New York: Newmarket Press, 1982, p. 75. Available at: www.mahatma.org.in/books/showbook.jsp?link= bg&lang=en&book=bg0012&id=1&cat=books.
4 Fischer, 1997, p. 117.
5 Gandhi practised sleeping naked with young women to test his vow of celibacy. This is discussed in the last section of this chapter.
6 Fischer, 1997, p. 167.
7 Gandhi in M.K. Gandhi, *A Gandhi Anthology*, Ahmedabad: Jivanji Dahyabhai Desai Navajivan Press, 1952, p. 50. Available at: www.mahatma.org.in/books/ showbook.jsp?link=bg&lang=en&book=bg0013&id=1&cat=books.
8 Fischer, 1997, p. 245.
9 Gandhi in *A Gandhi Anthology*, Book 1, p. 44.
10 Gandhi in *Young India*, 8 December, 1921.
11 Gandhi in D.G. Tendulkar, *Mahatma*, 2nd edn, Ahmedabad: Navajivan Publishing House, 1960, Vol. 5, p. 265.
12 Gandhi in Prabhu and Rao (eds) *Mind of Mahatma Gandhi*, 3rd edn, Ahmedabad: Navajivan Publishing House, 1968, p. 405. Available at: www.mkgandhi. org/momgandhi/momindex.htm.
13 Gandhi in M.K. Gandhi, *The Collected Works of Mahatma Gandhi*, The Publications Division, Ministry of Information and Broadcasting Government of India, Ahmedabad: Navajivan Trust, 1960, XXV, p. 577.
14 Gandhi in Prabhu and Rao, 1968, p. 405.
15 Gandhi in *The Collected Works of Mahatma Gandhi*, XXV, p. 351.
16 Gandhi in *The Collected Works of Mahatma Gandhi*, XXVI, p. 292.
17 Fischer, 1997, pp. 310–11.
18 The five obligations or 'pillars' of Islam are as follows: swearing that there is only one God called Allah and Muhammad is his prophet (known as the *Shahadah*), praying five times a day (known as *salah*), undertaking the pilgrimage to Mecca (know as the *Hajj*), fasting during Ramadan (known as *sawm*), giving charity (known as *zakah*).
19 Gandhi's spoken and written output was enormous; it included speeches and addresses at numerous public occasions and political events, regular contributions for the weeklies *Harijan* and *Young India*, and his autobiography *The Story of My Experiments with the Truth*.
20 Gandhi in A.T. Hingorani (ed.) *Our Language Problem*, 1998, p. 2 at: www.mahatma.org.in/books/showbook.jsp?id=13&book=bg0019&link=bg&la ng=en&cat=books.
21 Gandhi in A.T. Hingorani, 1998, p. 101.
22 Gandhi in Attenborough, 1982, p. 13.

23 Gandhi in *Story of My Experiments with the Truth*, Ahmedabad: Navajivan Mudranalay, p. 229.
24 Gandhi in Fischer, 1997, p. 584.
25 Gandhi in Tendulkar, 1960, Vol. 2, p. 341.
26 Ibid., p. 6.
27 Ibid., p. 318.
28 Gandhi in Prabhu and Rao, 1968, p. 295.
29 Gandhi in *The Collected Works of Mahatma Gandhi*, XXVI, p. 273.
30 Gandhi in V.G. Desai, *Satyagraha in South Africa*, *M.K. Gandhi*, Ahmedabad: Jitendra T. Desai and Navajivan Mudranalay, 1928, p. 106.
31 Gandhi in Tendulkar, 1960, Vol. 8, p. 9.
32 Gandhi in Fischer, 1997, p. 102.
33 Gandhi in *The Collected Works of Mahatma Gandhi*, XXV, p. 558.
34 Gandhi in Tendulkar, 1960, Vol. 5, p. 83.
35 Gandhi in K. Kripalani (ed.) *All Men are Brothers: Life & Thoughts of Mahatma Gandhi as Told in His Own Words*, Ahmedabad: Navajivan Publishing House, 1960, p. 3.
36 Trial of Mahatma Gandhi, Ahmedabad, India, 18 March 1922.
37 Gandhi in *The Collected Works of Mahatma Gandhi*, XXV, p. 489.
38 Gandhi in Tendulkar, 1960, Vol. 7, p. 147.
39 Gandhi in *Young India*, 5 November 1931, p. 341.
40 Gandhi in Tendulkar, 1960, Vol. 4, p. 159.
41 Gandhi in *Young India*, 2 April 1931, p. 54.
42 Gandhi in *The Practice of Sayagraha, Selected Writings*, Ahmedabad: Navajivan Mudranalay, p. 79. (Said at a speech in Calcutta January 19, 1902.)
43 Gandhi in Kripalani, 1960, p. 164.
44 Gandhi in Attenborough, 1982, p. 75.
45 Gandhi in *Ghandi: An Autobiography or My Experiments with Truth*, Ahmedabad: Navajivan Publishing House, p. 432.
46 These were selected from *Quotes of Gandhi* by M.K. Gandhi, compiled by Shalu Bhalla and epigrams from Gandhi compiled by S.R. Tikekar at mkgandhi.org/epigrams/a.htm.
47 Gandhi in Tendulkar, 1960, Vol. 5, p. 111.
48 Ibid., p. 116.
49 Ibid., Vol. 4, p. 278.
50 Gandhi in Tendulkar, 1960, Vol. 4, p. 280.
51 Gandhi in Prabhu and Rao, 1968, p. 130.
52 Gandhi in Tendulkar, 1960, Vol. 5, p. 91.
53 Ibid., p. 243.
54 Ibid., p. 242.
55 Gandhi in *The Collected Works of Mahatma Gandhi*, XXVI, p. 374.
56 Gandhi in R.K. Prabhu (ed.) *Truth is God*, Ahmedabad: Navajivan Mudranalay, 1955, p. 39.
57 Gandhi Tendulkar, 1960, Vol. 5, p. 169.
58 Ibid., p. 135.
59 Gandhi in Prabhu and Rao, 1968, p. 113.
60 Gandhi in Tendulkar, 1960, Vol. 8, p. 140.
61 Gandhi in Tendulkar, 1960, Vol. 5, p. 80.
62 Ibid., p. 170.
63 Gandhi in R.K. Prabhu (ed.) *The Message of the Gita*, Ahmedabad: Navajivan Mudranalay, 1959, p. 14.
64 Gandhi in *The Collected Works of Mahatma Gandhi*, XIV, p. 299.
65 Gandhi in Tendulkar, 1960, Vol. 5, p. 130.
66 Gandhi in Prabhu and Rao, 1968, p. 153.

67 Cf. J. Charteris-Black, *Politicians and Rhetoric: The Persuasive Power of Metaphor*, Basingstoke and New York: Palgrave-Macmillan, 2005.
68 Gandhi in Tendulkar, 1960, Vol. 2, p. 131.
69 Gandhi in Tendulkar, 1960, Vol. 2, p. 42.
70 Gandhi in Tendulkar, 1960, Vol. 5, p. 304.
71 Gandhi in Prabhu and Rao, 1968, p. 277.
72 Gandhi in Tendulkar, 1960, Vol. 8, p. 176.
73 Gandhi in Attenborough, 1982, p. 86.
74 Gandhi, 2 December 1946 in *The Collected Works of Mahatma Gandhi*, III, pp. 86, 196.
75 These concepts were also shown to occur in the *Koran* (cf. J. Charteris-Black, *Corpus Approaches to Critical Metaphor Analysis*, Basingstoke and New York: Palgrave-Macmillan, 2004, Chapters 8–10).
76 This was based on a survey I undertook of 50 of his sayings.
77 Gandhi in Prabhu and Rao 1968, p. 108.
78 Gandhi in Tendulkar, 1960, Vol. 3, p. 128.
79 The full title is 'The grievances of the British Indians in South Africa: an appeal to the Indian Public'.
80 Gandhi in *Cape Times*, 5 July 1891.
81 Gandhi, address in Madras, 26 October 1896.
82 Gandhi in *Natal Mercury*, 5 March 1896.
83 General Smuts, October 1906.
84 Gandhi in *The Natal Advertiser*, 23 September 1893.
85 Gandhi in Kripalani, 1960, p. 20.
86 Gandhi in Tendulkar, 1960, Vol. 3, p. 182.
87 Gandhi in *The Collected Works of Mahatma Gandhi*, XXVI, p. 245.
88 Gandhi in Tendulkar, 1960, Vol. 2, p. 51.
89 Ibid., p. 230.
90 Gandhi in Kripalani, 1960, p. 159.
91 Gandhi in *Young Ind*ia, 312-12-31, 426, 427.
92 Gandhi in *Story of My Experiments with the Truth*, p. 436.
93 Fischer, 1997, p. 398.
94 Gandhi's message to Shanit Sena Dal, 5 September 1947, *Collected Works of M. Gandhi*, III, p. 156.
95 Gandhi in *Collected Works of M. Gandhi*, III, p. 12.
96 Ibid., p. 19.
97 Ibid., p. 18.
98 Ibid., p. 22.
99 Ibid., p. 29.

5 Nelson Mandela

1 The governor was named Badenhorst.
2 A. Sampson, *Mandela*, London: HarperCollins, 2000, p. 225.
3 Sampson, 2000, p. 159.
4 Sampson, 2000, p. 281.
5 Quoted in Sampson, 2000, pp. 191–2.
6 Sampson, 2000, p. 190.
7 B. Mtolo, *Umkhonto we Sizwe. The Road to the Left*, Durban: Drakensberg Press Limited, 1960, p. 40.
8 Mandela, speech 10 December 1993.
9 Mandela, speech 1 May 1997.
10 Mandela, speech 1 May 1997.
11 Mandela, speech 5 February 1999.

12 According to a communist architect Rusty Bernstein (May Day 1950) Mandela 'appeared to be heckler and disrupter-in-chief ... He stood out from the gaggle of jeering, heckling Youth Leaguers, partly by sheer physical presence but mainly by the calm authority he seemed to exercise over them', Sampson, 2000, p. 61.

13 Sampson, 2000, p. 59.

14 *Manchester Guardian*, 27–29 May 1961.

15 P.G. Northouse, *Leadership Theory & Practice* (3rd edn), London: Sage, 2004, p. 190.

16 Sampson, 2000, p. 411.

17 C. Mennell, *Memoir on Mandela*, unpublished, 1995.

18 Fatima Meer interview with Sampson, July 1996.

19 Kathrada *Star*, 17 July 1998.

20 N. Mandela, *Long Walk to Freedom*, London: Abacus, Vol. 1, 2002/2003, p. 469.

21 Mandela, 2003, Vol. 2, p. 76.

22 Mandela, 2002, p. 264.

23 Mandela, op. cit., pp. 375–6.

24 Sampson, 2000, p. 179.

25 Mandela, speech 11 February 1990.

26 Sampson, 2000, p. 407.

27 de Klerk, BBC radio interview, London, 15 September 1998.

28 Mandela, 2002, Vol. 1, p. 31.

29 Held at Durban on 22 June 1952, prior to the Defiance Campaign. Mandela, op. cit., Vol. 1, p. 184.

30 I discuss Martin Luther King's style in J. Charteris-Black, *Politicians and Rhetoric: The Persuasive Power of Metaphor*, Basingstoke: Palgrave-Macmillan, 2005, Chapter 4.

31 Mandela, 2003, Vol. 2, pp. 350–1.

32 Mandela, 2003, Vol. 2, p. 69.

33 Sampson, 2000, p. 83.

34 Sampson, 2000, p. 136.

35 See Chapter 6 for a discussion of Castro's slogans.

36 Mandela, 2002, Vol. 1, p. 236.

37 Cf. Charteris-Black, 2005; J. Charteris-Black, *Corpus Approaches to Critical Metaphor Analysis*, Basingstoke and New York: Palgrave-Macmillan, 2004.

38 Mandela, speech August 1952.

39 Mandela, speech 21 September 1953.

40 Mandela, speech 9 May 1994.

41 Mandela, speech January 1962.

42 Mandela, speech 12 September 1997.

43 Mandela, speech 20 April 1964.

44 Mandela, speech 6 February 1998.

45 Mandela, speech 5 February 1999.

46 See Charteris-Black, 2005, Chapter 2.

47 Mandela, 2003, Vol. 2, p. 272.

48 Mandela, 2003, Vol. 2, p. 233.

49 Mandela, speech 6 February 1998.

50 Sampson, 2000, p. 62.

51 Sampson, 2000, p. 275.

52 Mandela, 2002, Vol. 1, p. 335.

53 Mandela, speech 4 September 1998.

54 Jail Memoir. Unpublished memoir.

55 Mandela, speech 10 December 1993.

56 Mandela, speech 11 February 1990.

57 Charteris-Black, 2004, p. 74.
58 Mandela, speech 5 February 1999.
59 Mandela, speech 5 February 1999.
60 In Charteris-Black, 2005, I identify and analyse the use of journey metaphors by Winston Churchill, Martin Luther King, Margaret Thatcher, Bill Clinton, George W. Bush and Tony Blair.
61 Mandela, speech 27 April 1999.
62 J. Campbell, *The Hero with a Thousand Faces*, Princeton: Princeton University Press, 1949, p. 30.
63 Mandela, 2003, Vol. 2, p. 435.
64 Mandela, Jail Memoir.
65 Mandela, speech 10 December 1993.
66 Mandela, 2002, Vol. 1, pp. 385–6.
67 Mandela, 2003, Vol. 2, p. 110.
68 Mandela, speech 20 April 1964.
69 Mandela, speech 12 September 1997.
70 Mandela, speech 9 May 1994.
71 Mandela, speech 10 December 1993.
72 Mandela, speech 10 December 1993.
73 Mandela, speech 12 September 1997.
74 Mandela, speech 5 February 1999.
75 Mandela, 2003, Vol. 2, p. 437.
76 Mandela, speech 10 December 1993.
77 Mandela, 2003, Vol. 2, p. 180.
78 Mandela, 2003, Vol. 2, p. 199.
79 *Star*, 7 July 1998.
80 Mandela, speech 21 September 1953.
81 Cf. Rivonia trial transcript, Pretoria Supreme Court, 1963–1964, p. 15,791.
82 Mandela, speech January 1962.
83 Mandela, speech 10 December 1993.
84 Mandela, speech 6 February 1998.
85 Mandela, speech 12 September 1997.
86 Sampson, 2000, p. 421.

6 Fidel Castro

1 Castro, speech: 1 June 2004.
2 Castro, speech: 1 June 2004.
3 Castro, speech: September 1960.
4 T. Szulc, *Fidel: A Critical Portrait*, London: Huthinson, 1986, p. 371.
5 He spent a period of four months with Castro while he was leading the insurrection against Batista while working for Paris Match.
6 Szulc, 1980, p. 46.
7 L. Coltman, *The Real Fidel Castro*, New Haven and London: Yale University Press, 2003, p. 116.
8 R.E. Quirk, *Fidel Castro*, New York and London: WW Norton & Co., 1993, p. 1.
9 Castro, speech: 6 November 1938.
10 Castro, speech: 26 July 1967.
11 Castro, speech: 20 January 1981.
12 Castro, speech: 20 May 1960.
13 The aim of this was to bring down the dictator of Dominican Republic – General Rafael Trujillo.
14 Coltman, 2003, p. 35.
15 Coltman, 2003, p. 159.

16 For the purposes of researching Castro's leadership I have made use of a wide range of sources including biographies; and a web site 'Castro speech Data Base': www1.lanic.utexas.edu/la/cb/cuba/castro.html. This is a database of records in the public domain containing the full text of English translations of Castro's speeches, interviews, and press conferences. It is based on the records of a US government agency, the Foreign Broadcast Information Service (FBIS), that is a responsible for monitoring broadcast and print media in countries throughout the world. It does not claim to be a complete record of all his spoken output but is certainly a very considerable resource.
17 Castro, speech: 2 September 1960.
18 Castro, speech: 24 October 1965.
19 Castro, speech: 23 May 1963.
20 Castro, speech: 20 May 1961.
21 In Coltman, 2003, p. 295.
22 In Coltman, 2003, p. 308.
23 Castro, speech: 30 August 1960.
24 Castro, speech: 23 April 1961.
25 Castro, speech: 16 January 1983.
26 Castro, speech: 20 May 1970.
27 Castro, speech: 21 June 1975.
28 Castro, speech: 26 September 1960.
29 Castro, speech: 2 November 1991.
30 Castro, speech: 26 March 1995.
31 Castro, speech: September 1960.
32 Castro, speech: 2 December 1978.
33 Castro, speech: 16 May 1961.
34 Castro, speech: 5 January 1961.
35 Castro, speech: 27 May 1991.
36 Castro, speech: 9 May 1994.
37 Castro, speech: 22 June 1994.
38 Castro, speech: 28 November 1959.
39 N. Chomsky, *Hegemony or Survival: America's Quest for Global Dominance*, London: Penguin, 2004, p. 206.
40 Castro, speech: 9 January 1959.
41 Castro, speech: 9 January 1959.
42 Castro, speech: 1 May 2004.
43 Castro, speech: September 1960.
44 Castro, speech: 5 March 1960.
45 Castro, speech: 2 January 1984.
46 Castro, speech: 28 November 1959.
47 *Moscow Tass*, 9 December 1984.
48 In Quirk, 1993, p. 132.
49 Ibid., p. 134.
50 Quirk, 1993, p. 159.
51 Coltman, 2003, pp. 184–5.
52 However a search of the Castro database showed no reference at all to Chomsky.

7 Ayatollah Khomeini and divine leadership

1 V. Martin, *Creating an Islamic State: Khomeini and the Making of a New Iran*, London and New York: IB Tauras, 2003, p. 59.
2 www.islamfortoday.com/shia.htm.
3 D. Brumberg, *Reinventing Khomeini*, Chicago and London: University of Chicago Press, 2001, p. 49.

4 Ibid., p. 96.
5 A. Nafisi, *Reading Lolita in Tehran*, London and New York: 4th Estate, 2004, p. 159.
6 A well known Shia saying attributed to Hossein's descendent Imam Ja'far ibn Muhammad as-Sadiq.
7 Khomeini, *Islam & Revolution* (translated and annotated by Hamid Algar), Berkeley: Mizan Press, 1981, p. 205.
8 B. Moin, *Khomeini: Life of the Ayatollah*, London and New York: I.B. Tauris, 1999, p. 133.
9 Ibid., p. 119.
10 Nafisi, 2004, p. 200.
11 Nafisi, 2004, pp. 167–8.
12 On November 1925 Ataturk was responsible for a new 'hat' Law that made wearing the fez, a criminal offence and European hats obligatory. (His opponents claim that these new hats were deliberately designed so that heads would not touch the ground during prayers). Efforts to end the wearing of the turban had raised similar issues regarding the symbolic significance of clothing in the nineteenth century.
13 Khomeini (January 1978): www.irib.ir/worldservice/imam/speech/Default.htm.
14 Ibid.
15 Khomeini, quoted in Moin, 1999, p. 135.
16 Nafisi, 2004, p. 244.
17 Moin, 1999, pp. 130–1.
18 Martin, 2003, p. 137.
19 Moin, 1999, p. 199.
20 Moi, 1999, p. 202.
21 T. Wells, *44 Days: The Hostages Remember*, San Diego: Harcourt Brace Jovanovich, 1985, pp. 123–4.
22 Khomeini, 1981, p. 38.
23 R. Wright, *In the Name of God: The Khomeini Decade*, London: Bloomsbury, 1990, p. 47.
24 Khomeini, 1981, p. 76.
25 This is the plural form of *faqih* that is usually translated as 'jurist'.
26 Khomeini, 1981, p. 112.
27 Martin, 2003, p. 111.
28 Ibid., p. 113.
29 S.H. Ruhani, *Basari va tahlili az nahzat-i Imam Khumaini*, Vol. 1, Tehran, 1356–1977, p. 26.
30 Moin, 1999, p. 93.
31 Nafisi, 2004, p. 97.
32 Khomeini, speech, January 1978.
33 Khomeini, speech, 1941.
34 Khomeini, speech 21 October 1978.
35 Khomeini, speech, 15 January 1979.
36 Khomeini, speech, 7 January 1979.
37 Ibid.
38 Ibid.
39 Ibid.
40 G. Lakoff and M. Turner, *More Than Cool Reason: a Field Guide to Poetic Metaphor*, Chicago and London: University of Chicago Press, 1989.
41 Khomeini, speech, January 1978.
42 Khomeini, speech, 9 October 1978.
43 Khomeini, speech, 3 June 1963.
44 Khomeini, speech, 26 January 1978.

45 Khomeini, speech, 25 November 1979.
46 J. Charteris-Black, *Corpus Approaches to Critical Metaphor Analysis*, Basingstoke and New York: Palgrave-Macmillan, 2004, p. 231.
47 The Koran, *The Dinner Table* (5.16): www.hti.umich.edu/k/koran/simple.html.
48 Khomeini, speech, 7 January 1979.
49 Khomeini, speech, 18 February 1978.
50 Khomeini, 1983, pp. 137–8.
51 Khomeini, 1983, p. 60.
52 Martin, 2002, pp. 152–3.
53 Khomeini, 1983, p. 117.
54 Ibid., p. 146.
55 Ibid., p. 59.
56 Ibid., p. 62.
57 L.W.L. Gardner and B.J. Avolio, 'The charismatic relationship: a dramaturgical perspective', *Academy of Management Review*, 23, 1.
58 Khomeini, 1983, p. 92.
59 Ibid., p. 35.
60 Ibid., pp. 139–40.
61 Ibid., p. 136.
62 Ibid., p. 142.
63 Ibid., p. 145.
64 Ibid., p. 147.
65 Ibid., p. 149.
66 Khomeini, speech, 17 February 1978.
67 Moin, 1999, p. 295.
68 Wright, 1990, p. 56.
69 Wright, 1990, p. 59.
70 Nafisi, 2004, p. 246.

8 Mahathir Muhammad

1 M.J. Gannon, *Understanding Global Cultures: Metaphorical Journeys Across 23 Nations*, 2nd edn, Thousand Oaks, London, New Delhi: Sage, 1994, p. 258.
2 Jayasankaran, 'Mahathir: the man and the PM', *Far Eastern Economic Review Reference*, 159, 14, p. 18.
3 M. Mahathir, *The Malay Dilemma*, Singapore: Times Books International, 1970, p. 116.
4 Khoo Boo Teik, *Paradoxes of Mahathirism: An Intellectual Biography of Mahathir Mohame*, Oxford: Oxford University Press, 1995, p. 7.
5 Bruno Manser is a Swiss Human Rights Activist who has defended the right of the indigenous Penan people against the destruction of their native habitat in the tropical hardwood forests in east Malaysia. He was declared an 'enemy of the state' by Sarawak's Chief Minister Abdul Taib Mahmud.
6 UMNO is the United Malays National Organization.
7 R. Adshead, *Mahathir of Malaysia*, London: Hibiscus, 1989, p. 65.
8 Khoo Book Teik, 1995, p. 272.
9 Supriya Singh, 'The man behind the politician', *New Straits Times*, 14 April 1982.
10 Mahathir quoted in ibid.
11 Malaysia was invited to be host of 1989 CHGM; to be Asia's representative to UN Security Council in 1988 and Chairman of G-77 in 1989.
12 Cf. J. Charteris-Black, *Politicians and Rhetoric: The Persuasive Power of Metaphor*, Basingstoke and New York: Palgrave-Macmillan, 2004, Chapter 4.
13 Hashim Makaruddin (ed.) *Globalisation and the New Realities: Selected Speeches of*

Dr Mahathir Mohamad Prime Minister of Malaysia, Subang Jaya: Pelanduk Publications, 2000, p. 56.
14 Ibid., p. 177.
15 M. Edelman in M.L. Geiss, *The Language of Politics*, New York: Springer Verlag, 1987.
16 Adshead, 1989, p. 53.
17 Khoo, 1995, sees *The Malay Dilemma* as structured according to 'the methodical way that doctors solve medical problems'. It begins with a pathologist's report on 'what went wrong' 'the Government was no longer able to feel the pulse of the people' (15) and ends with a therapeutic diagnosis of 'the Malay value system and code of ethics' (172).
18 His views on ethnic factors and social and economic progress were shared by Lee Kuan Yew (cf. pp. 000).
19 Mahathir, 1970, p. 56.
20 Ibid., pp. 56–7.
21 Ibid., pp. 60–1.
22 R. Scollon and W. Scollon, *Intercultural Communication*, Oxford: Blackwell, 1995, p. 134.
23 Mahathir, 1970, p. 61.
24 Ibid., p. 94.
25 Ibid., p. 116.
26 Ibid., p. 120.
27 Ibid., p. 103.
28 Ibid., p. 147.
29 Mahathir, speech, 14 July 1967.
30 Musa Hitam, 'Malaysia: the spirit of '46 rises again', *Correspondent*, November 1987, p. 19.
31 Hashim Makaruddin, 2000, p. 16.
32 Ibid., p. 105.
33 Ibid., p. 77.
34 Ibid., p. 116.
35 Mahathir, 1970, p. 160.
36 Ibid., p. 171.
37 Ibid., p. 172.
38 Ibid., p. 172.
39 Ibid., p. 172.
40 Hashim Makaruddin, 2000, pp. 36–7.
41 Mahathir, 1970, p. 173.
42 Ibid., p. 103.
43 Ibid., p. 162.
44 Ibid., p. 158.
45 Ibid., p. 163.
46 Ibid., p. 167.
47 Ibid., p. 171.
48 Ibid., p. 173.
49 M. Mahathir, *The Challenge*, Kuala Lumpur: Pelanduk Publications, 1986, p. 103.
50 Ibid., p. 91.
51 Ibid., p. 47.
52 Khoo Boo Teik, 1995, p. 68.
53 Ibid., p. 182.
54 S.H. Alatas, *The Myth of the Lazy Native*, London: Frank Cass, 1977.
55 Mahathir, speech 'Vision 2020: the way forward' at the Vision 2020 National Congress, Pealing Jaya, April 1997.

56 Hashim Makaruddin, 2000, p. 27.
57 Ibid., p. 44.
58 Ibid., p. 45.
59 Mahathir, 1970, p. 126.
60 Previously they had formally recognized the legal authority of the Malay sultans in the states of the Malay Peninsula.
61 Ibid., p. 136.
62 Ibid., p. 132.
63 Ibid., p. 140.
64 Ibid., p. 141.
65 Ibid., p. 147.
66 *ra'ayat* may be translated as 'subjects'.
67 Mahathir, 1970, p. 170.
68 The first Prime Minister of Malaysia was Abdul Rahman, affectionately known as 'the Tunku' because he was a prince of the Kedah royal family.
69 Khoo Boo Teik, 1995, p. 23.
70 J. Minchin, *No Man Is an Island: A Study of Singapore's Lee Kuan Yew*, Sydney: Allen & Unwin, 1986, p. 72.
71 Mahathir, 1970, p. 10.
72 Mahathir, speech at 39th session of the UN General Assembly.
73 Khoo Boo Teik, 1995, p. 301.
74 *Hari Raya* means literally 'Great Day' and occurs at end of the Islamic month of *Ramadan* that is known as *'Puasa'* in Malaysia.
75 Ibid., p. 302.
76 R.M. Stogdill, 'Personal factors associated with leadership: A survey of the literature', *Journal of Psychology*, 25, 1948, pp. 35–71.
77 Karim Raslan, Asiaweek, www.asiaweek.com/.../0,8782,174684,00.html.
78 This is a translation of *'kepimpinan melalui teladan'*.
79 Mahathir 'Whither Malaysia', Paper presented at the Keio International Symposium on Asia and Japan, Tokyo, 7–11 November 1983 quoted in Khoo Boo Teik, 1995, p. 200.
80 Rehman Rashid, 'Why I took to Politics', *New Straits Times*, 5 July 1986.
81 He was not the originator of the concept of 'Melayu Baru', 'the New Malay', but a strong proponent.
82 A full list of such paradoxes is given in Khoo Boo Teik, 1995, pp. 9–10.

9 Lee Kuan Yew

1 Lee Kuan Yew attended Raffles College and went on to Cambridge where he was awarded a double first in law.
2 Lee Kuan Yew, *The Singapore Story: Memoirs of Lee Kuan Yew*, Singapore: Times Editions, 1998, p. 211.
3 Legislative Assembly 27 April 1957 (column 1757), quoted in M.D. Barr, *Lee Kuan Yew: The Beliefs Behind the Man*, Richmond: Curzon Press, 2000, p. 168.
4 This was the name given to the Chinese who were loyal to British government.
5 Lee Kuan Yew, 1998, p. 74.
6 Ibid.
7 Ibid., pp. 538–9.
8 T.J.S. George, *Lee Kuan Yew's Singapore*, London: Andre Deutsch, 1973, p. 113.
9 Lee Kuan Yew interview with Cai Xi Mei of Xinhua News Agency, 25 August 1992 in Lee, Senior Minister's Speeches, Press Conferences, Interviews, Statements etc. Singapore: Prime Minister's Office, 1991–1995.
10 Lee Kuan Yew, 1998, p. 185.
11 Chewing gum was banned in 1992.

12 Barr, 2000, p. 83.
13 Lee Kuan Yew, 1998, p. 538.
14 Speech at multi-party symposium, Kuala Lumpur 28 August 1964.
15 Lee Kuan Yew, 1998, p. 487.
16 Ibid., p. 488.
17 George, 1973, p. 9.
18 Lee Kuan Yew, 1998, p. 302.
19 Ibid., p. 488.
20 Ibid., p. 486.
21 Broadcast 9 August 1965.
22 George, 1973.
23 Lee Kuan Yew, 1998, p. 322.
24 Ibid., pp. 278–9.
25 Ibid., p. 343.
26 Barr, 2000, p. 146.
27 Ibid., p. 61.
28 Lee's address to the Singapore Union of Journalists, 16 August 1959 in Lee Prime Minister's Speeches etc.
29 Lee Kuan Yew, 1998, p. 186.
30 Question and answer session after address to the Political Association of the University of Singapore, 23 December 1977, reported in the *Business Times* (Singapore), 31 December 1977.
31 Lee Kuan Yew, 1998, p. 300.
32 Ibid., pp. 354–5.
33 Ibid., p. 497.
34 Barr, 2000, Interview with Maurice Baker 25 October 1996.
35 Lee Kuan Yew, 1998, p. 615.
36 Lee's address at the opening of the seminar on 'Education and Nation Building', 27 December 1966. In Loy Teck Juan, Seng Han Tong, Pang Cheng Lian (eds) *Lee Kuan Yew and the Chinese Community in Singapore*, Singapore Chinese Chamber of Commerce and Industry and Singapore Federation of Chinese Clan Associations, 1991, p. 29.
37 George, 1973, p. 170.
38 'Stars' web site. National Archives of Singapore: http://stars.nhb.gov.sg/public/index.html.
39 Prime Minister's National Day Rally speech, 15 August 1993.
40 Party conference, 15 November 1982.
41 Ibid.
42 Interview, 25 November 1981.
43 J. Charteris-Black, *Corpus Approaches to Critical Metaphor Analysis*, Basingstoke and New York: Palgrave-Macmillan, 2004, p. 245, identifies LIFE IS A STRUGGLE FOR SURVIVAL as a general concept key for political discourse.
44 Speech in parliament, 23 February 1977.
45 Speech at the Commonwealth heads of government meeting, London, 8 June 1977.
46 Speech at the joint meeting of the United States congress, 9 October 1985.
47 Interview with Alan Ashbolt in ABC studios, Canberra, 24 March 1965. In Lee Prime Minister's Speeches etc. Quoted in Barr, 2000, p. 194.
48 Prime Minister's National Day Rally speech, 18 August 1996.
49 Speech at Queenstown Community Centre, 10 August 1966.
50 Speech at the Inaugural dinner, University of Singapore Business Administration Society at the Mandarin Room, 27 August 1966.
51 Speech at the annual dinner of the Singapore Employers' Federation, held at the Conference Hall, Trade Union House, 31 May 1967.

52 Prime Minister's National Day Rally speech, 15 August 1993.
53 Speech at NYUC seminar on 'progress into the 80's' held on 6 November 1979.
54 Terry McCarthy, *Time Magazine 100*, 23–30 August 1999, Vol. 154.
55 The President's speech to Parliament, January 1989 cited in Government of Singapore Shared Values: White Paper 1991, Singapore: Singapore National Printers, 1001, p. 1.
56 Conference on 'Global strategies: the Singapore partnership', Raffles City convention center, 24 October 1988.
57 Chua Beng Huat, *Communitarian Ideology and Democracy in Singapore*, London and New York: Routledge, 1955, pp. 193–4.
58 M.D. Barr, 'Lee Kuan Yew: Race, Culture and Genes', *Journal of Contemporary Asia*, 29, 2, 1999, p. 60.
59 Lee to Malaysian student, London, 10 September 1964, in Lee, *One Hundred Years of Socialism*, Singapore: Ministry of Culture, 1965, pp. 37–8.
60 Lee Kuan Yew, 1998, p. 208.
61 The use of disease metaphors to describe communism has been traced back to the influence of George Kennan.
62 Speech at the Victoria Memorial Hall, 22 September 1963, after announcement of the general election results.
63 For a discussion of American Cold War metaphors for communism see K.L. Shimko, 'The Power of Metaphors and the Metaphors of Power'. In F.A. Beer and C. De Landtsheer, *Metaphorical World Politics*, East Lansing: Michigan State University, 2004.
64 Extempore remark at the Commonwealth head of government meeting, Melbourne, Australia, 1 October 1981.
65 Debate on East–West relations at the Socialist International Conference Council on 3 September 1964, Brussels.
66 Lee's press conference at the broadcasting house, Singapore, at 12 p.m. Monday, 9 August 1965.
67 Speech to the Cantonese and other civic organizations, 14 March 1964.
68 L. Wee, 'Divorce before marriage in the Singapore-Malaysia relationship: the Invariance Principle at work', *Discourse & Society*, 12, 4, 2001, pp. 535–49.
69 Under Malay–Muslim custom, a husband, but not the wife, can declare 'Talak' ('I divorce thee') three times and the woman is divorced.
70 Lee Kuan Yew, 1998, p. 192.
71 Ibid., p. 193.
72 Ibid., p. 286.
73 J.R. Meindl, 'On leadership: an alternative to the conventional wisdom'. In B.M. Staw and L.L. Cummings (eds) *Research in Organizational Behavior*, Vol. 12, Greenwich: JAI, 1990, pp. 159–203.
74 Lee Kuan Yew, 1998, p. 303.
75 This has continued to be performed in Chinese communities in southeast Asia such as Penang for a long time after the Cultural Revolution terminated its celebration in China.
76 Lee Kuan Yew, 1998, p. 398.
77 Ibid., p. 492.
78 Ibid., p. 496.
79 Prime Minister's National Day Rally speech, 18 August 1996.

10 The design of leadership style

1 E. Goffman, *The Presentation of Self in Everyday Life*, London: Allen House, 1969, p. 2.
2 Goffman, 1969, p. 220.

3 S. Scollon and W. Scollon, *Discourse in Place: Language in the Material World*, London and New York: Routledge, 2003, p. 56.
4 Goffman, 1969, p. 74.
5 B.M. Bass, *Bass and Stogdill's Handbook of Leadership: A Survey of Theory and Research*, New York: Free Press, 1990, p. 192 (citing Downton 1973).
6 R. Darnton, *'Peasant tell tales', in the Great Cat Massacre*, London: Penguin, 1985, p. 26. Quoted in R. Burns, *Erving Goffman*, London and New York: Routledge, 1982, p. 124.
7 R. Finnegan, *Communicating: The Multiple Modes of Human Interconnection*, London and New York: Routledge, 2002, p. 226.
8 Goffman, 1969, p. 221.
9 Bass, 1990, p. 197.
10 Ibid., p. 91.
11 Goffman, 1969, p. 222.

Bibliography

Adshead, R., *Mahathir of Malaysia*, London: Hibiscus, 1989.

Alatas, S.H., *The Myth of the Lazy Native*, London: Frank Cass, 1977.

Applbaum, R.L., Anatol, K., Hays, E.R., Jenson, O.O., Porter, R.E. and Mandel, J.E., *Fundamental Concepts in Human Communication*, New York: Canfield Press, 1973.

Atkinson, J.M., *Our Masters' Voices: The Language and Body Language of Politics*, London: Methuen, 1984.

Attenborough, R., *The Words of Gandhi*, New York: Newmarket Press, 1982.

Ball, M.A., 'Political language and the search for an honourable peace: Presidents Kennedy and Johnson, their advisers, and Vietnam decision making'. In C. De Landtsheer and O. Feldman (eds) *Beyond Public Speech and Symbols: Explorations in the Rhetoric of Politicians and the Media*, Westport and London: Praeger, 2000.

Barr, M.D., *Lee Kuan Yew: The Beliefs Behind the Man*, Richmond: Curzon Press, 2000.

Barr, M.D., 'Lee Kuan Yew: race, culture and genes', *Journal of Contemporary Asia*, 1999, 29, 2.

Bass, B.M., *Leadership and Performance Expectations*, London and New York: The Free Press, 1985.

Bass, B.M., *Bass and Stogdill's Handbook of Leadership: A Survey of Theory and Research*, New York: Free Press, 1990.

Bennis, W., 'Leadership transforms vision into action', *Industry Week*, 31 May 1982, pp. 54–6.

Bennis, W. and Nanus, B., *Leaders: The Strategies for Taking Charge*, New York: Harper Row, 1985.

Bormann, E.G., *Communication Theory*, New York: Holt, Rinehart and Winston, 1980.

Brumberg, D., *Reinventing Khomeini*, Chicago and London: University of Chicago Press, 2001.

Bryman, A., *Charisma & Leadership in Organizations*, London: Sage, 1992.

Bull, P., 'New Labour, new rhetoric? An analysis of the rhetoric of Tony Blair'. In C. De Landtsheer and O. Feldman (eds) *Beyond Public Speech and Symbols: Explorations in the Rhetoric of Politicians and the Media*, Westport and London: Praeger, 2000.

Burns, J.M., *Leadership*, New York: Harper Row, 1978.

Campbell, J., *The Hero with a Thousand Faces*, Princeton: Princeton University Press, 1949.

Charteris-Black, J., *Politicians and Rhetoric: The Persuasive Power of Metaphor*, Basingstoke and New York: Palgrave-Macmillan, 2005.

Charteris-Black, J., *Corpus Approaches to Critical Metaphor Analysis*, Basingstoke and New York: Palgrave-Macmillan, 2004.

Charteris-Black, J. and Musolff, A., 'Battered hero or innocent victim? A comparative study of metaphor in describing Euro trading in British and German financial reporting', *English for Specific Purposes*, 2003, 22: pp. 153–76.

Chilton, P., *Analysing Political Discourse: Theory & Practice*, New York and London: Routledge, 2004.

Chomsky, N., *Hegemony or Survival: America's Quest for Global Dominance*, London: Penguin, 2004.

Chua Beng Huat, *Communitarian Ideology and Democracy in Singapore*, London and New York: Routledge, 1955.

Coltman, L., *The Real Fidel Castro*, New Haven and London: Yale University Press, 2003.

Conger, J.A., 'Charismatic and transformational leadership in organizations: an insider's perspective on these developing streams of research', *The Leadership Quarterly*, 1999, 10, 2: pp. 145–79.

Conger, J.A. and Kanungo, R.N., 'Toward a behavioural theory of charismatic leadership in organizational settings', *Academy of Management*, 1987, 12, pp. 637–47.

Cronin, T.E., 'Thinking and learning about leadership'. In W.E. Rosenbach and R.L. Taylor, *Contemporary Issues in Leadership*, Boulder, San Francisco and London: Westview Press, 1989, pp. 45–64.

Darnton, R., *"Peasants tell tales" in the Great Cat Massacre*, London: Penguin, 1985.

De Klerk, F.W., *The Last Trek: A New Beginning – The Autobiography*, London: Macmillan, 1998.

De Landtsheer, C. and Feldman, O. (eds) *Beyond Public Speech and Symbols: Explorations in the Rhetoric of Politicians and the Media*, Westport and London: Praeger, 2000.

Desai, G.V., *Satyagraha in South Africa, M.K. Gandhi*, Ahmedabad: Jitendra T. Desai & Navajivan Mudranalaya, 1928.

Downton, J.V., *Rebel Leadership: Commitment and Charisma in the Revolutionary Process*, New York: Free Press, 1973.

Erikson, E., *Gandhi's Truth*, New York: Norton, 1969.

Finnegan, R., *Communicating: the Multiple Modes of Human Interconnection*, London and New York: Routledge, 2002.

Fischer, L., *The Life of Mahatma Gandhi*, London: HarperCollins, 1997.

Flood, C.G., *Political Myth: a Theoretical Introduction*, New York and London: Garland, 1996.

Freud, S., 'Mass psychology and analysis of the "I"'. In *Mass Psychology & Other Writings*, London, Penguin, 2004.

Gandhi, M.K., *A Gandhi Anthology*, Ahmedabad: Jivanji Dahyabhai Desai Navajivan Press, 1952.

Gandhi, M.K., *The Collected Works of Mahatma Gandhi*, The Publications Division, Ministry of Information and Broadcasting Government of India, Ahmedabad: Navajivan Trust, 1960.

Gandhi, M.K., *Ghandi: An Autobiography or My Experiments with Truth*, Ahmebad: Navajivan Publishing House, 1927.

Gannon, M.J., *Understanding Global Cultures: Metaphorical Journeys Across 23 Nations*, 2nd edn, Thousand Oaks, London and New Delhi: Sage, 1994.

Gardner, William L. and Avolio, Bruce J., 'The charismatic relationship: a dramaturgical perspective', *Academy of Management Review*, 1998, 23, 1.

Gardner, J.W., 'The tasks of leadership'. In W.E. Rosenbach and R.L. Taylor, *Contemporary Issues in Leadership*, Boulder, San Francisco and London: Westview Press, 1989, pp. 24–33.

Geertz, C., *The Interpretation of Cultures*, London: Hutchinson, 1975.

Geiss, M.L., *The Language of Politics*, New York: Springer Verlag, 1987.

George, T.J.S., *Lee Kuan Yew's Singapore*, London: Andre Deutsch, 1973.

Goffman, E., *The Presentation of Self in Everyday Life*, London: Allen House, 1969.

Handy, C., 'The language of leadership'. In W.E. Rosenbach and R.L. Taylor, *Contemporary Issues in Leadership*, Boulder, San Francisco and London: Westview Press, 1989, pp. 235–41.

Hariman, R., *Political Style*, Chicago: University of Chicago Press, 1995.

Hashim Makaruddin (ed.) *Globalisation and the New Realities: Selected Speeches of Dr Mahathir Mohamad Prime Minister of Malaysia*, Subang Jaya: Pelanduk Publications, 2000.

Hingorani, A.T. (ed.) *Gandhi for the 21st Century, 13. Our Language Problem by M.K. Gandhi*, 1998.

House, R.J., 'Theory of charismatic leadership'. In J.G. Hunt and L.L. Larson (eds) *Leadership: The Cutting Edge*, Carbondale: Southern Illinois University Press, 1977, pp. 189–207.

House, R.J. and Singh, J.V., 'Organizational behavior. Some new directions for I/O psychology', *Annual Review of Psychology*, 1987, 38, pp. 669–718.

Jayasankaran, *Mahathir: the Man and the PM*.

Johnson, M., *The Body in the Mind*, Chicago: University of Chicago Press, 1987.

Jones, N., *Soundbites and Spin Doctors: How Politicians Manipulate the Media – and Visa Versa*, Guernsey: Indigo, 1996.

Jung, C., *Man and His Symbols*, London: Pan Books, 1964.

Khomeini, R., (translated and annotated by Hamid Algar) *Islam & Revolution*, Berkeley: Mizan Press, 1981.

Khoo Boo Teik, *Paradoxes of Mahathirism: An Intellectual Biography of Mahathir Muhammad*, Oxford: Oxford University Press, 1995.

Kress, G. and Van Leeuwen, T., *Multimodal Discourse*, London: Arnold, 2001.

Kripalani, K. (ed.) *All Men are Brothers: Life & Thoughts of Mahatma Gandhi as Told in His Own Words*, Ahmedabad: Navajivan Publishing House, 1960.

Kuhnert, K.W. and Lewis, P., *Transactional & Transformational Leadership: A Constructive/Developmental Analysis*. In W.E. Rosenbach and R.L. Taylor, *Contemporary Issues in Leadership*, Boulder, San Francisco and London: Westview Press, 1989, pp. 192–205.

Lakoff, G., *Women, Fire and Dangerous Things: What Categories Reveal About the Mind*, Chicago and London: University of Chicago Press, 1987.

Lakoff, G., 'The contemporary theory of metaphor'. In A. Ortony (ed.) *Metaphor and Thought*, 2nd edition, Cambridge: Cambridge University Press, 1993, pp. 202–51.

Lakoff, G., *Moral Politics: How Liberals and Conservatives Think*, 2nd edition, Chicago and London: University of Chicago Press, 2002.

Lakoff, G. and Johnson, M., *Metaphors We Live By*, Chicago: University of Chicago Press, 1980.

Lakoff, G. and Johnson, M., *Philosophy in the Flesh: Embodied Mind and its Challenge to Western Thought*, New York: Basic Books, 1999.

Lakoff, G. and Turner, M., *More Than Cool Reason: a Field Guide to Poetic Metaphor*, Chicago and London: University of Chicago Press, 1989.

Lee Kuan Yew, *One Hundred Years of Socialism*, Singapore: Ministry of Culture, 1965.

Lee Kuan Yew, *The Singapore Story: Memoirs of Lee Kuan Yew*, Singapore: Times Editions, 1998.

Mahathir, M., *The Malay Dilemma*, Singapore and Kuala Lumpur: Times Books International, 1970.

Mahathir, M., *The Challenge*, Kuala Lumpur: Pelanduk Publications, 1986.

Mandela, N., *Long Walk to Freedom*, London: Abacus. Vols 1 and 2, 2002/2003.

Martin, V., *Creating an Islamic State: Khomeini and the Making of a New Iran*, London and New York: IB Tauras, 2003.

Maslow, A., *Motivation and Personality*, New York: Harper & Row, 1954.

Mauss, M., 'Une categories de l'esprit humaine', *Journal of the Royal Anthropological Institute*, 1938, p.67.

Meindl, J.R., 'On leadership: an alternative to the conventional wisdom'. In B.M. Staw and L.L. Cummings (eds) *Research in Organizational Behaviour*, 1990, 12, pp. 159–203.

Mennell, J. and Gibson, A., *Mandela* (film), 1995.

Miller, K.D., *Voice of Deliverance: the Language of Martin Luther King Jr. and its Source*, New York: Free Press, 1992.

Milne, R.S., and Mauzy, D.K., *Malaysian Politics Under Mahathir*, London and New York: Routledge, 1999.

Milton, G., *White Gold: The Extraordinary Story of Thomas Pellow*, London: Hodder & Stoughton, 2004.

Minchin, J., *No Man Is an Island: A Study of Singapore's Lee Kuan Yew*, Sydney: Allen & Unwin, 1986.

Mitchell, T.L., 'Print media coverage of the Murrah building bombing'. In C. De Landtsheer and O. Feldman (eds) *Beyond Public Speech and Symbols: Explorations in the Rhetoric of Politicians and the Media*, Westport and London: Praeger, 2000.

Moin, B., *Khomeini: Life of the Ayatollah*, London and New York: I.B. Tauris, 1999.

Mtolo, B., *The Road to the Left*, Durban: Drakensberg: Press, 1966.

Musa Hitam, 'Malaysia: the spirit of '46 rises again', *Correspondent*, November 1987.

Musolff, A., *Metaphor and Political Discourse: Analogical Reasoning in Debates about Europe*, Basingstoke: Palgrave-Macmillan, 2004.

Nafisi, A., *Reading Lolita in Tehran*, London and New York: 4th Estate, 2004.

Northouse, P.G., *Leadership Theory & Practice*, 3rd edition, London: Sage, 2004.

Prabhu, R.K. (ed.) *Truth is God*, Ahmedabad: Navajivan Publishing House, 1955.

Prabhu, R.K. (ed.) *The Message of God*, Ahmedabad: Navajivan Publishing House, 1959.

Prabhu, R.K. and Rao, U.R. (eds) *Mind of Mahatma Gandhi*, 3rd edition, Ahmedabad: Navajivan Publishing House, 1968.

Quirk, R.E., *Fidel Castro*, New York and London: W.W. Norton & Co, 1993.

Rosenbach, W.E. and Taylor, R.L., *Contemporary Issues in Leadership*, Boulder, San Francisco and London: Westview Press, 1989.

Ruhani, S.H., *Basari va tahlili az nahzat-i Imam Khumaini*, Vol. 1, Tehran, 1356–977.

Sampson, A., *Mandela*, London: HarperCollins, 2000.

Schlenker, B.W.M., 'The charismatic relationship: a dramaturgical perspective'. In

W.L. Gardner and B.J. Avolio, *Academy of Management Review*, Jan 1998, Vol. 23, Issue 1.

Schnell, F., Terkildsen, N. and Callagan, K., 'Symbolism and social movements: how US political debates are shaped and citizens' attitudes influenced by symbolic communiques'. In C. De Landtsheer and O. Feldman (eds) *Beyond Public Speech and Symbols: Explorations in the Rhetoric of Politicians and the Media*, Westport and London: Praeger, 2000.

Scollon, R. and Scollon, W., *Intercultural Communication*, Oxford: Blackwell, 1995.

Scollon, S. and Scollon, W., *Discourse in Place: Language in the Material World*, London and New York: Routledge, 2003.

Shimko, K.L., 'The power of metaphors and the metaphors of power'. In F.A. Beer and C. De Landtsheer, *Metaphorical World Politics*, East Lansing: Michigan State University, 2004.

Stein, R.T. and Heller, T., 'An empirical analysis of the correlations between leadership status and participation rates reported in the literature', *Journal of Personality and Social Psychology*, 1979, 37, pp. 1993–2002.

Stogdill, R.M., 'Personal factors associated with leadership: A survey of the literature', *Journal of Psychology*, 1948, 25: pp. 35–71.

Stogdill, R.M. and R. Ashby (eds) *The Process of Model-Building in the Behavioural Sciences*, Ohio: Ohio State University Press, 1970.

Stohl, C., 'The role of memorable messages in the process of organizational socialization', *Communication Quarterly*, 1986, 34, pp. 231–49.

Szulc, T., *Fidel: A Critical Portrait*, London: Hutchinson, 1986.

Taran, S., 'Mythical thinking, Aristotelian logic, and metaphors in the parliament of Ukraine'. In C. De Landtsheer and O. Feldman (eds) *Beyond Public Speech and Symbols: Explorations in the Rhetoric of Politicians and the Media*, Westport and London: Praeger, 2000.

Tendulkar, D.G., *Mahatma*, 2nd edition, Ahmedaba: Navajivan Publishing House, 1960.

Tosi, H.L., Rizzo, J.R. and Carroll, S.J., *Managing Organizational Behaviour*, New York: Harper Row, 1990.

Weber, M., *The Sociology of Religion*, Beacon: Beacon Press, 1922.

Weber, M., *The Theory of Social and Economic Organization*, T. Parson (trans), New York: Free Press, 1924/1947.

Weber, M., *The Sociology of Charismatic Authority*. In H.H. Mills and C.W. Mills (eds and Trans) *From Max Weber: Essays in Sociology*, New York: Oxford University Press, 1946.

Wee, L., 'Divorce before marriage in the Singapore-Malaysia relationship: the Invariance Principle at work', *Discourse & Society*, 2001, 12, 4, pp. 535–49.

Wells, T., *44 Days: The Hostages Remember*, San Diego: Harcourt Brace Jovanovich, 1985.

Wolpert, S., *Gandhi's Passion: The Life and Legacy of Mahatma Gandhi*, Oxford: Oxford University Press, 2001.

Wright, R., *In the Name of God: The Khomeini Decade*, London: Bloomsbury, 1990.

Zaleznik, A., 'Charismatic and consensus leaders: a psychological comparison'. In W.E. Rosenbach and R.L. Taylor, *Contemporary Issues in Leadership*, Boulder, San Francisco and London: Westview Press, 1989, pp. 95–110.

Zhisui Li, *The Private Life of Chairman Mao: The Memoirs of Mao's Personal Physician*, London: Arrow Books, 1996.

Reference work

Hoad, T.F. (ed.) *Oxford Concise Dictionary of English Etymology*, Oxford: Oxford University Press, 1986.

Web sources

Chapter 4

Mahatma Gandhi Research and Media Services – Archive – Writings. Online. Available at: www.gandhiserve.org/information/writings_online/writings_online.html (accessed, 6 September 2004).
The Words of Gandhi, selected by Richard Attenborough, New York: Newmarket Press. Online. Available at: www.mahatma.org.in/books/showbook.jsp?link= bg&lang=en&book=bg0012&id=1&cat=books (accessed, 12 September 2004).
A.T. Hingorani (ed.) *Gandhi For 21st Century 13, Our Language Problem*. Online. Available at: www.mahatma.org.in/books/showbook.jsp?id=13&book=bg0019&link= bg&lang=en&cat=books (accessed, 10 November 2004).
Quotes of Gandhi by M.K. Gandhi, compiled by S. Bhalla. Online. Available at: www.mahatma.org.in/books/showbook.jsp?id=1&book=bg0032&link=bg&lang= en&cat=books (accessed, 25 November 2004).
Epigrams from Gandhi Compiled by S.R. Tikekar. Online. Available at: mkgandhi. org/epigrams/contents.htm (accessed, 30 November 2004).

Chapter 5

Nelson Mandela: 'Mandela Speaks'. Online. Available at: www.anc.org.za/ancdocs/ history/mandela/ (accessed, 2 December 2004).

Chapter 6

Fidel Castro: 'Castro Speech Database'. Online. Available at: www1.lanic.utexas. edu/la/cb/cuba/castro.html (accessed, 19 January 2005).

Chapter 7

Ayatollah Khomeini: 'Imam Speech'. Online. Available at: www.irib.ir/worldservice/imam/speech/Default.htm (accessed, 20 February 2005).
Sayings of Imam Khomeini. Online. Available at: www.geocities.com/Tokyo/Spa/ 7220/khom-quds.html (accessed, 10 March 2005).
Islam for Today. Online. Available at: www.islamfortoday.com/ (accessed, 20 March 2005).
The Koran. Online. Available at: www.hti.umich.edu/k/koran/simple.html (accessed, 25 March 2005).

Chapter 9

'Stars' National Archives of Singapore. Online. Available at: stars.nhb.gov.sg/ public/index.html (accessed, 2 April 2005).

Index

Page numbers in *italics* refer to illustrations.

Index of conceptual metaphors and metonyms